Look To The Sky

Look To The Sky
LOOK TO JESUS

Dorothy Ann Johnson

authorHOUSE®

AuthorHouse™
1663 Liberty Drive
Bloomington, IN 47403
www.authorhouse.com
Phone: 1-800-839-8640

First published by AuthorHouse   01/03/2012

ISBN: 978-1-4634-3861-6 (sc)

Printed in the United States of America

Any people depicted in stock imagery provided by Thinkstock are models, and such images are being used for illustrative purposes only.
Certain stock imagery © Thinkstock.

This book is printed on acid-free paper.

This young man is my mother's baby brother.

Mr. Precious Debney

Precious has since died, we was told his wife had him killed.

Michael
Brown

Acknowledgment

I WOULD LIKE TO give my acknowledgment to some wonderful people, some since have left us to soon however, they not forgotten. *I like to thank my beloved grandmother the late Miss Cara Suggs, my mother Maybelline Brown; my Aunt Annette Matthews, both still living for sharing the stories of our roots with me. Our roots make up the blood that runs through our veins. In addition, I like to thank the police officer that carried my ID to my mother's house and asked about me that was so nice of him to do so. I like to thank everybody who prayed for me when I needed it the most. I know there are families whose love ones are in the war I like to say there is no word to express thank you for figh ting and dying for our freedom. I like to take time out to ask everybody please give what you can to our disable veteran of American because what he are she given us we cannot give back to them. In addition, I like to thank them who tried to keep my spirit up. Also I like to thank my doctors and nurses for their tender loving care they given me the hold time I was in the hospital and I like to thank all the peoples who came to see my family and me in Bakersfield and San Francisco. In addition, I want to thank my family for being there for me starting with my mother Maybelline Brown and my stepfather Michael Brown Sr. My brother Michael Brown Junior and his wife Lahaska, and their children, starting with Mikesha and Fineness and Chantaira and Nicole and Aquarius and my sister Louryette Greene and her children starting with Dairies Briggs and Michael and Nay Nay and Kay Kay and Kataira and my sister Dana Greene and her daughter Marquita S. Mackey and my Aunt Annette and her family starting with Charles and his wife Mary and family Mary lost a sister 4-22-2005 to bone cancer just like I lost a cousin in January 9-2006 just nine months apart, both so young. Please put the family in your prayers and may they rest in peace. In addition, I like to thank my cousin Roy for coming to visit me with his sisters Beverly and her twin daughters Vesha and Taleka and my cousin Verlean. Acknowledgment goes out to other members of my family such as my cousin Torino and his family and my cousin Junior, and my cousin Verlean and her husband Marvin and son Devan and my cousin Carolyn and her family and Beverly and her family and my cousin June and her son Tony. And my aunt Martha Greene and family starting with brother Chuck Green, daughter Pam and Kelly sons Darrel and Calvin and Todd and Martha and Chuck's brother which is an original member of the group the platters which later has pass away. During this time while writing my book in January of 2006 we lost my cousin Diane Fisher at age 43 to liver cancer in the early morning hour on January 9 2006. I am doing a tribute to her at the very end of my book. In addition, I like to thank my grandmother the late Miss Cora Suggs for telling me all those funny jokes and giving me the family I have to day because this was her and my grandfather during" In addition, I know my grandmother is looking down on me as I write my book and saying Dorothy well done. And I like to thank the best group known to mankind Mr. Otis Williams (AKA) big daddy, the only original Temptation living and his Temptations for coming to Bakersfield his smile can light up the darkest room. I would like to take time out to thank some wonderful people at the Career Services center who bended the rules for me so I could write my book. I thank you people. When a person does something nice for you, they should be appreciated, they do it from the heart and not because they have to. However little of much be appreciative because it is a blessing. In addition, this goes out to Mr. Tony the young man who fixes my computer and did not charge me a dime, I like to tell you thank you ever so much you are what a man is about. To the people at the center which is a blessing to know. And Mr. Christ Frazer In, addition, Mr. Larry Baker and Mr. Charles West who went to see Otis Williams (AKA) big daddy, and his temptations and did not forget to bring me back some pictures of them. In addition, Mr. Peter and Mr. Pete and Mr. Sam Townsend and Miss Denise Pete and Mrs. Deborah Lovell and Mr. Manual and Mr. David and Mr. Tom and Mr. Henry and Mr. Ken and Mr. Ravon and the ones I do not know your names but you know who you are. In addition, here is a young woman who is starting her own design business and she needs some customers so why not give the little woman a call at (661) 835-8380 I am sure she would love to hear from you. That is Mrs. Crystal Corbin of Serenity by Design and that is right here in Bakersfield California. I like to thank the Maintenance man who I met when I was in the hospital up in San Francisco California that told me that day when I was crying and he asked me what was wrong. I told him I do not know why I gotten my leg shot off. He told me to look to the mountain look to the sky, but don't look back and don't ask why. Now little did we know, one day I would be writing a book using his words. So now, you know where I got my book title. I like to thank Mr. Daniel Rodriguez who is staying in the same apartments as I who wish me well. Sadly, while writing my book Mr. Daniel Rodriguez pass away due to cancer. I had given Daniel a ring made from a nickel one day and Daniel put it on his finger and never took it off. The night Daniel died his ring had gotten tangled up in the bedcovers when he notice his ring wasn't on his finger. His family didn't know his ring was tangled up in the bedcovers while they were pulling the covers up on him. While his family was pulling his covers up his ring broke due to the covers pulling it. The first time his ring had ever been off his finger since I give it to him. Well that night Daniel passes away. He had a dog he named her sister; he knew he was passing and sister was a very old dog, he had her for many good years. However, just before he passes away he had sister put down. Now Daniel and old sister are together once more. Daniel and sister you are missed by your family and friends and I know you still buying sister that fried chicken she so dearly love. You were a friend to all who knew you. I sure miss seen you and Ike sitting on that big rock by the mail box. It was a long time before Ike could bring himself to sit there. He was so hurt he couldn't go to your funeral he wanted to remember the happy times. We miss you and may you rest in peace my friend. In addition, Marilyn Townson and family and Shirley and family. Marilyn M-Christian and her friend Big Patrick F. Gannon and Enique Ceruantes and his mother Ms. Ana Gomez. In addition, family. Mr. Carlos Adolfo Avalos. In addition to my friend the Late Mr. Danny Delona, may you rest in peace. Mr. Danny got in a car with a drunk driver one night the person was speeding down the street and lost control of his car and hit head on in to a tree. The car went airborne and Danny was killed on impact. The person who was driving Mr. Danny home that night was hurt but did not die. Danny had his seat belt on. And with this I like to tell people please don't drink and drive and people please don't get in a car with a person you know that been drinking and I can't say this enough the life you may save one day just might be your own. In addition, to Mr. Danny family I like to tell you all we all loved and respected Danny and we miss him each passing day. There's other people names I don't remember that got faith in me and wishing me well I can't tell you what that means to me. I like to thank everybody else who is living in our apartment complex for wishing me well. I like to thanks everyone from the temptations fans web site I am sure; you all remember me by the name, Dorothy Ann Johnson {AKA} Dann and Otis Ann in 1999-2006. In addition, (AKA) Taztales whose real name is Mr. Robert Hogan who once was the temptations security guard. Tell me Mr. Hogan, who once said I come all the way from Bakersfield California to Oakland California to meet Otis? I still laugh about that you know its funny how people can meet. I was like everybody else thought I could get away and never be found out. You know I have to say this' it is funny the way people can meet. In addition, we never will forget Miss Jackie (AKA) Lyrics who died in the New York treads center in the 911 RIP. In addition, my friend whom passed away due to AIDS last year you still in my heart. I like to thank all my doctors here in Bakersfield for their fine work starting with Dr Brenner My bone doctor, Dr MANOHARA my psychiatrist, and Dr. BHANGOO who treat me for high blood pressure. I like to thank the doctors and nurses and the nurse's assistants, here in Bakersfield California. I like to thank the cooks for the good food and the housekeepers and janitors for the well up keeps of the hospitals the hold time I was there. And I would like to thank my family in Chicago starting with my sisters and brothers for calling and checking on me starting with my sister Betty Darrough and her family, my sister Gwen Darrough and her family their mother Mara Darrough, and my brothers Frank Darrough Junior, Kenny Darrough, Tank Darrough, Wayne Darrough. In addition, all of my uncles and aunts start with Aunt Mara Nash who done pass away now and who want get a chance to read my book and I like to take the time to say hello to her children. In addition, I would like to say hello to my aunt Rube Darrough, Uncle Johnny Darrough and my uncle Fred Darrough whom just pass away, and his wife Ann and family of ARK. If I forgotten some names please forgive me and if I misspelled your name. I like to thank you all for calling and checking on me. I didn't forget you. You know, I never dream I would ever be saying this, but last but not least, I like to thank all the people who told me when I was a little girl that I will never amount to anything because I couldn't sing nor dance and I have a learning disability. Because you all giving me the strength I needed to write my book and to make it in life, see some times you can say things to hurt a little child feeling and as that child grow they never forget about the things that been said to them and they must prove you wrong as I did. However, what you were doing was judging me, and I prove you all wrong. I must say this; at times I would stop and say going back in time to them unhappy days is too painful for me. However, in my mind I could hear you saying you will never amount to anything just as I said you would not. In addition, of all people you writing a book, dumb oh you, No way. In my mind, I can hear you laughing at me. Therefore, I would get back to writing my book to prove to myself I weren't as dumb as people thought I was. However for that I want to say thanks guys I thank you all for your unkind words because if it weren't for them I would not have the will to go back in time to them days and go in to memory to write my book. Therefore, I have to say thank you all ever so much and may god always bless you.*

> *This is a pre write up of look to the sky: Than I'll get to look to the sky. I decided I'll do it this way so you can understand better where I'm coming from instead of jumping on into my story. I wanted to write a short story about myself. I met Dorothy there at Camarillo State Hospital, this story is about her; I'll tell a little about myself, but this is her story Dorothy was there with me all the way through Camarillo State Hospital.*

When I was release from Camarillo State Hospital in September of 1968; a week or so later my mother and I had to go to this clinic, I never did know what kind of clinic it was, nor did I ask. I just remember my mother and I pulling up to this building and getting out the car, and entering through these double doors and we walking up this long hallway and in front of us was another double door, but it was open. Entering through this door, to our right was this big round wooden table where two men and two women were sitting. One of the men seen my mother and I at the door and told us to come in and take a sit we did. That same man looked at me and asked me how was I feeling? I answer I was feeling ok, which I lied, I weren't feeling ok, I was depressed as ever, and stayed that way the hold time after leaving Camarillo State Hospital, and still to this day, but a little better due to medication. It's amazing what medication can do. You can think that depression is gone, but unfortunately it comes back on you for no apparent reason at all. You can be depressed and not know why. Also you can be depressed and forget what you depressed about, and you have to think, what am I depressed about. Depression can make some people commit suicide. That's the reason when a person commits suicide that's the first thing the family is asked, were your love one suffering from depression? Depression is known to affect people in variety of ways. You may frequently want to sleep all the time, you may feel tired all time and you don't feel like getting out of bed. That's the way I use to feel when I was in Camarillo State Hospital. You may be happy for a while and you're going to come back down. There for depression can be a chemical imbalance. That's why medication is needed to balance the chemicals in your brain. A simple way to put this is by saying, chemical carry messages between the brain cells which they allow brain cells to talk to each other. I'm explaining this in a child like term, I'm not going to use big medical terms like everybody up on medical terms when I know they not. However, you have a happy input chemicals sent to the brain and the brain receives it, and you have an unhappy input chemical sent to the brain and the brain receives it. However, when the chemical in the brain are balance most likely you will feel normal. Now lest say you happy, which the chemical is called endorphin that makes a person happy. Now lest say something happen that makes you sad, the sad chemical coming over to the unhappy chemical, now what you think going to happen? The sad chemical going to give the unhappy chemical some of the sadness, now the unhappy chemical going to have more chemical in the brain cells than the happy chemical does in the brain cells, now what you think have happen? That's right, now you have what is known as a chemical unbalance. Now what can you do about it? Go to a psychiatrist and be put on medication to balance the chemical in the brain. That to would send you to a nut house for sure. Now look what happen to the person if they don't be put on medication, here comes the sadness, the depression, the anxious, and the person becomes unable to cope with life. Now to feel better you have to be on medication, however see how easy it was to go to a mental hospital back then.

Introduction

I MET A GIRL years ago, and to tell you the truth I can't say I liked her, and the reason why I say that I didn't stand up for her and I let people do and say whatever they wanted to her, now can you really say you care for a person you let that happen to? Even as years passed, she became a person I didn't respect, how can you respect a person that let people treat them the way she let other treat her? You can't, and I couldn't love and respect her and that's why other didn't. Now I had to do a story on her so you can see what I mean by the kind of person she was, yes I met her and I wouldn't want to be her.

She in up in Camarillo State Hospital that's where I met her at, why were I there? Just read the story, I'm sure you will be surprise.

Before you read my book, I like to say there's going to be skeptics, that's human nature to be skeptical of things you don't understand, if somebody else had written the same book and I was reading it I to would be skeptical, there for I understand where you coming from. Since it's my book and I know the stories are true, what can I say, I can't make you believe me, I'm telling things as I seen them and as I heard them it's up to you to believe me or not.

I like for you to meet a dear friend of mines, her name is Dorothy ;she is a very interesting person. However her life haven't been a bed of roses as you will be able to tell from reading her story. I taken everything I learn about her through the years with the help of her family and put her story together. Dorothy is the focus of this story because like you will see some very interesting events have happen in her life and yes, to her family also. However I'm focusing mainly on her and after reading her story you will be able to see why.

Here's the short story of Dorothy Ann Darrough life.

Look to the sky is telling the heartache, the abused; the disappointments, and the struggles in Dorothy life as a child and adult. However, through it all she met a person she learn to love and respect, that person was herself. Sometimes in our life we must learn to love and respect ourselves. Dorothy taking everything she went through in life to be her learning tree, which is the tree of knowledge. Her life has been nothing but disappointments "after" disappointments and abused after abused. However, most things that happen to us in life we let happen to us. Why I say this is because most things in my life I let happen to me, such as staying with men that abused me. God gives most of us commonsense enough to know when we're being abused. There for why stay with a person that abusing you? That's not love and never believes it is. A person don't love you when they abused you, take from you, cheat on you, anything a person do to hurt you that mean they don't love you. The abused was because she wouldn't stand up for herself and she would let people walk all over her. When you let people walk over you they want respect you. Dorothy had to meet Dorothy, She never met Dorothy. Dorothy had to learn to love and respect herself. She had to learn you can't love and respect yourself if you let people treat you the way she let people treat her. She had to learn if you mistreat a dog long enough it will find the sense to leave you. However, Dorothy know now no doubt about it that in its self is a mental disability and it played a Part on her being sent to the most famous Mental Hospital not just in California; however they say in the world. This at the time was Camarillo State Hospital. Yes the year was 1968. However, little did she know that day when the police officers come for her back in "2-11-1968" she would be on her way to the most famous mental hospital in the world, it I will tell you why later why it was so famous. Despite her difficult life as a child Dorothy still finish high school. She even was on the honor roll and she spent some time in collage. However, she didn't complete anything because it was hard for her to decide on what she wanted to do. Collage has so many classes to be offered, if you're anything like her it's hard to make your mind up about anything. You could spend ten years in collage and want had completed anything. That's another reason why people like herself stay in bad relationships because it's hard for them to make they minds up to leave. If they in love with a person they buy into what they telling them. Such as please don't leave me, I love you; please don't go, please stay. And they stay. People like her have to learn things the hard way, and two thing they have to learn is you can't buy love and you can't be nice to everybody, It's just a few people you can be nice to and they want take you for granted. People like her must learn to take care of their selves and love themselves enough to say enough is enough and not letting themselves be abused; Dorothy standing up for herself a little better now since she's older. Well after leaving Camarillo state hospital something happen, she never did think about that place again. It was like she never been there. Looking back over her life now, she can say she had blocked that place out of her mind; even when she married. She knows now that's why she didn't think to tell her husband she had been in Camarillo. Dorothy always heard put unpleasant things behind you and move on with your life and that's what she tried to do. Well you can't always do that, first before you can move on with your life, you have to let the world know whatever other people know about you, because that you don't tell there's always going to be somebody to tell it for you; and usually it's never the way it is, or they don't know the reason why it happen. Before you tell something on somebody that you shouldn't be telling in the first place; learn the hold story, than tell the reason why it happens, because there's a reason for everything. She don't mind people telling about her being in Camarillo, however they should know the hold story first. They should know what she went through that sent her there. This why I'm writing this book, She want the world to know why she was admitted to Camarillo State Hospital, and I'm putting it out there for the world to read and that way people will get the real story because nobody knows her story better than she and she should be the only one telling it. She don't care about anybody knowing her story and sure don't care about any man knowing, people think she do but she don't, because she been done wrong by men so much, that she never will feel the same by them anyway, because as soon as they know she have feeling for them here they go messing up on her and when things didn't work out with the woman like it usually never do, here they come wanting to come back until next time America when they see something else they think they want. When you try to do right by people where does it get you she asks me and I had nothing to tell her because I knew nowhere. Like some men can be good to women and treat them like ladies most women don't want that and men such as that usually get hurt and used. However take the men that treat women like dogs, the bad boys women call them has so many women they don't know what to do with them. Like the bad girls most men go for the bad girls, those that bag it back, shake it around; bring it out, and drop it to the ground. No room left for good kind people it seems like any more. You try to be a good kind person you get mess over ever time. Now I'm going to tell you something about me. I had a man that I loved and about four years into our relationship he met this woman and I tell you everything I didn't do she would do. That's another thing women will do and that is anything a man say his wife or woman want do, the other women going to make sure they do it. They going to act like they the best thing since slice bread, now let a man leave what he have at home, then he will see just how good they are. Some women can't cook, but men want know it until they leave what's at home. A man is thinking that woman can cook better than chef Boyardee and all the time she can't boil water. See when you go fishing you must use bait, and the better your bait, the more fish you bound to catch. That's women bait to pretend they're the better woman. If he likes a clean house she will clean and have her house smelling so good, he thinks she the cleanest little thing since snow and all the time that's the first time she clean house in months and Sundays. Yes she tells the man she going to fix him dinner. What she be doing is going to the store and buying that all ready cooked food. Everything you think she cooked for you are ready made. Before you come over she get herself a sack of flour and dip her hand in it and sprinkle some in her face and mess her hair up and you really think that woman went all out the way for you. Little do you know the cans and boxes are under the kitchen sink. See how women can fool the hell out of some men. yes I was happy he beat the hell out of that woman and broke her arm it was better for her arm to get broken than mine and then to she never let the phone get cool, she would ring it day and night and some time she would call and hang up all day till I unplug the phone. I mean he would beat her anywhere, see why you women can have our no good men. Now back to my story; yes Dorothy has been in a nut house. As I said she had blocked those days out her mind, that's why she didn't think to tell her husband before they married. However, it weren't blocked out of other people mind they told him for her. He never told her he knew. When she thought to tell him he told her he been told. I'm writing this book and letting the world know she's not ashamed of where she been and asking other that been in mental hospitals don't be ashamed because some things we can't help and anybody can go to a nut house and you don't have to be crazy. Just don't talk about people if things happen to them because the same thing can happen to you or worse and if you don't believe me just keep living because time can show you better than I can tell you. Life goes on and somehow we go on with it. Remembering Dorothy life as it happen I was able with the help of Dorothy mother, Maybelling Brown, and her aunt, Annette Matthew, and her grandmother the late Mrs. Cora Suggs by telling her their back home stories with they help I was able to put together my book.

Part One

My family's history

NOT TOO LONG ago there lived some people that would put red pepper in their shoes so the bloodhounds couldn't track their scent when they took that danger journey to freedom. Why did red pepper make it hard for the blood hounds to track the scent of the slaves? Only the slaves would know the answer to such question, which they were my ancestors. I say not too long ago because slavery wasn't a thousand years ago. However, this is where I come from; this is my roots which are the blood that runs through my veins today. However, the blood these people shed is the blood that made it possible for blacks to go to school which so many do not and they shed blood for other things we able to do today. These people are the reason why I'm here today and able to set here and write my book. These people alone with solders died for our freedom. They too died for days they would never live to see. They could be killed if they was caught trying to learn to read and write. However, if they got caught with a book they could be killed. At that time it was against the law for blacks to go to school. You know if it was still that way blacks would be fighting to go to school, now since they can many don't want to go. However that's being human, we want to do what we can't do and we want what we can't have. If only black kids knew the real history of slavery. Alex Haley roots were just a tip of the iceberg it goes much deeper than that. Nobody really will ever know just how badly slaves were really treated and it's good they never will. While writing my book two sprits that once was slave men told me their male genitals was cut off and stuff in their mouths, they wanted me to let it be known. Now again you may think I'm crazy but I most let it be know what they tell me while I'm writing my book if I don't I will have hell to pay. I don't know when spirits going to come to me while I'm writing my book however when they do come I just write down what they tell me to write for them like I will say again why me they come to I don't know I just write what they tell me to write, you don't ask spirits why this and why the other you just write what they tell you to get out there for them and let it be because if you don't they want leave you alone until you do what is asked of you, and after that you may not ever hear from them again.

1

Chapter 1

Dorothy family history
told from the stories I have heard.

BACK IN SLAVERY there were these teenager boys that knew black people was afraid of ghosts; there for they thought to themselves because they had gotten bored to death one night and being teenager it's not good for them to be bored. There for they decided to dress up in some scary masks and go around to the black people houses and scare the hell out of them. Well as time went on the word got around to some racist men that thought the kids had a good idea There for the men went and got some white sheets and guest what was born back in 1865-1874, can you guest? Yes that's right if you said the original KKK (aka) the ku klux klan. Like it or not they played a big part in black people history. These were the first kkk then in 1915-1945 come the second set of klans and on and on and haven't stop. Did you know the word Klan mean family? Yes they a family of racist people. Now they to have the right not to like who they don't like but they don't have the right to harm anybody. Now you know a little history of the kkk, yes they got the idea from something kids was doing for fun. Just for a laugh; something kids do all the time. Looking back on slavery I always have wonder what makes some people hate black people so when we was the one beaten to the inch of our life, hung; toes and limbs chopped off and taking from our family and sold and made to work in unbearable heat with little to no food and water. All was done to black people by other people. Now black people never did anything to anybody. I know it's said we not liked by some people because we're loud and so is other people. What people talking about or teenagers, Most grown black people do not act like teenagers, and they say we play our music loud, teens do play their music loud all teens do and so does grown people in every race. People say black people have big lips, not all black people have big lips most black people don't have big lips, than to other people go and have their lips pump up because they likes the way some black people lips look, and it's said black people have nappy hair, that's not true, most black people hair is not nappy most black have pretty, thick; black hair. Than to check it out, some people neglect their hair to get dreadlocks which is nappy hair and rarely do they wash it, and they hair look neglected and a mess. It's said we have big noses, that's not true most black people nose is not big at all, than to other people have their noses worked on to enlarge their nose. They say black people don't bath, there's some don't, but it's in every race and they say all black people want is a hand out, that's not true, there's some black people want accept anything free, than to when something is giving out free just take a look around. They say black people are lazy, that's not true some black people work two jobs, and it's said black women having babies for welfare. Count every race of kids that's all

I will say about that. And blacks do work however, on some jobs we're treated so badly even with us taking so much mess; we're still kicked out the door. And when we're working we better be a good butt kisser and we better work harder than any other race there. However, you can be the best butt kisser of all times that still don't get it. You still can be let go. Now when another black is pointed to be over other blacks don't think you going to get a brake because you're a lie if the truth not in you. Because that black person has to show other people that they don't give a dam about you ether. There for we dam if we do and we dam if we don't. Other things they say about black men that I want get off into, however you have a good idea what I'm talking about, I will put it this way, it's not the color of the bat nor the size it's all in the way you use your bat. Just because a bat may be big that don't mean the man will hit a home run, now on the other hand a bat may be small but a man can hit a home run every time. You just have to know how to use what you got to get what you want and if you get it you have to use what you have to keep what you have. Another thing if we're working on an easy job some people don't want to see us with that job and will make it hard for us by complaining to our boss about every little thing we do. Some people don't want to see other with nice things. The way some people will do others if a person working on a job and they buy something, I say a nice car. However that car must be made payment on. However that's all you have is that job, you starts working overtime so you can make payments on that car; check this out will you. They see you're doing ok for yourself, look like you coming up in the world; working overtime and all. One day you come to work, no time card; your being fired, no warning or nothing you have made plans on paying your car off soon, that way you will only have your house payment because you're buying your very first home. You building your future things are finally looking up for you you're somewhat happy now. However you want be for long because you soon to find out you're fired. Now back to my family history, I wonder, just how far does human history goes back. Where did it begin? If it started with Adam and Eve does that mean everybody is kin? How was Adam and Eve really created? Why can't we take a man rib and make a woman? If god taken a rib from man then why man don't have one less rib than woman? Why we can't take a grain of sand and make people? Why can't we take a hundred pounds of clay and make a world? Were Adam and Eve ever babies? A lots of things we will never really know the answers to will we? Well some things god showed and told me and I wrote them down in look to the sky. I was able to get some of the question answer by the master himself. I'm not god's messenger, I'm not special, I haven't been to church for a while. You don't have to be for god to bless you because church first has to start in the heart. Your heart must be right. I will pass on to you what god told me about different things I asked him later when I asked him why things happen the way they do just keep reading for now here's Dorothy's heartbreaking true story starting from childhood to adulthood and it telling how she taken her mishaps to be her learning tree, which is the tree of life.

Chapter 2

Dorothy Ann Darrough

IT WAS JUNE 21 1955 when god blessed a little girl baby to be born at 9: pm weighting eight pounds and eight ounces to a 17 year old single mother named Maybelline Dabney who lived in a far off little run down wooden shack out in the woods in Little Rock Arkansan with her mother, and sister and her sister two little boys, where the poorest of the poor black family lived. Dorothy mother had been chopping cotton in the hot sun all that day when her water broke. Still she would keep on working till she had made her day and she would go home and the baby girl was born at 9: pm that night. Dorothy Aunt Annette would name her Dorothy Ann Darrough. After the movie star Dorothy Jean Dandridge. Doing that time if the parents weren't married the child would go in the mother's maiden name. No if, ands; buts, about it, that was the law and that was all it was to it. However, Dorothy father wanted to marry Dorothy mother. However, Dorothy grandmother didn't care for Dorothy father; there for she wouldn't put her x on the papers so Dorothy parents could be married. Dorothy had to go in her mother's maiden name which is Dabney. As we all know that not the way it is today. Today a woman can have her baby put in a married man name and have the child support papers sent to his wife house, that way if the wife doesn't know about the kid she will then. Just like they will give a married man some nasty sexually transmitted disease and send him home to his wife to give it to her. That's if she's lucky, because like the health department people told my friend Dorothy, it could have been aids, Yes people Dorothy low down good for nothing second husbands could had giving her aides. When she confronts him about giving her gonorrhea, he told her yes! And the thing was good. I just put it a little nicer than he told her. And she was pregnant at the time. Yes he had gotten her pregnant with gonorrhea. When they went to the health department to see if the gonorrhea was gone he told her to ask the doctor how did he get it, she told him she knew there's only one way, he said no they told him he gotten it another way, ask him he told her again. It's only one way she told him again. He said ask the doctor. He will tell you. All the time he knew how that doctor would talk to his wife. However, she seen this white head doctor; she called him over to her to shut her husband up. She told him what her husband had said and asked him have they discovered another way a person can contract gonorrhea because her husband wanted that doctor to tell her he didn't get it through sex which she knew better. She knew there was only one way. However, if there was some miracle way a person could get it that she didn't know about she wanted to know about it. The way that doctor talked to that poor woman. I think he was gay and all the way and hated women. However I think I will leave it as that. Her husband laughs at the way that doctor talk to his wife. She was so hurt. Here she was pregnant with gonorrhea and feeling down as one could be. A woman hormone is all out of control anyway when she's

5

pregnant. And she's easily to get very emotional anyway and just think something such as that going on. She was showed no kind of compassion and care that day. However all she could think about was her unborn baby. The baby she had prayed and cried when her monthly come on because she knew her dream didn't come true that month. The baby she would dream she was giving birth to, too only wake up to find it was only another brokenhearted dream she had so many times before. Now she was bless she thought to finally have her prayer answer to only be taken away. What happen to Dorothy? She doesn't live here anymore. Some women can know they have VD and give it to a man to take home to his wife and tell her friends if that bitch doesn't know, because the wife is always the bitch. Anyway they say if that bitch doesn't know her man is fooling around she will know, because I gave the fool VD and when she starts burning when she pisses she'll know something up. Now how can you enjoy a person after them giving you some low down mess such as VD? However each time Dorothy husbands gave her that mess they got smart with her. Her first husband told a dam lie and told people she gave it to him. People that knew her knew he was telling a dam lie and told him so. Your feeling for that person will never be the same. Now never in her life have she ever had VD. She never contracted VD till she got married. Her first husband gave her VD and pubic lice. She never had lice before. Lice are crabs in the pubic region and it's very uncomfortable and itchy like hell. What married person would give they husband or wife such mess as what this woman husbands gave her. This why I will tell anybody when you envy somebody you think is happy as a lark because you don't have any idea what goes on behind closed doors. If only you knew you would be happy it was them and not you that had that person that was doing the other one so bad. Yes you woman can have them low down good for nothing nasty men. Now it hurts like hell to find out your man is messing around on you but one thing is certain a person can only hurt you only once, think about it you think they can hurt you over and over again, but they can't. Once they hurt you they can't hurt you again. When a person hurt you bad enough to make you cry, you don't know it, but each tear that fall that's less love you start to have for them. A person may feel good by knowing they hurt you bad enough to make you cry, however like I said; you don't know it, but your heart is healing. That's why crying ease the pain because you letting your emotion go and you going to feel relief. It's better to let your emotions go than keep it inside. The main person that's hurts the most believe it or not is a man, yes the world may never know this because what man want this know, and I'm sure not telling it. However, the reason why the world thinks its women because we the ones always crying and men most likely be the ones to fool around, however if a woman fool around on her man and hurt him somebody most likely going to die. Some women will kill also but we all know not to hurt a man not if you want to live, on the other hand if you ready to die that's a dam good way to go. No matter how bad people treat you whatever you doing for them they want you to keep on doing it; they want you to keep on being the fool you are and when you get sick of being a fool that's when they want to hurt you. Now the way they treat you they don't want to be treated like that and they wouldn't do anything for you if you treated them the way they treat you. All you did was love a person and tried to show them how much you cared for them. Some people don't have sense enough to appreciate a good kind decent person and people say all the time I wish I had a good man or good woman and one happen to come your way you mistreat them. A good kind person you mistreat can and will turn on you to the place you won't know them and they never be the same by you and once they turn on you forget about ever trusting them because that's gone that person is not the person you once knew and never will be again. That's what happens when you mistreat a good caring nice sweet person that loves you.

Chapter 3

don't blame the other woman

WOMEN ALWAYS BLAME the other woman for braking up her home; look can't anybody brake up your home; your home has to already be in the process of braking up. If the two of you have a strong bond between you, can't anybody break that up. Why would anybody step out their marriage and risk braking up what they have going for their self. If a person say they don't love the person they mess up with and they love the person they have at home then why would a person risk losing a person they love for somebody they don't love that's crazy to me and it don't make any sense. I think a person like this don't know who they want.

When a woman man messes up on her she shouldn't blame the other woman, blame the man; he's the one should respect you enough not to mess up on you. Before a person get in a relationship they should know what they want and who they want. If not don't bother anybody by getting in to a relationship with them because people has feeling and most likely they feeling can be hurt and they saying to themselves please don't break my heart. They want tell you but inside they hoping you want hurt them. When Dorothy husband's gave her gonorrhea I she can't remember to this day getting on the bus and going to the health department because she was so grief stricken with all that pain of thinking what going to happen to her unborn baby. She cried till she cried herself sick. She never blames it on the other woman. She knew the woman and knew where she lived, but she had nothing against the woman and still don't. She knew to lay the blame on her husband. She knew if a man love you he want mess up on you, if a man love a woman he want mess up on her. However if I was the kind of woman that mess up on a man, the man should check me, not the other man because he don't know what I told that man. I could have told him I don't have anybody like people will do. However Dorothy husband told her the woman gave him VD to give to her and she was pregnant. She told him look, she blame him! Not that woman. She says to him, if he was the man for her he wouldn't have mess up on her. She says if he cared for his baby and her he wouldn't had put they life in damager like he did. That was it! He didn't care about her nor they baby they had made together. By this time she was yelling and crying he was trying to hold her and kiss her, she didn't want his hands on her she told him to go and hold that woman. She told him; you should have cared for your baby and me and not look for the other woman to care. It was you who wanted to fool around, don't put the blame off on the woman. See a man not like a woman, a woman can go to bed with ten men and not care for one, she don't have to get ready. Unlike a man he have to be ready and stay ready because he will fall, not us we can make like we want it and can make like we're enjoying it and knowing we not and a man can't tell. However with a man he can't fake it because, well he just can't. When the woman seen Dorothy, Dorothy told her she have no beef with her and Dorothy didn't. Dorothy knew if her husband didn't want to fool around he wouldn't. If it hadn't been that woman she knew it would have been another one. There for both Dorothy husband fooled around on her and both gave her gonorrhea. Yes that's right two no good men gave her gonorrhea. She never had any STD's till she married. That's why she give them they walking papers. However for as myself concern, If a man give me something like that he can't love me and I don't want to hear baby I made a mistake, that's not a mistake 1+1=3 that's a mistake. When a man has sex how can that be a mistake? This mean his manhood mistakenly got ready to have sex, he mistakenly had sex with the woman. Don't be no fool a person don't mistakenly have sex and being a man a woman don't rape a man. Now back to Dorothy. At age one Dorothy mother would move her out west to California and Dorothy would never see her father till age 35 which would be the first and last time she would see her father that she can remember because he would die after that. Dorothy father's mother never wanted her father to have anything to do with her because she didn't care for Dorothy family there for she didn't care for Dorothy. However, Dorothy father would marry another lady and Dorothy father and his wife would have children. Dorothy father mother like her other grandchildren and told Dorothy sister Betty to let it go when Betty heard they had an older sister out west, but she didn't give up until she found her big sister Dorothy. At age three Dorothy would start seeing ghosts. However, through the hard and unhappy life she would have at school with the abused and all she would become a "12 "year old patient at Camarillo State Hospital. On jobs and with men through the years the abused continues. At age 38 Dorothy would fall victim to a drive by shooting which taken her right leg above the knee. Dorothy never believes in near death. However, it happens to her which she never knew she had experience because her near death experience wasn't anything like she ever heard. Doing the time Dorothy was in the hospital she was crying one day when a maintenance man came in her room and while he was mopping the floor he asked her what was wrong? She answers I don't know why this had to happen to me. He told her to look to the mountain, look to the sky, but don't look back and don't ask why. Little did Dorothy know one day she would write a book using that maintenance man words for the title of her book, which is look to the sky. Now since I told you a little about Dorothy let me introduce myself, my name is Dorothy AnnDarrough. My father was a 19 year old man by the name of Frank Darrough Junior. This is my true story. However, I hope you enjoy my story and I hope it's a book you will be talking about for a long time to come.

Chapter 4

That day we had to buy
my grandmother's funeral dress.

MY GRANDMOTHER HAD passed away and my mother and I had to buy her something to be buried in. We Had decided on buying her things at the funeral home, I could see they tried to make it less painful as they could and we was grateful for that. We was trying to hold up it was so hard on everybody. My mother and I were looking through the clothes for a dress to put my grandmother away in. However while we was looking over the dresses it hit me hard! My grandmother is gone! And we buying her a dress to put her away in and that's when I lost it. I couldn't do it, no god. I couldn't buy my grandmother her last dress to be buried in no! My God! I couldn't do that. I remember she telling me one day at age sixteen she wanted me to see to it when she's gone that she be put away in a pink robe there was no robes there at the funeral home, there for we had to have her put away in a white dress I tell you I don't know why God let us go through things such as putting love ones away. Why can't we just get to thirty-five and stay there, we never grow old and sickly we just live forever no sorrow no death no sickness we just live in a nice clean happy world forever, why can't our life be that way, why death?

At my grandmother's funeral

How could I said goodbye

My god, here we sit god at my grandmother's funeral, here I sit crying, it's time god it's

Time to tell my grandmother goodbye, how can I god, please tell me god how can I.

How do you tell a person goodbye that been with you all your life, How can you tell a person goodbye that would cook something good only for you even when they didn't feel like cooking, how do you tell a person goodbye when it's the last time you going to see them. If anybody knows would you please tell me.

Dorothy Ann Johnson

That day I looked down on my grandmother lying out in her coffin, I started reminiscing over the wonderful times we shared together, laughing and talking about her younger days. I tell you she had so many interesting stories to tell. Sometimes I think she would be so far off in her stories that she could relive those days over in her mind. Oh how I miss them days talking with her. I asked myself looking down on her that day at her funeral; where have the time gone? Seem like it was only yesterday she was running us kids with bullfrogs and making tea cakes and cooking all the good food we kids loved to eat. Why did it have to end? Lord why did she have to go? I would listen to everything she had to say. With older people if you just take a little time out and sit down and listen to them you can learn a lot from them. Like I said you have to listen to them like I use to listen to my grandmother. As l looked down on her, seem like I could hear her saying Dorothy one day I'm going to get sick and you all going to say mama doing better and all the time I'm going to had close my eyes and go to sleep. God it happens just the way she had said it would. Dorothy I'm going to sleep. She didn't have to tell me what she meant I knew all so well and I didn't like for her to talk that way because it would kill me in side. I knew that day had to come but, I was hoping I wouldn't live to see it. However here she lay. I couldn't believe she was gone. I couldn't believe my grandmother was lying in her coffin and I wouldn't see her or hear her sweet voice any more, I couldn't believe I wouldn't hear that familiar cough I heard all my life from the snuff she would dip. God I just couldn't believe I wouldn't hear her stories any more. Somehow I made it through her funeral. However my hold family from back home had many interesting stories to share with me. However my grandmother had the best because she was the oldest family member from back home. I taken the best stories along with some of my own and turned them into my book. I hope you all will find our stories as interesting as I did.

Chapter 5

my special ability to see spirits

MY BOOK IS covering my life and my special ability to see spirits and it started when I was around three years old "however" at the time I was so young I never knew what I was seeing wasn't real people. They would look like you and I. It was later as I got older that I realize what I was seeing was not real people. Another time I seen spirits was the night I gotten shot back in June 29 of 1993 at 11: pm. I have seen them long before than however I just say back then. I hope by reading look to the sky you will understand you can have a mental disability without knowing it and you will realize that everybody that goes to a mental hospital is not mental the way people think they is. just read my book and ask yourself do you fit anything I'm talking about and if you can answer yes to anything just think, at that time when I went to Camarillo you could had went also. My story is true, however some of the things I be telling you I will understand if you don't believe all what I be saying because if somebody was telling me these same things I'm telling you, I wouldn't be so quick to believe it. However it happens to me there for I have to believe it. I will start with age three. I was sitting down at the table eating a plate of spaghetti one day when I started playing with my food as kids would do. I pulled one spaghetti up and was pulling it a long in my plate and when I let go it started crawling like a worm I never said anything about it I didn't think anything about it. We were living on Texas Street. At age 6, I seen this human eye in my egg when I call for my mother it disappeared. At age 38 I would fall victim to a drive by shooting and I seen people that was spirits. It was doing this time I had my near death experience. Now I will ask you this because this happen to me there for I want to ask you if the same thing happens to you what little I told you that happen to me what would you do? What would you do as a 12 year old child locked away in a mental hospital and they give you a shot that have your mouth twisting to the side and your teeth lock down on your tong and nothing you can do to stop it and blood and meat from your tong be in your mouth because your biting your tong off. I'm talking about 3B the mental ward right here in Bakersfield California back in 1968. However, when you go ask the nurses to help you and they do nothing and your teeth is biting down on your tong so hard you have a mouth full of meat from your tong and blood and nobody do a thing until days later when they got ready. I ask you what you would do. Now if you can tell me what you would do please tell me because I didn't know then and still don't till this day. I just thought I ask you that because people tell me I been in a nut house and the things I went through I wanted to see what would you do if you was put in that same situation? What would you do if kids were fighting you every day at school and when you went for help nothing would be done about it? And what would you do if the teacher sic kids on you to fight you and they all out number you? Wouldn't that depress the hell out of you? There for before you judge me first see where I'm coming from. Then ask yourself what would you do? Never judge a person until you walk a mile in their shoes. Then to god said judge not unless you want to be judge, also I say before you criticize somebody first walk a mile in their shoes. They say god doesn't give us more then we can bear. Is that true? It don't always seem like that's the case do it? It makes you wonder if that's the case why some people end their life over some things and why some people in up on drugs and alcohol? It makes you wonder don't it. Well I don't have the answer to that question, god only told me some things I asked him and that's all. However, I will share with you what little he told me. Stress and depressions and worry are something some people been dealing with all their life and other people never had to deal with such things. I was stressed out in Camarillo but, some people there was happy. If a person can be happy in a nut house then they must be crazy and that's all it is to it. I will tell you Camarillo state hospital was a place I don't wish up on nobody, that and being an amputee and being not able to have children when you want them. People should stop telling women about adoption like they don't know that's what they can do. That don't solve the problem you still can't have children just don't say nothing at all if that's all you can say because I know I would feel like telling people off when I was told that. Another thing stop asking woman do they have children and they tell you no, and you tell them their lucky, That's not luck, being not able to have children is a medical condition and what's lucky about having a medical condition? I won the lottery that's luck! Know that different, its luck when you can have them and you're unlucky when you can't and you could have been lucky if you call that luck, if you had kept your legs close if you didn't want a baby. You didn't have to have a baby. And don't try to tell me that was a mistake. Opening your legs and having sex is no mistake. Anyway as I said we women who can't have kids don't want to hear about adoption because we know about it. Women like me want to feel our child move and kick inside us and you don't get that with adoption, we want to give birth, however people don't seem to understand that. People don't care that you can't have children. Look what my husband done to me, I would have never done that to him no way I'm not that low down and dirty. I care too much about people feeling, that man had no feeling for me. If a person doesn't have any feeling for people why would they bother a person about marriage. What kind of man would go out and get a baby with another woman because his wife can't have kids and take the kids around the wife family in hopes they tell the wife. What kind of human can do that? Now what dam good do people think adoption would do? You have not given birth to the baby. But the other woman has, she done given birth to your husband baby but you can't give birth. Now she had something you been dying to have, something you been trying for years to have. Your husband has been trying to get you pregnant for years however no baby yet. Than the first time he has sex with the other woman a baby, now why not you? Oh yes this where you can adopt what good would that do you when some other woman done had your husband baby and you can't. That's why don't talk to people about your problem like they care because they don't. I will tell you we know about adoption we know about all the unwanted kids out in the world we don't have to hear it we know it and we know where to go and get them. If the doctor tells a woman you were not born with a uterus or ovary or they had to be remove that's another thing. However as long as there's some kind of hope if you want your own child I say go for it. As I said if that's all you can tell a woman she can adopt don't say nothing at all and I'm speaking for all women around the world that can't have children and want them. I'm going to tell you something else women that can't have children they pretends to be ok around a pregnant woman. However, they want tell you how they really feel, they want tell you they would give anything to be in your shoes, they want tell you how they hurts inside when they see a pregnant woman or when they go into stories and see baby things and they want tell you how mad they gets when you say if it's a girl you don't want it when they would be happy with whatever god bless them with. No they won't tell you these things. They would rather die than to tell you how hard it is for them to have dreams they giving birth to a child and they so happy in that dream and they saying in the dream god please don't let it be a dream and in the dream it seem so real. However you wake up and finds it was nothing but that same old dream you had so many times before. Now you tell me what good will adoption do when you want to give birth to your own baby. If anybody that have adopted a baby if they told you the truth and don't care what anybody think of them like I don't they will tell you they still want their own child and they will tell you that's a dream they will never get over.

And women should speak up and speak out and tell people they don't want to adopt a kid if that's not what they want and forget about what people say about you spending money on trying to have your own child tell them to kiss where the sun don't shine don't go adopt a kid if that's not what you want.

Don't let people make you feel guilty for wanting your own child that's normal for you to want your own child. Why would any woman let people make them feel guilty because of all the unwanted kids in the world when they didn't put one out there. If anybody should feel guilty it should be the one that put them out there not you and I can tell you the one's that put them out there don't feel guilty there for why should you let people make you feel guilty. You go have your own child if that's what you want and I pray you do. Now people may say I'm cold but I don't care people didn't care about me. Check this out. Another thing that happen to me when I had my second ectopic pregnancy I was put on the ward with women that had their big fat pretty babies and I would lay there crying because I knew I was on the ward with babies and my baby was gone. Late one night I had cried myself to sleep and soon after I had gotten to sleep a nurse come in my room calling my name Dorothy here's your baby I said I have no baby. I didn't cry because all the tears in me were gone. See people that works in them hospital don't have feeling for women such as myself there for I'm telling you don't look for them to care about your feeling look to hear you can adopt that's all you going to hear so look to hear it and after all else fails if you do adopt you will still want your own child because you haven't given birth to a child. There for don't lie to yourself and pretend you're over your dream because your dream will never perished. Another thing don't be going out and buying things for baby showers if that's not what you want to do. Think about you because nobody else will. Tell me this do anybody ever tell you I'm going to get some people together and we going to get you the money you need so you can have your baby because we know how much you want your own child I can tell you no, just tell the truth why don't you. Only you can adopt right? Anyway when it was time for me to leave the hospital after my last extoped pregnancy the nurse come in my room and ask me where was my baby I told her I have no baby and I said crying now I'm so ready to get up out of here. She said because of the babies? I answer yes, she then told me about the times I be in stores I will see the babies she didn't understand that had nothing to do with it, I just didn't feel that I should had been on a ward with women having babies and I couldn't have my baby but still I was on the same ward with all them babies that the mothers had giving birth to and I never would. I feel for any woman who wants children that can't have them. You not going to have nobody to talk to that cares about you I will say again all your going to hear is that dam adoption and treatment is so high but to me it's worth every dime and more if that what it takes to make your dream come true. Every woman in the world should have a chance to become mothers if that what she want. If they can spend millions on a gold toilet set for an airplane why want they give women that trying to have a child a chance to have one, help with the cost of infertility treatments. Why women born here in the USA have to suffer like that? Why they have the cost of the treatment so dam high? And no help you get. And if you try to save up for the treatment about time you save up the money you too dam old they'll tell you and it shouldn't be an age limit on your dream. I pray no woman won't have a dog for a husband like I did, go out and get a kid on you, no woman shouldn't be done like that. It should be a law ageist a man doing his wife like that. I never was showed any kind of care at all at any time. If anything good happen to me in life I'm long over do. When I lost my last child I was put on the birth word where women was having babies lord that was so dam painful for me I never get over that god how can I? The day I die I take that to my grave no way could I do a woman like that that's inhumane to do anybody like that my god, That was too much on me and them dam doctors and nurses didn't gave a dam about me nor my feeling and no woman should be done like I been done yes that's is very emotional on a woman and no uses in saying anything because nobody cares about you nor your feeling. I wish somebody had let me know what to expect as I'm letting you all. Don't pretend to be happy for nobody. I have to get off this subject because I can feel tears building up in my eyes. Something like what happen to me can be the reason for some women to go to a mental hospital. That has been reason for women to kill themselves. Back to Camarillo, Camarillo State Hospital was three miles south of the city Camarillo. There were older girls in the dorm with us younger girls I would lay in my bed pretending to be asleep and watch the older girls getting it on if you know what I mean. That was a lonely place with mountains and trees surrounding the hospital and far away from anything. I would watch my mother going around them lonely looking mountains. At that time that was the only way to come and go which now you go the back way. Man I tell you seeing my mother going around them lonely looking mountains was the saddest thing to me. I tell you nothing at that time would look as sadder. I can recall for some unknown reason ever time my mother was about to leave somebody would put that sad song on by Gladys Knight and the pips it's time to go now. I only remember very little of the song this just to give you an idea the way it went. It's time to go now, so it's time to run it really been fun but I have to go, I got to go now. How in the name of god do you keep your 12 year old heart together hearing that song when your mother leaving you at a far off place such as that. Now I ask you can you see why I blocked that place out my mind. I was only a child and I didn't kill anybody to be sent there, so why couldn't I put it behind me and move on. About time I got out of Camarillo State Hospital, I was far beyond other girls my age. That's what a place such as that do to you. The stress I went through and other stress in my life never ended. However, I was told by my doctor I have been this way for so long that I will always be this way. However, I'm on medication but as we know medication can do so much and the rest is up to us. We must get out there and do things we like. Little things such as walking and talking with people we enjoy being around. Whatever makes us feel better, little things that don't "cost money" because that's something most of us have little of.

Now I will tell you a little about near death which I never believe in. You will notices that I will repeat some things and the reason for this I will tell you.

> Because it's so hard to believe some of the things that happen to me and some things have been so bad that it helps to get it out. There for I know I do repeat myself a bit. I must explain this because when you take to do something positive people is just waiting in the wings to say something negativity about it. I want you to know I never been a believer in near death experiences and the bright light people say they see doing near death and the people they say they see that long ago had passed away and so on. I had my own near death experiences and I will tell you mine weren't anything like I had ever heard. I didn't see people had long ago passed away. However, what I did see was shadow like people. They were all the same weight and size with long black hair and they weren't male or female and they seemed very protective of me. All I felted was love and peace and no pain. I was in such a lovely place, no time, no negativity; there weren't anything to envy no one about because everybody looked the same. One thing I notice no one had eyes nor ears nor mouth. I will tell you a little about what happen before I get all the way off in my story.

14

Back in June 29, 1993 at age 38 I was shot beside my right knee with a shotgun which I was an innocent bystander of. I had always heard people speaking about near death experiences. When I got shot I was standing up on this high porch and after I got shot I jumped down off the porch, jumping with a leg that had six inch of bone shot out of it. Today I don't understand how I jumped off that high porch with six inch of bone shot out my leg. I sit on the ground looking up at the people standing all around me however, they was the people I was telling you about they seemed very protected of me, where I was it was dark but that night it looked day I didn't understand this. Then I heard somebody say stay with us Dorothy stay with us, it was a policeman bringing me back. I never knew I had passed out and I had had a near death experience. I didn't want to come back I wanted to stay where ever this place was. When I came back seem like I enter hell its selves. I'm also telling ghost story and many more stories I think you will enjoy.

Chapter 6

Are there any books on Camarillo State Hospital?

ME BEING A formal patient of Camarillo State Hospital at age twelve I have not been able to find any books on Camarillo State Hospital which that hospital was once said to have been the most famous mental hospital In the world. Camarillo is located in Ventura County which is a little town out from Los Angeles California. It was famous because once up on a time it had house the famous musicians Charlie yard bird Parker whom had a nervous breakdown in1946 and was admitted to Camarillo State Hospital from June 29,1946 and released January 1947. However while during time at Camarillo State Hospital he wrote a song called relaxing' at Camarillo. However if you're interested in reading about him

You might be able to find books on Mr. Yard bird Parker at your local library he is worth reading about. I was a patient at Camarillo from February 11, 1968 until September 1968. I had suffered physical and mentally abused at the hands of teachers and students in junior high school. In high school, the abused was only from students. In high schools we are trying to be all we can be and a little more. However, some of us never make it to being the poplar kids whom others love to be friends to and hang with. There's the ok kids them the ones not poplar or a nerds, misfits, losers but ok. There's the anything goes kids them the ones sky's the limit they do anything just to be seen, There's the want to be, them the kids that want to be popular but not', they just put their self off on the poplar kids and do whatever they asked to do just to hang with them. There's the nerds them the ones that's smart makes all A's dresses funny and don't look to pleasing to the eye and the misfits them the kids that don't fit in anywhere they in a world of their own. And last but not least there's me the one with the big L tattooed on my forehead which stood for loser. I was the one nobody wanted to hang with because if they did they would be considering the same as I. I was the girl no young man took to the prom; I was the girl that was home alone on weekends, holidays, and no date for my sweet sixteen birthday party. I did have some friends later and they were consider as losers as I. However, they didn't care and they were very good friends to me. I was invited to parties but not for the right reason. I was only invited because the other kids thought I would make a fool out myself by trying to sing and dance which I was not going to do. I knew the reason why I was invited I was not that dumb. Now it is doing this time in your young life that you learn what true friends are. Such as a true friend will tell you the truth if you were going to make a fool out yourself doing something you think you can do but you can't. Let's say if you wanted to inter a talent contest because you thought you could sing now a true friend would tell you not to do it I know it's hard for some people to tell you the truth about something such as that because you might get mad or they may hurt your feeling which the truth sometimes hurts. A true friend will not tell you unnecessary things to hurt you, a true friend want tell you personal things around other people that should only be told in private. A true friend doesn't want to see you hurt in any kind of way and they want only the best for you. Now how many people can say they have a true friend not many I know. Now back to me being a loser. Now I was not the only loser however, at the time it seems like I was. When you are having it hard seem like you're the only one. Seem like I was in a world of my own. I did not know and didn't care I wasn't alone. Now as you will see in my story I'm not pulling any punches I'm telling you the truth and I'm telling you things the way god told them to me to tell you. Yes that's right god told me these things to tell you. However I'm not god massager I'm no saint nor anything such as that why me you may ask? Your gust is just as good as mine. You don't have to be a saint for god to give you something. Remembers Noah he was an alcoholic and god still gave him the ark. We will never really know god reason for doing thing. Even if you don't believe what I am telling you god didn't tell me you were going to believe me he just told me what to tell you. However I had to write down what five dead brothers told me to write down in order to get them to stop shaking my bed and hitting my wall inside and out and my window. You may think I'm ready for the nut house again. However that's ok to. I don't know why to this day I was the one god and they wanted to tell things I'm just telling it. look to the sky is a true heart breaking story from my childhood on into my adulthood. However today I'm doing ok thanks to my doctors and medications because when you going through what I been through that's something you can't go through along believe me, I tried.

Chapter 7

Bad news is usually the truth

People like for you to tell them what they want to hear and that's good news. However, the truth is hardly ever good news, in this life time we have to

PUT A HARD shell around our hearts to be able to cope in this world because not too much good news any more. Also there's more negativity around these days then there are positivity. It's hard to be a positive thinking person when everything around you is negative. However, to tell you the truth about life and what it holds for most of us is not good news. However, we must accept that most of our dreams won't come true; and that's what god told me and I won't lie to you. Most of us going to have heartache, and sorrow in life, most of us won't find true love and happiness no matter what some fortune teller or card reader have told you, it want happen for most of us, and later I be telling you why. However, my dreams never came true no matter how hard I prayed. Happiness and richness is something most of us won't know. God given us the necessities for life; he given us food, water; air, the rest we have to try and get it on our own with little to no success. Now if he sees we're helping ourselves, he will make it possible for us to have some of the things we want if he sees fit for us to have them. When it comes to our dreams of having many nice things, and love and happiness; don't look forward to all if any coming true. Most of us have to work hard just to get the common things rich people takes for granted. I'm sure most of you know this already, however if not I'm here to tell you most of us have to look forward to hard times, hard work; and never getting a head. Look forward to having only enough money to get by on. This is what life holds for most of us. The way some people get their money is by stealing, and cheating poor people out what little money they have and never look back. That kind of person does not have a conscious, there for people that have a conscious such as me will never have the things in life what a person without a conscious have. A person without a conscious will enjoy all the finest things in life, when a person with a conscious will work hard and never get a head. If you're not the kind of person that can walk all over others to get a head in life look to have very little of everything, If you're not the kind of person that can lie, and take from others you will stay where you're are in life it's sad but that's the price you pay for having a conscious. tWhen you have a conscious look to be used, look for people trying to get over on you. I just wanted you to see why some people have the finest things in life when others do not. If you cannot do just anything for money, you most likely will not live on top of the world; well what they call on top of the world. To me you are on top of the world when you have a nice clean place to lay your head and food to eat, family, and friends that love you and you all with good heath that is a blessing. Where we cannot lie, cheat, and steal from people we must stay poor. If a person can do these things to get ahead, stay away from that person. God blesses us to bless others he don't bless us to keep it all that's why he will bless some of us with lots of money. I said with god blessing taking from others that is not a blessing and believe me the poor will come out on top because the person that living wrong one day be found out. I said I want tell you no lie. Look to the sky covers many unhappy events in my life. Such as me dealing with infertility and the unwanted advice people was giving me about I could adopt which is not for me and my husband going out and getting a baby on me with another woman because I couldn't have kids he could have divorce me first I wouldn't had wanted him to stay with me if he wanted a child and I couldn't give him one it's just that he didn't have to do me that cold. And me as a twelve-year-old girl on unit 575 in Camarillo State Hospital, being the only black girl on the unit, I have to tell you I experience some racism back then. You would think by that being a mental hospital people wouldn't have sense enough to be racists oh but they did they knew the word Niger. I just thought I mention Camarillo State Hospital because you cannot find books on Camarillo. There for I just decided to let the reader know that I been in Camarillo State Hospital and I have a small write up about it to let you know there's nothing to be a shame of if you been in a place like that anybody can go and you don't have to be crazy. Back then all it had to take was a husband or wife wanting a divorce from the other one and if they didn't want to give it to them all the person had to do that wanted the divorce was to have the other person declared mentally unstable and have them put in a mental institution and it was no problem in getting the divorce as simple as that. Back then I heard now I don't know how true it is but the word was out when you had a person put in a mental hospital you were paid three hundred dollars. Now as I said I don't know how true it is. If that was true look at the people that was put away back then for nothing. I really do hope other people out there in the world that been in Camarillo would do a write up about it because that's a place worth writing about. I know I seen on the internet a person was asking people that been in Camarillo to write in about their experience at that hospital which I must tell you the formal patients weren't going to get a dime for sharing the time they spent in that hospital and not everybody crazy that spent time at Camarillo I don't think they knew that there for that person was going to make money off the one that didn't know any better than to sharing the story with that person and not getting a dime out it. See how people takes avenged on mental ill people. I decided to write my own book because nobody knows our story better then the people that been there and nobody should be paid for they story other then the people that lived their life there. I was there for six long months since I'm telling my story I have to live it over in my minds and I tell you it's not easy looking at that place on the internet. However as times goes by it don't get any easier. Whoever said time heals all wounds is wrong. You know the old saying there's somebody in the world for everybody; well I'm willing to bet you many people don't feel that way because they haven't found that somebody yet. Well to tell you the truth not everybody going to have true love and happiness because it all has to do with the energy that is surrounding us call auras and I will explain them to you. When we're young we may go for looks, however, as we get older we learn looks not that important anymore now we start to realize what is. We start to realize it's what's inside a person heart that counts. Also it has to do with auras. Now I will get into them.

Chapter 8

Introduction you to auras

THERE ARE DIFFERENT kinds of auras one is colors, and there is human energy fields, which is migraine aura that is migraine headaches and other neurological and image aura. The image aura is the aura that makes you a certain way and it attracts certain people to you. Now we have two image auras a positive aura and a negativity aura. Now some people may only set off their negativity aura because that's the energy surrounding them. The image Auras are the energy that is surrounds the person. If it's positive or negative you have no control over it. However if your energy not too strong and if you grow up in a positivity environment with negative energy sometimes you can kind of rise above it however not always more not then do. In addition, if the energy surrounding you is negative then you will only attract negativity people to you. Now we have no control over the kind of person we attract. It is not as if we go out looking for negativity people to treat us badly. Therefore, do not let anybody make you feel him or her is a better woman or man then you. Their no better then you it is the energy surrounding them is positive and yours is not. In addition, we may not ever have positive energy surrounding us. If not we will only have negative energy and negative energy will attract negativity to you. When your energy in negative you will have negative thoughts and you will have learning disability you will suffer from depressions you will have move swings you will have low paying jobs you will tend to draw negative people to you, you will tend to have low self-esteem. You will think less of yourself. You will feel you are never good enough. You will attract them that misused you and treat you badly your health won't be that well. On the other hand, if your aura is positive things will be the opposite. That's the reason why not everybody going to find true love and happiness no matter how hard you try, it just not for everybody and we must face facts, that's part of being an adult and that's being able to except what's not to be. However I know there's going to be negativity about my book how I know because

No matter what you do and how well you do it always look for more negativity then positivity because there's so many negativity giving people in the world. However, they not going to do anything expect voice their negativity opinion. Pay them no mind, just do your best and forget them.

Chapter 9

don't you know marriage
is not for everybody?

YES IT'S TRUE. Have you ever known of any one that been married more than three times without their spout dying and they always end up divorce? Don't matter what the reason may be, not everybody cut out for marriage. You cannot make it with a person that's not the husband and wife kind of person. Some women try forcing a man to marry them and that's the wrong thing to do, because you can't force him to stay with you. And don't try that I'm pregnant trick on him and if he marry you and as time goes by you not showing than you have to lie and say you miscarried. Whatever you do, don't be like the women my first husband use to have. Check it out, when my first husband and I got married I will say a week later my husband went out and when he come home he had some mess to tell me and that was a woman told him she had a two year old daughter by him. Now the kid she told him was two. I asked him don't that look funny a woman going to tell you she has a kid by you soon after we marry don't that look funny to you. I didn't want to hear no mess such as that, they was starting already. I couldn't have kids so they were starting up and the ink on our marriage license weren't even dry but it had started. Now we divorce. Now she said she never had a kid by my husband see there. Men don't fall for that same old out dated lie because it will happen it always do so look for it. There for men I will tell you this, if you marry a woman and some old use to be comes up to you telling you she have a kid by you soon after you marry don't go to your wife with that mess because first and most your wife don't want to hear it. I will tell you now it will be a lie. No woman waits two to three years before she tell a man she's pregnant, that's the first thing she will tell him and I mean if she's one day late she will tell him she's pregnant. Like I told my crazy forty one year old husband and you would think at that age he would be up on things but he was dumb and people knew it and they knew he would fall for anything age don't make you have any sense I found out. If some women don't have nothing going for themselves they will try everything there is to try if you two not together anymore and you have moved on and have somebody else and look like you two is happy, here she come trying to brake you two up. But nobody can break you up if you two is meant for each other. Marriage is not for everybody, everybody won't have children and some people dreams will never comes true no matter what you may have heard I'm being for real I wouldn't be writing this book and telling you just anything as long as I feel this what you want to hear just so you can buy my book. However, if you don't care to know the truths don't bother reading my book please, now on the other hand if you want to know the truth than here it is. Now I will tell you how negative people mind works. Some mothers have raised their sons in the right way and that's to be true to their woman or wife and if he has kids to do the best he can by his wife and kids. Now a man like that usually will get a woman that her mother have told her if you find a sucker bump his head, if you find a good one bump it twice. However, a negative thinking person they aura sets off negative energy. Now just because her daughter blessed to have a good man the mother feels her daughter's man is a sucker. However, the mother telling her daughter to used the hell out of him. I mean she going to used him up. Now this happens to a person when they try to do right by a negative thinking person. Now this turns a person off from wanting to do right by the next person. See when you have been use for a sucker, you going to make sure it won't happen again. The reason why it's so hard to find a decent person, because people don't know how to treat decent people and they don't appreciate them. Others feel if you do right by them you must be a sucker. That's what men taken me to be the biggest sucker of all time. That's what my own husbands thought about me, and I was only trying to be a good wife. However, nothing I ever did was good enough. I just stop trying. I just gave up and when I stop trying my love was gone. Once a person looses love for you it's not coming back. There for, the only thing to do is move on; because once the love is gone the respect leaves also. When there's no love and respect in a relationship the relationship in over, done with; you should move on. I refused to be use as a sucker by men again. Some people you can't be nice to because they will take you for a sucker every time. That's a true saying, there's a thin line between love and hate. Two people with positive energy with positive thinking the two of you may have something in common with each other. In order to make a relationship work the two of you have to have something in common. However, you cannot pretend for too long you have something in common with a person when you don't. Lying to get into a relationship or to stay in a relationship will not work for very long because you will get tired of pretending to like something when you know you don't. Just be honest with yourself and the person. if you don't like something tell a person and don't be afraid to tell a person you don't like something thinking if you don't go along with what the other person likes they going to find somebody else that likes what they likes. That's what they should do and you should find somebody like yourself that likes the same things as you. After reading my story I hope you see things clearer than before. I am an amputee due to a drive by shooting; however this how look to the sky came to be. I will be explaining things to you the way God explained them to me when I asked why bad things happens to good people, asking about myself. I'm not saying I'm a good old god fearing woman and every time the church door open I'm in it no I'm not saying that, however I am saying I don't do people wrong, I don't take what's not mine ; I don't tell things on people not true. Now some people can do all the above and living the kind of life some of us only dream of. However, I had to remember the old saying god doesn't like ugly and he's not crazy about pretty, this why bad things happen to good people. I asked God why some people has a happy childhood, when others do not, and why some people has so much money they don't know what to do with it; when others don't have enough money to hold them over from one month to the next. Why are there's people living in a sixteen bed room mansion, when some people are homeless and works so hard when the person that living in the mansion not working at all and has everything they ever wanted and need. I kind of explained that to you. However, in some people childhood they only knew the best things in life when others all they knew was hungry cold days and nights and so cold and hungry at night they couldn't get to sleep. But still they had to go to school because they knew with god and their hopes and dreams maybe they would have a better life a head. Our childhood is the most important years of our life it can have a lot to do with the kind of adult we become. Our childhood should be happy and care free with no worries in the world because we're going to have enough of that in our adulthood such as getting in relationships and jobs.

With some people their childhood are the worst years of their life. My story covers a lot of abused which nobody shouldn't let themselves go through, You should love yourself enough to stand up for yourself and stand up for what you believe is right no matter what others may and may not believe. I will tell you any kind of abused as a child can have a major affect on your mind and having you thinking other people are better than you and whatever is said about you as a child can have a major affect on your mind in your adulthood. If people told you that you was dumb and useless as a child some people will grow up believing they is dumb and useless and no good for themselves and nobody else. On the other hand, if you were told positive things about yourselves such as your smart and you can be whatever you want to be as a child you will think highly of yourself as an adult and you will be a positive person. You must learn at a very young age to think positive as well as negative. However, whichever one you are it will show in everything you do and say and it will show in the company you keep. A positive thinking person not going to have a negative thinking person for a lover because they know that kind of person don't have anything in comma with a positive thinking person. Positive+ negative = what? However positive plus positive=positive and negative plus negative=negative see what I mean. You must keep with a positive person if you are a positive person. In addition, my story covers ghost stories I mean real ghost stories, there for if you never believe in such thing as a ghost then maybe after reading my book it will make you think twice. I want to tell you before I get deeper in my story: *Life for some reason we will never understand it, but that is ok because if God wanted us to understand his reason for things we would. In addition, I wanted to let children see what all I been through and I still made it through high school. I want them to see what hell I went through without having the proper education it takes to get a good job and to know how I was treated on jobs and how I was made to feel like I was a nobody. Don't ever let anybody make you feel that way. You were somebody the day you were conceived. This why I say please get your education so can't nobody ever tell you that you in no position to tell them anything and you can be gotten a dime a dozen that's all your worth to them ten people for a dime and two free. Other words what they saying is your worth nothing and after being told that you have to go back to work and even if nothing you do is worth anything you still must work like a dog and try to forget about what you been told and do your best every day with all that mess on your mind and you must hold back the tears and never let the boss see you cry, never let him or her know how much they hurt you. I can remember one day I was so hurt that I couldn't hold back the tears and I seen the glow in this nurse eyes when I cried this why I said don't give nobody the satisfaction in knowing how much they hurt you, just keep your head up and think about happy things while they talking to you so that way you want cry. In addition for as ever smiling if I did it was said I was not doing my work and I was told something to bring me back down they thought, however little did they know every day of my life I was down and as down as one could get. A person can smile without being happy a person can smile and be ready to do some harm. I was not smiling because I was happy, I was never happy. If my book can get just one child back in school I will feel that my book have done some good. I been in a mental hospital and I made it through high school there for I know you can I have faith in every one of you I know you can do it and I know you can go to college and make something out of yourself. In junior high school I was consider a loser, you know I caught hell. In addition I also want parents to know when your child comes and tell you what's goes on in his or her school you believe your child. In addition, never believe any teacher or another child over your child because teachers and kids will lie and never get on your child for taking up for themselves.*

As long as your child don't fight back and let kids beat on them nobody will call you to tell you your child don't fight back now as soon as your child get fed up and knock the hell out of the bully look for your phone to ring but never stop your child from standing up for themselves because if they don't nobody going to do it for them. Make your child feel good about his or herself and tell them no matter what they just as good as anybody else and tell them while their young don't wait until the child is grown before you tell them these things because by then what ever way they feel about themselves is the way they always will feel. See when a person feels good about themselves they will never be a follower they will always be a leader. When people feel good, about themselves, they will take nothing off anybody, they will demand respect, and they will feel nobody is better than they are. When a person feels good about themselves it shows. However it shows in everything they do it shows in the way they carries themselves, it shows in the way they talk even in the way they walk and in the way they dress and that kind of person knows what they want and want settle for less. On jobs, they will speak up and speak out if they don't like something. They want let people walk all over them. Only kind of person that will take abused off anybody is a person that's afraid of a person or a person that doesn't think highly of his or her self. However, all this shows in a person and this is a very unhappy person. This kind of person is bond to have heart problem later in life due to all the stress of keeping their mouth close, remember a close mouth don't get fed. This by no means is good on your health. A person that tells a person where to get off tends to be a healthier and a happier person and nine time out of ten this person will outlive a person that keeps their mouth close. And people may think letting people run over them make other like them however I'm here to tell them it don't that only make them disrespect you and feel as your nobody. Also I like for parents to tell their children while they still young because they grow up so fast tell them that people will pretend to be their friend when they not. They must realize people don't always have their best interest at heart and not to have anything to do with that person. And to tell if a person your friend just see how they treat you when the two of you is by yourself and check out the way they treat you when others come up. Notice if they whistling things to their friends they don't want you to hear, see if they only invite you to things to make fun of you with their other friends. See if they always asking you for money and never paying you back. Do they only want you with people they laugh at because they think you're silly? Don't ever have anything to do with that person their no friend to you and never will be that kind of person will get you hurt just to get a laugh. A true friend wants the best for you they want to see you happy and want nothing you got they won't backstab you in anyway. There for we can't take everybody for a friend because they don't come a dime a dozen.

Chapter 10

My fondest memory of school

I MUST SAY, EVEN if I did have it tough back in school them fieldtrips, and art classes; and story time, was my most fondest memory back in elementary. Now at story time I can recall our teacher reading us children stories and no matter what the story was about the ending was always the same with they lived happily ever after. In addition, if it was a love story the woman would meet her prince charming and they marry and have the house with the white picket fence, and two kids; and a dog, and a cat. However, the stories were just fairytales. How well do we know in real life hardly does any woman meet her prince charming, hardly do she get the house with the white picket fence. Most marriages end in divorce, and hardly ever are there a happy ending. "We have to forget about the fairytale life we once knew as children, and welcome life as it is, which is the real life. In real life we have to play the hand we been dealt. Some people hand going to be better than the hand we been dealt, however that's life. No matter how nice some people may be, some people will have the worst luck in life you can imagine. This why the bible reads, god don't like ugly and he's not crazy about pretty. Which mean he not crazy about right doing. Now this may be confusing to some people, you may ask; if god not crazy about us doing the right thing then why god wants us to do the right thing? What this mean is god don't have favors. That's why I say and will tell people, no such people going to hell and no such people going to heaven; if there was a heaven, and hell ;since it's not, where do you think we will stay? You're right, if you said we will stay here on earth. However, no matter what kind of hand we're dealt in life we can't throw our hand back in. Imagine my life, at times it have seem like I had the worst hand ever been dealt to a person. However, I know now that never been the case. No matter how bad our life may be it can always be worse. I know that don't make you feel any better. As the old saying goes when life deals you lemons, you make lemonade. Well here's my recipe for the best lemonade in the world. This is experiencing life and experiencing hard difficult times. Now with these two things in my life being my lemons now here is my lemonade my book. See god let us go through hard times to learn to make our way out of them and to make our minds strong. Understand nobody comes in the world with a strong mind it's going through hard difficult times in life that makes the mind strong. Not everything in life can be easy we have to go through hard times to learn to appreciate the good and to learn to make it when times are hard. See take a person that always had an easy life and never had to work for anything they get, they get it just by asking. Now let's say that stops and now that person have to go out and work for what they want however times get hard for them do you think that person will have the knowhow to take care of their self? Maybe and maybe not however the person that been going through hard times all their life there's no doubt about it that person will know how to take care of their self that person will know how to make it. In addition, the person that always had to work for a living appreciates what they have. Now the person that never worked for anything nothing they get they usually don't appreciate what they get. That's why it's good to have a child work around the house for things they want that way they will learn to appreciate things. You have to learn to appreciated people and things. A hard life can turn out to be the best life after all and it can turn out to be our learning tree which in life can be our best teacher and our best friend a lone the way. When life is easy it teaches us nothing however when we makes mistake and go through hard difficult times that's when and only when we learn. Sometimes our mistakes can be costly sometimes we may lose things in the end but we have gain knowledge and knowledge is power. Now let me pour you a glass of my lemonade in look to the sky: which means look to Jesus.

LOOK TO THE SKY

Chapter 11

our family's history

OUR FAMILY HISTORY goes as far back when our family was slaves which they was our ancestors and they would work in them hot fields until their hands and feet's be red and blistered and bleeding from the hard back-breaking work they be doing and they would be in the hot sun all day sometimes they would feel they couldn't no longer go on and that's when they would sing to give them strength. Singing was telling the hurt and pain in their life, the hurt and pain only they knew. They knew they couldn't stop working even if their hands and feet's and backs and legs are hurting. There for our family not taking care of their blisters on their feet' they would be infected. If they had, what use to be known as sugar diabetics now it's known as a person being diabetes. Anyway, if the blisters on their feet were infected and if they had sugar diabetes they would have to have their feet's amputated. They had to use roots and plants for medication. They didn't know what a doctor or medication was. What others would do because some people didn't dip snuff but the ones who did would take the snuff out their mouth and rub it on the blisters and they would soon heal. Now I will tell you about some of the things our ancestors invented and built. Our ancestors builds the white house yes, they sure did, the slaves built the white house, even if they were not allowed in it they still built it. I'm going to tell children something they don't teach them in school. That is about our ancestors inventions. Slaves just about invented everything there is to invent. Yes, unbelievably our ancestors invented the self-starting gas engine, and in New York City where the Stock Exchange is located, run along what was once the wall of a fort built by slaves. Wall Street and much of the city's renowned financial district were built on the burial ground of African slaves. Slaves invented the Gas Mask, automatically oil machinery, blood transfusion, wash machine, the steam Boiler Furnace, The steam engine, Street Sweeper Supercharger for Automobiles, the first flush toilet, Toilet for Railroad Cars, Tricycle, Turn Signals, Typewriter, the OWERTY keyboard, Permanent Wave Machine (for perming hair) Postmarking and Canceling Machine, Printing Press, Propeller for ships, Refrigerator, Rotary Engine, Screw Socket for Light Bulb, Smallpox Vaccine, The traffic light, Self starting gen engine, the ironing board and the iron the rocking chair. This just some things our ancestors invented, there are many more things the slaves invented but it will take a while to write them all down. So this is to show our young black children that all people no matter who you maybe we all are very impotent and we all make up this world and no one is any better than anyone else. Even if our ancestors never went to school they were bless to have the knowhow to invent thing that is still useful to day. They all have pass on but their inventions lives forever. Now what our young people should do is think of one invention they like the most and think of ways to improve it to make it better so it can keep up with time. Now you see the slaves was very smart people but back in them days a slaves had no rights at all so there for they couldn't get a patent on any of their inventions, there for they would have their master go and get the patent for them and sometimes their master would have the patent put in their own name there for the master would take credit for the inventions. Then to if, the slaves could have the inventions put in their names they couldn't read or write and if they could, they couldn't let it be known by their master because they could be killed. See their masters knew knowledge is power and the masters didn't want the slaves have any knowledge they wanted to keep them dumb that way they could have control over them. As I said, knowledge is power if the salves didn't have knowledge they didn't have power. The masters had knowledge there for they had power. See why the masters didn't want the slaves to have any schooling. Now some of the young people today that can go to school but some don't. that means they want people to have power over them and they don't want knowledge they don't feel they worthy of knowledge. They feel they have to have somebody else that have power be over them and that came from slavery and I think they want to go back because they have all the opportunity to go to school and many don't, there for what does that tell you. I'm going to tell you something that they do not teach us in school and this is black slaves is not the original slaves there for who is? Caucasian people aka white people yes they was the original slaves however you have to look it up because the only slaves we will ever hear about is the black slaves. Anything negative about black people they teach you in school however if you want to learn about anything positive about black people you have to look it up or wait till you're in high school and take black history it's a shame however that's how it is. This why I told about the inventions our black people

Invented. Even today black people are still inventing different things. However like myself we can't afford the patent and the patent lawyer, we have to let it go and other people that can afford to have our invention patent they get them and have their names put on the patent and you will never know who really invented the things. Also I will tell you that the original cowboys was black, yes it's true. I know we were watching Roy Rogers the king of the west, this how black cowboys originated. We all know black men were call boy didn't matter if he was 80, it was still boy. However they road horses in the rodeo and they would jump off the horse and take the cattle by the horns. There for the black men= boy the cattle=cow. There for the cattle =cow+ the black man=boy, put cow and boy together you have cowboy. Do you know where the world cracker comes from? And I don't mean a cracker you eat. I'm talking about the word people call some people? Well you know that word come from slavery? You didn't well let me tell you how it came about. The slaves would be out in the fields working and if they stop and the bosses see they weren't working he would come with his whip which the slaves would call it cracking the whip when he be beating them, there for they would call the boss the cracker. They would look up and see the boss coming with his whip and say here come the cracker. Do you know where redneck comes from? It comes from the red scarf hillbillies would wear around the necks. See how harmless words can change. Gay once up on a time meant happy. I just want to let you know how harmless some words use to be. Boy is a harmless world however it's who you say it to and how it's used; now getting to my story.

Chapter 12

About the Author

MY NAME IS Dorothy Ann Darrough (AKA) Dorothy Ann Johnson some of the Darrough spell it Dorrough it don't matter it's just however you want to spelling it. I was born in little Rock Arkansas to a seventeen years old single mother named Maybelline Dabney on June 21, 1955. My father was nineteen years old. His name was Frank Darrough Junior. He since has passed away but I was blessed to meet him before his passing. I always have been overweight and in Grad School, I was picked on over my weight. Before I inter junior high school, I dieted and walked off twenty pounds. However, I went from being called fat to being called ugly and other names. That told me something and that was with true friends they will love you and except you just the way you are. You don't have to change a things. I learn that at an early age and this goes for true love as well. Love a person as they are and when a person love you they want you to be happy, your happiness means most of all they never want to see you unhappy they never want to see a tear in your eye and they don't want anybody to make you unhappy. When you unhappy their unhappy that's how truelove is. Now I know this is hard to believe but it is true so god help me. Teachers would provoke the kids when I was in junior high school to pick on me and they would just stand there and smile when the kids would be picking on me. Yes if the kids wouldn't be picking on me the teachers would start the kids picking on me. Now not all the kids would go for that they just look sad with their heads down and they would say don't cry Dorothy. Well I went through both emotional and physical abuse. Then depression took over my life just as it will do and with that I would withdraw from everything and everybody. There for I was sent to Camarillo State Hospital back in February the eleven nineteen sixth eight. How that place was? The only way for me to explain it is being dead or in a deep coma and never coming out of it is better than being there. Now that's the words for explaining that place.

Chapter 13

how my roots begin

IAM GOING TO *close my eyes and imagine I am going back in time, to a time before I was born, a time before my mother was born a time before my grandmother was born. A time before my great grandmother was born, a time when my family was slaves and they were given only one pair of shoes per year. However, in the wintertime, their feet's would be cold and bleeding from blisters that was on their feet's from the snow and the blisters would be infected and smelling. However, it would be blood all in the snow from my family feet's. It was at a time the slaves would designed quilts for secret maps for others slaves could follow when they took the danger route to freedom. However, it was at a time when they would name two lines of seven starts that was shape like the dipper they would use to dip their water with. One line of starts looked like a big dipper and the other looked like a little dipper gust what they named them? That's right the big deeper and the little deeper they both was made up of seven stars and was on the north side of the sky. Now this big star didn't look like anything but a stair this was the biggest star in the sky and it was on the north side of the sky and it would shine brighter than any star in the sky and the ones that didn't have quilts to fallow would fallow this star and it would guide them away from the plantation to the underground railroad where white families would hide them in their houses till night so they could start their damager journey to freedom. What was the name of this star? You're right if you said the northern star. It was at a time when they would tell time by the position of the sun. It was at a time when my family would have a secret song only they would know the meaning to such as sweet chariot the gospel song it went like this. Swing low sweet chariot coming for to carry me home swing low, sweet chariot coming for to carry me home. I looked over Jordan and what did I see coming for to carry me home a band of angels coming after me coming for to carry me home. If you get there before I do tell everybody I'm coming to coming for to carry me home. Now as I said this was a secret song only the slaves would know. Such as the part that goes I looked over Jordan which was the code name for the Mississippi River, and a band of angels coming after me. The band of angles was the Underground Railroad which was houses where white families lived that had hideaway places where they would hide the slaves until late at night until the slaves could get away and them people could be killed themselves helping the slaves to escape to freedom. The part that's goes if you get there before I do which mean if you get freed before I be freed tell everybody I'm coming to. Which mean tell everybody I'll be freed to. There for that was their journey to freedom. Another song they would sing was Michael row the boat ashore. Now who was Michael I was not told that because nobody knew any way this song was telling Michael to row his boat to the shore so the slaves could get on it to escape to freedom. My brothers and sisters is all aboard the river is deep and the river is wide milk and honey on the other side which means freedom on the other side. Jordan's river is chilly and cold chills the body and not the sold which means the body is cold as hell but they was going to make it to freedom no matter how cold it was because it didn't get to cold for them to not try because they sold was worm. You may call the slaves strong people however they was not strong they was determined people so determined that they would risk dying trying to make it to freedom. Now also I have to say they all tried so hard to make it to freedom now they have made it now their sold are free at last. They died for day's they would never see this is the reason why look to the sky was able to come in focus thanks guys and thank you Underground Railroad for helping my family to escape to freedom. Now this telling about my great great grandparents which was slaves back in slavery when it was ageist the law for black people to go to school they did not have the right to read and write. If they was caught doing so they could be killed. It was at a time when slaves couldn't leally marry what they would do was jump the broomstick. Where this came from people wasn't sure. They would jump the broomstick together. Their master wouldn't let them sleep together afterward. It was at a time when slaves were taken from their families and sold. It was at a time when most slaves didn't know who they were. They couldn't know who they were when most slaves didn't know where they were from. Such as a young woman who was my great, great grandmother whom names I forgotten meets a man everybody forgotten his name while she was working hard in the field in Birmingham Alabama. The man was pulling a mule a long with two big water cans tied to the mule's back. The man was taking the others slaves' some water. My great, great grandmother and the man meets and they likes each other and after dating about two years they jump the broom that means to married in the slave's terms. After a year or so my grate, grate, grandmother gives birth to a baby girl she names Lonnie. Lonnie grows up and meets a young man name Charles Reels and they hit it off well. There for a year on in their relationship they jump the broom. A year later Lonnie gives birth to a little baby girl she name Cora Lee Reels on June 3th 1903. Cora father dies while she is still very young so her mother meets another man and at this time, Cora is five years old. My grandmother mother puts my grandmother Cora in school, which she was in the first grad because back in them days there was no kindergarten so at age five you was in the first grad. After only one day of school when my grandmother Cora comes home, her mother would have some sad news to tell my grandmother Cora and that was her stepfather says she cannot attend school another day. I tell you that really did hurt my grandmother. Therefore, she never learns to read, write, and count. However, nobody could beat her out of one red cent. Even if she could not count, she knew when somebody miscounted her money better than I, and I spent a little time in collage. In addition, my grandmother was a smart lady she may not had school knowledge however, she had street knowledge and I tell you the little lady could stand eye to eye with the best. Well anyway, my grandmother Cora grows up and moves from Birmingham to Little Rock ARK taking her mother with her. By this time, her stepfather had passed away do to stomach cancer. Now while in Little Rock Cora meets a man name Joe Dabney one hot summer day on Sunday while she was attending church. In addition, they liked each other, and sometime later they would marry, and out of the marriage 12 children was born with my mother Maybelline Dabney being the 12th child. However at age fifth teen my mother meets a man by the name of Frank Darrough Junior while she was at a friend's home. They like each other however they would never marry because my grandmother who was Maybelline mother did not care for my father. However I was conceive two years later my mother was seventeen and my father was ninth teen now here is my story. I was born Dorothy Ann Dabney to Maybelline Dabney and frank Darrough JR in Little Rock Arkansas on June 21-1955 at 9: pm the first day of summer. This is the longest and the hottest day of the year. My mother was in the hot field chopping cotton all that day when her water broke. She started having labor pains with me. An old man told her to go home because I was on my way. However, she keeps on working and when the day was over she went home and I was born at 9: PM that night. After I was born, she would take me to the field with her. She would lay me down on her cotton sack and pull me along when it was cotton picking time and talking about people backs hurting because they had to bend over to pick cotton. I remember a lady that had picked cotton for so many years that her body was bended over in the way to pick cotton. She had lived to be an old lady and still in her mind, she was still picking cotton. She was in the rest home and she would not eat unless we tell her she had already paid for the food. It was hot in them fields and the work was hard with little pay. The cotton choppers pay was four dollars per day two dollars in the morning and two dollars in the evening and cotton pickers were paid by the pounds of cotton they would picked. There were not any free money nothing was free accept hard times now they got more than they could handle.*

Everything they got they had to work hard for it. I can remember my grandmother telling me about the time when she was a little girl she recalled her mother taking her to work with her and her mother was working in these people house even if she was a midwife she only worked when there was babies to be delivered in the meanwhile she would do house work. Grandmother told me she would witness her mother cleaning out them people outhouse restroom with her necked hands, I do mean the stool in the outhouse, and after work she had to go home and cook dinner now imagine that. Why cleaning that outhouse with her necked hands never made her sick, no one knows. I do not remember anything about Little Rock Arkansas because I was so young, there for all I can tell you is the stories my family told me and I know every one of the stories was true because every one of the stories been told to me over and over again by different members of my family. Then to my family wouldn't lie about back home and I have seen things on TV my family have talked about. And my family and other people from back home had not too happy stories to tell me about back home because people was so poor and times was so hard back there. There for I have put together their stories one by one and I'm telling them the way they were told to me starting with my mother because she had the most to tell. My mother told me back home in Little Rock Arkansas during this time where they lived there was no school buses for the black students there for they had to walk miles to school in the rain in the snow whatever. My mother told me the white students would pass the black students by in their school buses and call out to the black students Niger! As far as they could see the black students and at this time all schools were segregated. However when blacks had to go to the store they had to inter from the back of the store and black people couldn't buy coca cola because it was said to have had cocaine in it and it might make the Niger's go crazy and they may kill up the white people the white storeowners would say. However I have white people in my family I'm just going by the way the story was told to me and then to this was the way people talked back then because they didn't know any better you talked according to the way you was raised, I wanted to write my book the way the stories was related to me. In addition, when Blacks went to the store to buy sunbeam bread if the blacks just ask for sunbeam bread the white storeowner would ask them what did you say? If you want this bread, you had better say miss sunbeam or little miss sunbeam do you hear me Niger? Or boy if you was a man didn't matter if you were an 80 year old man it was still boy white people didn't have any respect for black people. In addition, there were some nice looking black men in Little Rock Ark and some of them had wives and didn't fool around on their wife. However, there would be some white women that would have their eyes on them black men and they went after them black men. The black men would turn the white women down and the white women would tell the black men I'm going to tell you rape me Niger! There for they would have to get the hell out of Little Rock Ark if he wanted to live. I was told we had a good looking cousin back there and many white women just was in love with him. He use to ride a motor cycle and one nigh he was on his way home and some white men in an old truck that had pitch folks and drove them in him pulling his guts out and he died on the road where he was left. Since I'm on the subject of black people and school I just decided to let people know what they never told student back then in school and not even now. Let me tell you this first then I will get to the rest. Now first I know it always been said George Washington was the first president of the United State of America however he was not. He was actual the eighth president of the United State. During this time, there was no Constitution of the United State of America. However when the Constitution of the United State was written by Gouvemeur Morris of Pennsylvania that made George Washington be the first president under the Constitution. However believe it or not the first president of the United State was a black man by the name of John Hanson however you may not be able to find his name because it may be lost in history however he was the first President of the United State from 1781 till 1782 AD. However, they didn't know at the time that John Hanson was a black man. There were many black people then that pass for white there's movie starts today that's black but pass as white. I know people thinks that president Obama is the first black President of the USA however, he is not. He's the only one they know about and even being the president of the USA it's still a different in the way he being treated. Another thing God told me to tell people it's not true what being said about why black people are black because of the cursed Noah put on his son when Noah was drunk and he lay asleep in his tent butt naked when his son seen him that way he laughs at his father nakedness and as a result Noah cursed his son and told him he's less than other white people. God tells me no truth in that he said he created all man equal and he told me that some of his people is bless to have dark skin yes he said it's a blessing to have dark skin he said depending on where you lived in the world the sun is hotter and he put a shield over the skin to shield you from sun burn. He said man destroyed the bible and put what he wanted to put in it he destroyed it just like he destroyed the world. Back to my story, you may still be able to find John Hanson and read about him if you don't believe me.

Do you know how the word lynching was originate

If not I will tell you, back in slavery in the 1700 there was this kkk man by the name of Charles Lynch, and he would hang slaves. There for the other kkk take the name lynch from Charles Lynch for hanging slave back in slavery. There for they would say we going to lynch a runaway slave today kkk brothers.

Another thing, I just thought I add in this don't have anything to do with school but it have something to do with a song I know most of old school have heard. And that's the song of Frankie and Johnny: However what I know you have not heard and that is the really Frankie and Johnny were two black lovers from New York. Yes they were "black" I know it was played by Elvis Presley and Donna Douglas.

Chapter 14

However, they were not white; well here's how the real story goes.

SURE FRANKIE AND Johnny was lover and I tell you Johnny was bad with a knife and people were afraid of him because he didn't take any mess. However Frankie was a little woman and Johnny would mess over her with other women and he would go all the time living Frankie at home alone. Well one night Frankie decided

She would go out; well she went to this club where Johnny was now she didn't come to start any mess she didn't know that Johnny was even there. However somebody called out to "Johnny" Johnny! Here come Frankie, Well Johnny

Come out side where Frankie was and pushing on her to go home because he would beat the hell out of her and she knew this, there for she had went and both her a gun because she was fed up with Johnny beating on her so that night he started in on beating her and that's when she came out with her gun and shot him she didn't mean to kill him but he died. However she was still living when somebody comes out with the story Frankie and Johnny. Frankie told them to tell the story right because that was not the way the story goes. However, they never did and Frankie ended up in a mental institution from losing her mind because the real story was never told. Now that's the real story of Frankie and Johnny. But, what you didn't know that the real Frankie and Johnny were black.

Chapter 15

Back to my roots

BLACK FAMILIES WAS so poor and even back then there were single blacks mothers left alone to fend for themselves and their kids the best they could because my grandmother were one of them mothers left alone with kids to do the best she could with little of much. That's the reason white women would call black women strong and tell them they couldn't do it alone like black women and how do they do it? In addition, say if I had to do it all by myself I couldn't make it. My god you black women are so strong. Black woman was not strong back then just like they not today it's just that you do what you have to do and you cannot say what you can't do unless you put in that situation because you just might one day find yourself during what you said you couldn't do.

Chapter 16

What my mother told me

MY MOTHER TOLD me when she was a little girl they were so poor they didn't have toys at any time. In addition, at Christmas she told me she would take cornstalks and make her dolls. Now with times being as hard as they were back there some men would still leave their family to make it the best way they could. My mother father left them to take care of another woman and her kids and dam his own. The other woman use to be friends to our grandmother. The way my mother found out that their father was going with their mother best friend the woman daughter told my mother that their father would come to their house and go to their mother bedroom window and take his trouser off and leave them on the ground outside her mother bedroom window and climb in bed with the mother. Now when their father was home he didn't buy any food until Sunday and that's when that woman was coming over. After my mother father left them one day she was over the woman house and she overheard the woman mother asking her what you see in Joe? He's black and ugly what do you see in him? The woman answers see mother he's so good to my kids and me. My mother told her father what she had heard and he beat her butt. One day my mother was crying about something and the woman asked her what you caring for I should be the one crying after what you told your father. When my mother and aunt would go over their father house the woman kids would be outdoors playing and my mother and aunt would be setting on the porch not playing and the woman would tell our mother and aunt you guys not playing like my kids because you guys to hungry to run and play like my kids. Now their father was taking care of some other woman kids and his was without everything no food, shoes, clothes no decent place to stay wife didn't even have pads to hide the blood from her monthly. One day my mother went over his house and asked her father for a little money to buy food for the house hold he tells her he had a family to take care and that would be the other woman and her kids. My mother and my aunt Annette had worked in the fields all summer to buy a bedroom set and their father moved it out the house from them and gave it to his wife for her kids. My mother brother left for the army and he would send money back home to his father to give to his mother for my mother and Aunt Annette. When he comes home from the army and asked his father about the money he sent home for his mother and his sisters his father told him he didn't have it because he had spent it on his wife and her kids. When my mother was a little girl in school she said she would take one sock, cut it in half, and make two socks out of one sock and people would give her mother old shoes they did not want. The shoes would be for women and they would have high heels so my mother told me she would cut the heels off the shoes, there for the toe of the shoes would stick up but that never matter to my mother she was happy to have some shoes. Back then most people done the best they could with what little bit they had and they felt bless to have it. Back in the days, most people believed in god and prayer. That was all they had, god and prayer and their faith in god and their hopes and dreams of a better life.

Nevertheless, flew people would take their faith and hopes and dreams with their believed in god and turn them in to reality. Now unlike my family they took their hopes, dreams, and their believed in god and made a better life for themselves. It is good to pray however, you must get up off your knees and do something to help yourself. Other words you must do something about what you is praying for. See god help them who help themselves. When you make one-step god makes two. Now the things my mother told me they would see living in the woods when she was a little girl such as big hairy things that would come in their house would chill you to the bone. My family told me one night when they was all in bed they seen this woman appear in a long black dress and the woman run her hand over my grandmothers' face. My mother told me about the time they all stayed in this old shotgun house far back in the woods. That's where poor black families would live far back in the woods in old shotgun houses, Or chicken coups, they were not chicken coups, but that's what my mother told me kids would call their old house. She told me the way the kids found out where they lived because they never did let the other kids know where they lived because at the time they didn't know how bless they was to just have a house to live in because some people didn't have that. Well one day some people was having a hayride for the kids and my family was asks to come alone and they told the kids no because they had something to do that day, they didn't but they didn't want the kids to know where they lived. Well luck would have it that day of the hayride my family would be outdoors and the kids was going for their hayride when they pass by my family house and seen my family outside and they all pointed and laugh and said they lived in a chicken coup. Now when I said shotgun house I know some people don't know what kind of house that is so I will explained what kind of house that is or was because nobody knows for sure if that kind of house still exist today. However a typically shotgun house has one room leading into the next room without hallways this style of house is particularly well suited for hot climates and the houses didn't look that well however nevertheless people took care of what little bit they had no matter what it was or how it looked. If it was yours, you took care of it and were glad to have it. The boards on my family house were so far apart that they could look out doors. Their house had dirt floors and talking about the snake's man, I tell you there were so many snakes in poor family's houses. Anyway late one rainy night when my family were home my grandmother was sitting under this window in the living room when something hit this window and the board fallen off and hits my grandmothers behind her neck and like to broken it. Whatever this thing was looked through the hole where the board uses to be and was trying to talk. I tell you my family told me it was hell living in Little Rock Arkansas benign poor as they were. My mother told me they would pick cotton all day and the sack they put their cotton in would be the same sack they would sleep on that night. My mother told me when people said they were going to hit the hay they meant it because some people would sleep on hay

> *Because everybody didn't have a bed, People didn't think about what they didn't have, they just tried to keep body and soul together and what I been told that was hard for the people that had little to no education because the only kind of work it was for them was field work, or cleaning house if you was lucky or babysitting.*

Now as I said there was snakes back there and I will tell you about the one they called the chicken snake why they called it the chicken snake nobody know. However one day my mother had went fishing and she had taken me alone and she had laid me on my blanket beside her while she was fishing and she happen to look down over at me and here was a chicken snake headed for my throat. She picked me up and start running and the snake was running behind her and a woman that was out fishing also had her hole with her for snakes and she ran behind the snake and killed it. Little rock Arkansan had all kind of snakes back there and even in fields where the worker would be working but people had to work no matter what they still had to take care of themselves and their family didn't matter if you was a woman left by yourself with kids you had to work your but off taking care of your kids the best you could. Women couldn't depend on men like most can't today. There for they had to hit those hot fields like men's in the summer and there were field rats, which the snakes would eat. Some things my family told me about back home they were joking which I found out after I was grown, now I will tell you one. I would say I was around sixteen and I was looking

Dorothy Ann Johnson

through this book that had back home houses where black families lived. However I notice all the houses was build on top of bricks. I ask my family why that was. My family would tell me back home white people would build the black people houses on top of big bricks so when a strong wind come up it would blows the Niger's away. I always believe whatever they told me until I start working in the Convalescent hospital. Now this what happen one day while I was working in the Convalescent Hospital a patient was looking through her family albums and when she laid it down I seen white families' with their houses built on top of big bricks also, there for I asked her why was the houses built on bricks she told me when a rain storm came up I said look out to myself I gust black people use to live there and white people moved in and they didn't take the houses off the bricks for the white families I said to myself. She explained when a rainstorm came the water would go under the house if the water weren't too deep there for your house wouldn't be swept away. That's when I realize my family was only joking. Also my family told me about the kind of fishing which is known as Niger fishing now what this is when you cast your line out in the river and you take your pole and stick it up in the grown and put rocks around it to hole it up this the lazy way to fish this why it called Niger fishing which is for lazy Niger's because black people was called lazy and there for it was said that's how black people fish which I have seen many people fish like that because they would have many fishing poles and they couldn't hold all of them there for that's how they would have them. As I said, anything that had to do with something negative it was blame on blacks then and now. AIDES mostly in the black race it always have been said. That's the reason why young white kids didn't think they could get it because all they ever heard were it mainly was in the black race. There for believing such thing they would bed down with many people without practicing safe sex as long as their partner weren't black they thought they were safe. However, all the time they never did think about if that was true other races mix all the time. Telling a person this is very misleading.

Chapter 17

the snake the called the joining snake

I WAS TOLD ABOUT the snake they called the joining snake. They called it the joining snake because when you hit it; where ever you hit it, its body would come apart then join back together. If you hit the head the snakes head go roaming through the field looking for its body if the snake couldn't find it's body because some people would dig a hole and put the snakes body in it and cover it up so the head couldn't find it's body there for the snake would die. Yes you would see a snakes head looking for its body addition, if the snake finds its body, the head would join back on to its body but if the snake did not find its body, the snake would die does that sound scary. My family told me just some back home ghost stories and by the way I will be telling some ghost stories myself and believe it or not my ghost stories is about right here in Bakersfield California yes its places here is haunted as hell I know. One story my family told me about back home was about a light they would all see in their house. I'll tell you the story. I was told when our family was little they would see this mysterious light that would change shapes that be moving around in their house when there was no light in their house that could give in the count of that light. Other words no light they ever seen then and now put off the reflection that light put off that night. The only light they would have would be kerosene lamps and that light did not put off the reflection of a kerosene lamp. They told me about the night all of them was in bed when my mother seen this woman appears with no head. One night both my grandparents and my mother, my aunt, uncle, were on their way home. And there was this light called a jack-o-lan-tern that lead my grandmother to a hole and she fallen in, however she didn't hit the bottom, she held on to the outside of the hole and the family pulled her out before she could hit the bottom. When you hit the bottom, the hole closes up and the light guides somebody else to a hole. Other words you is buried a life. My family told me about a tall man with no head that would dot passes them late one night when the family was on their way home from a friend house. My mother would later tell me about the time when she was a little girl she seen this big yellow dog in the kitchen under the table grinned back looking at her and disappeared. She told me about a little girl she would see looking like an angle behind the garbage can outdoors wanting to play with my mother. My mother told her mother about it and her mother told her she was her sister whom had died years before my mother was born. In addition, my mother told me that she and her sister and brother seen this horse one night when they was on their way home from playing with their cousin at their house. She said this horse was the tallest horse they ever seen and look as if to them this horse was trying to climb a hill when there was no hill to climb. In addition, my mother told me about the time when she and my aunt and uncle was children they was going over their cousin house to play. Before they left, their father told them to go to the well and get some water before they come home. But when they went to play they stay to long and night came they went home without the water and their father made them go back to get the water. That night they heard something grunt they looked up and here stand *the tallest man they ever seen, he was taller than any tree there. My mother told me she dropped her pail and they run like the wind. Now I'm going to tell you two more I have others however, I will leave the best for last, just before I get to the end of my book. Now since I been grown my mother told me a true story about two men an older man and a younger man which was working in the coal mine and one day they gotten trap inside the coal mine with no food nor water nothing the only thing they had was the light on their hats and it was dark as hell at night and they didn't burn what little light they had all night because there was no other light; oh but it was, little did they know just keep reading. Now at nigh the younger man would fall asleep because he just knew they would die in that mine. The older man couldn't sleep there for he would pray all night. After they had been trap in that mine about two days is when the older man seen a man he knew had died years before. In addition, the man would open up a door that had light in the room and he would have food and water and candy with him. However the hold time the man come the younger man would be asleep the hold time. The older man would wake the young man up and there would be all kinds of food and no way could the older man tell where all that food come from. They was trap in that mine for two week before they was rescued. People just knew they would be dead however they was well and looking good and they was taken to the hospital and they was checked out by the doctor and the doctor wanted to know how did they get food and water in that mine because the doctor knew they had to have food and water no way they could have lived without it. The older man just answered we didn't. Another story my family told me was about the plant they call the peeping tom plant I will tell you the story the way it was told to me. My family told me back home there was a woman that lived on a back road and miles from anybody she had no kids her husband left her because he thought he wanted this younger woman and she wanted him there for he left his wife but wanted her back. But no way in hell would she take him back and I don't blame her because no way in hell would I take a man back now after leaving me for another woman, that's meaning you going behind another woman that your man left you for because he thought he wanted that woman and maybe the woman got to the place she didn't want him anymore and she put him out now he tuck his tail like an old dog, because he has nowhere else to go and he has a dam good idea the cost clear at your place. Now here he comes bags and baggage's. Hell no it's not that good to me anymore that I'm going for that not now I'm not that's when I was younger and cared a lots for men now them days is over I don't have to have any man in my life now and god bless menopause. Now back to my story at this time she lived upstairs on the first floor in an old rundown apartment building. Below her window was a plant, she could look down at it from her apartment window. Through the years, the plant got taller and taller until it was at her window. She would undress now the plant I will say it face would turned facing her window and she wasn't looking out her window when she undress there for she wouldn't see the plant when it would turn around when she undressed till one night it was raining cats and dogs and she was looking out her window while she was undressing and this when she seen the plant turn around facing her, this went on about two months till she called the police to cut it down and they asked her why do you want us to cut down that plant in your window? She told them over the phone that when I undress that plant turns around facing my window and they thought she was crazy however they came out anyway. They say to the woman you clams when you undress the plant turns around looking at you other words right? She answers that's right yes I mean every time I undress that plant turns around facing me the policemen just looked at each other when she asked you want me to undress they said lady! She says that's ok I'm undressing on my own free will and that's what she did and sure enough just as she said the plant turned facing her, that was everything the polices ever seen then they knew the woman was not crazy they seen if first hand. They asked her could they shop the plant down she says yes please do so there for they did just that and that plant bleed as if it was human. This just some of the stories my family would tell me. Anyway, my mother and her sister Annette my aunt decide we move to Los Angeles California when I was a year old. There for a month later my aunt Annette left Little Rock Arkansas moving to the big city of angel Los Angeles California. We all stayed behind. As always, Little Rock was hard. Nobody was able to help anybody because people hardly had enough of anything for themselves. My mother was out on the back porch one day washing what flew clothes we had when this big black and white hunting dog came up to her. By this time she was hanging clothes out in the back yard. That hunting dog walked up to my mother carrying a big fat rabbit in his mouth. Boy! My mother was happy to see that big fat rabbit. My mother tells me she takes the rabbits from the dog, cleans it, and cooked it up and the dog and we all eat it. Nobody never thought about the rabbit might have rabies or the dog might have rabies or something. Everybody just ate and worried later. My mother names the dog Pup. Boy was he a good hunting dog. Anyway, two months later my mother was out back hanging out clothes she had wash because we was leaving for California in two days when a big wind come up and blew all the clothes on the grown and she had to wash them all over. She didn't mind because as poor as everybody was everybody had a washer and dryer. See who ever was washing they was the washer and the sun or wind was the dryer. It was on a Thursday when we said good-bye to Little Rock for the last time. In addition, it was cold and pouring that day. My mother had given old pup to a friend because the friend wanted old pup anyway because he knew he would have himself a dam good hunting dog. We were standing out in front of the house waiting for a friend to come and take us to the bus station. Soon he pulls up and we all got in his car. Well about ten minute later, we were pulling up to the greyhound bus station and our bus pulled up about an hour later. Boarding that bus that day were my mother and our grandmother and my aunt two boys and myself. We said good-bye to haunted Little Rock Arkansas and hello California. We just had two fairs because my cousins and I would ride free.*

Chapter 18

Moving to Los Angeles California

WE HAD NO food and no money to buy any. But we was bless with this army man to be on the bus whom mother had given him a bag of fried chicken and he given it to my mother and she let us kids eat it and her mother and her didn't eat anything the hold three days and nights in to Los Angeles. Maybe the ride to California was ok because nobody said anything about it. Well three days and nights, we were on the road. The day we arrived in Los Angeles California, there was Annette my aunt and a friend waiting for us. My mother said they had to learn the life of the big city of Los Angeles. When my family first comes to California, they did not know how to use a phone. They did not know which in to talk in. My aunt had gotten us all a house on 103rd street in watts and she got my mother a job with her cleaning houses when we got there. From that to any other work, they could find. Later on, my mother gotten jobs at the car wash were she had to pass as a man. She worked so hard on that job and was so good at it that nobody could tell that she was not a man. My mother told me she could remember when Charles Wright and the 103 rd street watts rhythm band was just getting together and she said they all would meet up at Griffin Park when they was very young men. Charles Wright is the man who put out express yourself in 1970 and Charles Wright and his band use to be called the Wright sound. In addition, Charles Wright is the uncle to the late eazy e. Eazy E was a gangster rapper whose real name was Eric L. Wright. He died of AIDS twelve years back which was so sad he was so young. Nevertheless, I loved what he done on his deathbed he wrote a letter to his young fans telling them not to live the life he lived and AIDS is real. Also my aunt and mother met Gene Allison which real name was Verse Eugene Allison, he was the man who song this is dedicated to the one I love and you can make it if you try. My mother and aunt met him that same day as he was going in the recording studio to record this is dedicated to the one I love. He was in loved with my aunt Annette. My family told me he had tried to kill himself by stabbing himself in the stomach and we heard he was on drugs bad and that was the reason why my families stop him from coming to our house. My aunt Annette told me late one night which was Easter Sunday a knock came at the door and when she open it here stood Gene Allison with one Easter egg in his hand. In addition, he would take the shoestrings out of his shoes and tie his pants up with them. So as I said they stop him from coming over to our house. In Los Angeles during the 50's my family met so many singers before they even became singers. Gene Allison died since we been in Bakersfield California. He died from liver and kidney failure on February the 23 2004 he was 68 years old still so young. He would sing me to sleep singing this is dedicated to the one I love. The blues man Buster Brown liked my mother and wanted us to move to Chicago where he lived my mother told him no. A dear friend of the family dated a young man by the name of Sam Cook, she loved the hell out of him I was told but he would drank too much for her, other than that he was a good man. Watts is better known as South Central L.A this was where we were living when that somebody gives my poor grandmother that poison watermelon. My aunt Annette told me after our grandmother eaten that watermelon she would have fits like a dog. My aunt told me our grandmother would come out the bedroom with her fingers curly under and her face would be pulled to one side and she would hit the floor while grind back showing nothing but the white of her eyes and she would be moving in a dog like fashion while she would be growling and howling. The ambulance was called and she was put in the hospital for a while then she was ok. We stayed in Los Angeles for a year. Our great-grandmother that was my grandmother's mother had been killed in Little Rock ARK where we had left. We heard all kinds of stories about how she died. In addition, one of them was some white men came in her house, cut her head off, and set her house on fairer. We never knew which was true. Nobody told my grandmother about what had happen to her mother because she was sick and just getting out the hospital. Nobody had to tell her because after she gotten better she told my mother and my aunt that her mother come in her hospital room and she told my grandmother that she was gone now. Our grandmother knew what she meant. Since I'm on this subject, I will add this in. When Our grandmother was in her last days it was a time I would not had been able to write this, anyway as I was saying when she was in her last days my aunt Annette told me one day she told Annette her mother is sitting right over there in that chair and she would called all her kids names that had long ago passed and she told Annette here come my baby boy riding up on a horse. And here come God and he's telling my baby boy I'm not ready for her yet so her baby boy road off on his horse because he had come to carry my grandmother away. It was a blessing my grandmother never gave my cousin and me some of that watermelon. From then on, she never would eat anything anybody would give her again expect for the family not even friends because she knew it had to be a so call friend that given her that poison watermelon. Any way my aunt and mother use to come to Bakersfield to work in the cotton fields. There for they had to ride one hundred and ten miles each way. This when they decided to move to Bakersfield California where all the field work was in the summer that way they could be right here where they work and didn't have to trivial so far to work and that worked out better for everybody. They wouldn't have to travel over two hundred miles a day to work and back home. Then to my family didn't care for Los Angeles anyway because just coming out of Little Rock ARK life was a little bit too fast for them then to Bakersfield was much slower and much smaller and wasn't as many people in Bakersfield like it was in Los Angeles. That being a city it was going to be bigger. They were use to the slower life. The People in Los Angeles were city people and lived in the fast lane. My mother and aunt just felt out of touch with the city life. Bakersfield is more of the country life as they were used to. The people were more of their speed and they felt more at home then in Los Angeles. The men in the big city were much faster and my mother and aunt didn't let the men there take advantage of them being country girls. They were up on things in that way. I gust men thought they were silly women just coming out of Little Rock. However my mother and aunt fool the hell out of the men they may been out of Little Rock Arkansas, however they by no means was they dumb. And sure was nobody fool. Some city people use to think back home people was all dumb and they didn't know much, if they didn't know much they couldn't do much. However, they found out they was wrong when they met my mother and aunt.

They by no means was they dumb, they was very young women coming out to California but they was up on life they still had things to learn about the city life

But what they didn't know they soon learn. They didn't have much to learn.

Then again, nobody ever will know it all; as you live there always going to be more things to learn. Even a doctor and lawyer still learning different things and for as a doctor, they never stop learning because something new always popping up that they have to learn about. We learn as life goes on, we learning when we don't realize we're learning, as long as your brain working you're learning and what a joy it is to learn.

Chapter 19

Moving to Bakersfield California

THE YEAR WAS 1958. Now Bakersfield is one hundred and ten miles north of Los Angeles and back in the fifties and sixths, this used to be the place to come and party down on the weekend. Yes, Bakersfield was the place to come if you wanted to get your party on. Talking about the singers who would come here Bakersfield had it going on back then. People all around California would come here to party back then. People still come here by the hundreds to see Kern River and hundreds of people have drowned in it. Kern River is said to be the fastest running river in the world. Now I do not know how true this is but that is the word around town. In addition, people come to see all the different flowers and fields. Just about everything, you like to see farm work related we have it here in Bakersfield. Now the things other people come from all over to see we see it every day so it is nothing to us. However, we understand if you have not seen this stuff before we know it can be exciting. We first stayed in a one-room motel room on Lakeview Ave called the Lakeview Inn. That motel since been torn down and Lakeview Ave since has been name Martin Luther King Boulevard. Now as I said we all stayed in this one room motel and it was my grandmother and mother, aunt, and her three boys now because Torino was born in Los Angles California and me. I grown up with mostly all boys and playing with boy toys with the boys. That was why I use to love toy cars and toy trucks, and toy guns and I loved to climb trees and climb up on houses and jump off. I could fight to because the boys made me fight that's why I shouldn't let kids pick on me like I did because I could beat the hell out of some of the boys I would play with and they was all bigger and taller than me. It is fair to say I was a tomboy for a while and we tomboys known for fighting. My aunt gave me a doll and I did not like her I wanted a fire truck. I think we stayed in that motel room for a year nobody remembers for sure. Then we moved on Texas Street.

Chapter 20

Living on Texas Street:

THE HOUSE WE all lived in on Texas Street was a big white and green house with a small living room and dining room with two bedrooms and with the restroom in the middle of the two bedrooms and a back kitchen leading to the back porch where cats used to be. In addition, up the street on 607 Texas Street would be the first school I would attend which was John C. Fremont Elementary School. In addition, I am three years old at this time. However, I can remember that being a haunted house for sure. Some people by the name of Mr. and Mrs.Flentroy both died there. They would let us know in no certain terms that were their home and we were guests in their home in addition sometime unwelcome guests depending on how they felt some days. I still can recall all those cats on the back porch the mother cat and her kittens. I never liked cats but at the time I, thought the kittens were cute. Therefore, I wanted to hold one. I would go up to one and try to pick it up but with no success. Never could I touch the kittens. With me benign a child, I never thought anything. One day when my grandmother was living, I asked my grandmother did she remember those cats on the back porch on Texas Street. She told me she did and asked the one nobody could ever catch. I said yes! She told me they were not cats they were ghosts. My aunt and her three boys founded a place of their own on Milham Drive just up the street and around the corner from where we lived. My grandmother stayed with my mother and me. I cannot recall how long my aunt and her boys lived with us. I recall my Mother telling me about the time we went to visit her sister and my mother had not made up the bed before we left. In addition, we stayed longer then we intend. When we returned home, it was dark. My mother would later tell me many years later when we stepped up on the front porch she could hear somebody trying his or her best to get up off the couch. Somebody that was very big and heavy. She said she sat on the porch and I set down beside her. We sat there until my mother got up enough nerve to go inside. After I was grown, she told me what she had heard in our house that day. She told me when she stepped up on the porch that day she told me she could hear something running through the living room. She told me we sit there on the front porch for a while longer then we got up and went in. For some reason I can recall looking up to the ceiling that day and seeing the name Flentroy written in cursive. Now looking back, I wonder how in god's name anybody could reach that ceiling high as it was. In addition, when we went in the bedroom the bed had been made up. We thought maybe my grandmother had come home and made our bed up because one thing my grandmother couldn't stand was a house that was not neat as a pin. Anyway, we took our baths and put our nightgowns on and went to be. Back then, most houses had the lights hanging from the ceiling and we did in both bedrooms. Anyway, we would sleep with the bedroom light on in our bedroom and I want tell you way because I think you know. However, my mother and I was about to go to sleep; when we heard this somebody walk up to our bed and turn the light off. Now I was only three, but I can remember this and the light from the moon was shining bright that night in our bedroom and my mother and I both witness this. My mother pulled the light back on and somehow we went to sleep. We didn't remember going to sleep because we both were so afraid that night. Later when we went to sleep and woke up the bed was just the way we had left it. In addition, one day my mother was over her sister house and she told her sister that she would hear somebody tearing paper in the living room and they would be taking their own dear time tearing the paper. We had this old wall heater in the living room and it sounded like somebody would slide down it all the time my mother was telling her sister. Now this I do remember even if I was a little three year's old little girl. Because being a child or not some things just stay with you and this did. My mother and I was sitting in the living room early one morning and in the restroom we could hear somebody using the toilet sound just like somebody would urinate in the toilet, then flush, wash his or her hands, come out, and pass us by and out the living room door. I was a little three-year-old girl but I can remember that so well as if it just happen to day. I recall people telling my mother that they would see a man sitting on the side steps of our house and when they went to speak to him the man would disappear. We heard later that a man and his wife both died in our house. People told us that there was money hidden away somewhere in our house and that is why things went on in our house the way it did. If that was so, back then knowing what we knew about that house and the people who died there we would had let that money stay in that house. We had this big tall tree in our front yard and people would tell my mother they would see the wife of the man who died in our house in the tree in our front yard, which the wife had died also in our house. We stayed on Taxes Street a year or so then, my sister Louryette was born April 12-1960. I have to tell the truth I was jealous that I was no longer the baby anymore. I use to want my mother to give her back to the doctors so I could be the baby again. However, I soon enjoyed having a little sister around. She was about eight months I'm just gusting I know she was walking around the time we moved from Texas Street to Milham Drive. We just couldn't take that house anymore on Texas Street any longer there for we moved just before I inter school. When she started walking, I would take her out doors walking with me and we would walk around in this old vacant lot. I remember one day I had taken her walking with me in this vacant lot for some unknown reason I looked down and here was this old black fifty-cent coin. I picked it up and taken it to my mother and she put it up on top of the refrigerator in a bowl. We had this woman staying with us, I do not recall when she moves in with us or when she move out and where she moved. Anyway, we had a man friend that would come over every now and then. One day our mother thought about the coin and showed it to the man with the woman there and asked him what he thought the coin was worth? The man answers I don't know but I can tell you this much its worth lots of money. That was it one day our coin took legs and walked off and we never seen it again. Now we had nothing but what little we had our mother made that woman welcome to it and she ripped us off what a shame. That was not the last time she stole from us another time was when our mother got her check for us two little girls and she stole all of it and said it was I. A five-year-old child, I guess if my little sister Louryette was old, enough she would have said it was she but she was only nine months. I ask the woman what could I do with eighty dollars with me only being five years old. She answers go buy candy, sure a five year old buying eighty dollars worth of candy back in 1960. Now even today if a five year old child go into a store with eighty dollars if the store person was the right kind of person he or she would write the child a note to take home to the parent wanting to know why a five year old child coming to the store by themselves with eighty dollars. In addition, after that she moves out. A little while later, we move from Taxes Street. Now see what some people do to you when you is kind and try to help them. Now that woman did not have a job and no money she did not have a pot and our mother welcomes her in our home with no way to help with the bills. In addition, that was the thanks she gave my mother for taking her in our house. Not only she did not have any family here in Bakersfield she did not know anybody but us and everybody in our family was good to her. I do not recall if my mother told any of the family about what that woman did or not I just do not remember.

Chapter 21

my first year in grammar school

NOW HERE IT was September of 1960. By this time, we had move in the same house my aunt and her boys use to live in on MIL Ham Drive. Now I am still five years old school age now. My mother and my aunt enroll me in kindergartner at John C. Fremont School on 607 Texas Street. I am afraid of being away from my mother for the first time. In addition, this school looked so big. Here were kids I did not know and this teacher. Oh how I cried when my mother and my Aunt left me at this school. I was five years old my first day in Kindergartner. One day my teacher name Miss Chapman where playing the piano, she had this round very colorful thing on the side of her piano, and we kids where sitting on the floor singing. In addition, I where in front and some kid reach over my shoulder and swirl it around. She stops playing the piano, and got up and asked who done that. The kid said me. She came over where I was sitting and kicked me on my leg. I already was afraid being away from home for the first time. I went home and told my mother, I can tell she did not believe me. She wrote the teacher a note and my teacher wrote back saying she never kick me. Now that's one thing I never did and that was to lie on a person. If I tell you somebody done something, they did that. God is my witness that teacher kicked me. I can remember that so well just like it just happen yesterday. In addition, I can recall one day we got this new boy, his mother came to class with him because he was crying his little eyes out. While his mother was in the classroom Miss. Chapman picked the little boy up and sits him on her lap. Now soon as his mother left the classroom Miss. Chapman tells the little boy you get out my lap pushing the child out her lap. After that year was up my mother decided to move to Omaha NE. that was where my sister Louryette father Chuck Green lived. Therefore, at age six we would move to Omaha NE. Nobody else stayed in that house on Texas Street after we moved. We were the last people who live there and the yard was even stomp in after we moved. However, many years later they did put up another house in the same spot. However to this day that house is up for sale as always and the price is so low nobody ever lived there any link of time. Well after school was out our mother and my baby sister and I moved to Omaha Nebraska. Early one morning in July our family, come to take us to the bus station, which was on eighteen street, which it is still today.

Soon we were pulling up to the bus station. Man I tell you I sure did not want to move to Omaha. I was feeling sick at my stomach. Everybody got out the car so we could hug and said our good buys. Our grandmother didn't come, now I know why it was because she couldn't stand to see us go away then to it would have been too much for me. It was already heard enough on everybody. That was a very emotional day for everybody.

Saying good-bye can be heart breaking for some. People were all line up to board their bus. In addition, we looked up to see the bus to Omaha NE was not there yet so we went and had a seat in the bus station. Our family had left by now. About an hour or so, later our bus was pulling up and we all boarded on headed for Omaha NE. I looked up to see my mother wiping her eyes. I asked what was wrong she told me nothing she just had something in her eye I know now she was crying. It took three days and nights to make it to Omaha. Man I tell you the ride was fun. Now looking back, I was six years old and my sister was one year old. Now we did not make a sound on that long ride to Omaha. People on the bus were crazy about my sister and me. Man talking about the candy I tell you my sister and me would get so much candy. In addition, we knew how to say thank you when people give us something. We could go anywhere and we did not scream and keep people awake all night. That's why people enjoyed us and would give us so much candy it's all in the way you raise your kids. Kids don't have to be a problem when they go places. Our mother would tell us what time it was before we went any place and she would explained to us she didn't have any money so don't be asking for this and that and we knew not to. In addition, yes people would enjoy us on our long bus ride and it didn't matter if our mother had much money or not because we would get all kinds of stuff and we would be the only kids on the bus. In addition, by all the stuff my sister and I would get you would think our mother had money

Running out her ears.

Chapter 22

when my sister Dana was born

THIS WAS IN the early sixths and going to Omaha Nebraska was not all fun and games. We went through towns that did not care for black people at all and they didn't mind letting us know. Now doing the first day on the bus, we were the only black people riding the bus. My mother was the only black grown up and we two little girls my sister and me. Now that next day two black men's board. Now my mother will stand her grounds with anybody. Back then if a person went in the restroom while the bus was running the restroom door would lock on you and the only way you could get out of the restroom the bus driver had to pull the bus over and stop it so you could come out. Well like kids, my sister and I had to use the restroom no matter what, whatever was going to be a problem kids have to do it and we was no different. Therefore, sure thing my sister and I went in the restroom and the door locked on us. My mother went up to this big tall bus driver, I do mean he was big and tall and even them two black men I think was afraid of him I know they asked like it. My mother asked him in a nice tone of voice, would he please let us girls out the restroom. He told my mother no! She then says please sir let my children's out the restroom. He told my mother look! I told you no! Now go sit down! With no respect for our mother at all and he talked to her though she was a child. My mother had to stop being ladylike and let the man part come out. See to spell woman, man is in the spelling. Therefore, when that came out he pulls the bus to the side of the road and let us out the restroom. One black woman had that bus driver pull that bus over and let us out. Another time I remember was one night a white lady boarded the bus now my mother was holding my sister Louryette and I was sitting in a seat next to my mother when this white woman boarded. My mother was told by the bus driver to hold me to. I do not like using the world white woman or white man but back in the days that's the way most black people, talked like black people was called Niger and still is. However Niger just means dark skin but it's the way it's used remember it's not always, what you say but the way you said it and who's saying it. However our mother tells the bus driver no! She was not going to hold two kids with all that room was there for the woman to set down. In addition, our mother stood eye to eye with him and she the woman told the bus drive there's enough room for her to sit down. She was a nice woman. All the people on the bus were nice to us. There is good and bad people in every race. Back in slavery there was white people that help slaves to escape to freedom and also some march beside blacks in the freedom march and they was beaten and killed right alone with the blacks. Those kinds do not have anything to do with what the bad ones done. Now back to the bus ride to Omaha. A man in the back roll had reached his destination so my mother had me to move to his set. I was in the back of the bus sitting between two men. One on my left was a black men and the other one to my right was a white man. Now this white man started patting my legs, I told him to stop and take his hand off me! In addition, I moved his hand off my leg he stated patting my leg again. This time I got up and told my mother and she had me to sit in her set and she went back in the back where I had been sitting and sat down beside the man and told him to pat her leg, which he did not. My mother had to hold her own with men. Now when the bus driver would stop in towns where black people were not welcome and we would order food white people would throw the food to my mother and us. She would tell us not to eat the food and throw it back. Nice people on the bus would take their money and tell us how sorry they were and buy the food for us. Our mother would try to pay them but they would not take the money. As I had said it sometimes was hell, I will say this and proud to say it, now my mother is one lady that will stand up for herself and us and anybody else that's in the right still to this day. She did not look for them black men to stand up for her. And we girls are the same way, not only we do not look for men's to stand up for us we do not look for anybody to stand up for us. We like the cheese in the children song the farmer in the dell we stands alone and that is the way my mother is to this day. And when we was all at home my mother was the mother and father both and she ran her house like a strong man, and she would tell anybody where to get off and she wouldn't bite her tong. Well three days later, we arrived in Omaha NE. I tell you I did not like Omaha because I missed the hell out of my family in Bakersfield California. We lived in a basement when we first arrived there. I do not recall how long we lived in the basement. My baby sister Dana would be born when we move on Maple Ln. However, it was a while yet before she is born. So anyway, after living in the basement we moved right above the basement in an upstairs apartment in the alley. Nobody could tell me that was not a spooky place. I knew better and nobody could tell me differently. Until this day, I still say and will tell anybody that was a hunted place. See Omaha was not too far from Little Rock Arkansas where my family and I use to live. There for no wonder it was so haunted. Now I was old enough to remember more things now. We were staying up stairs in an apartment. The grammar school I went to call Lake School had no Cafeteria at this Time. Therefore, everybody had to come home for lunch. One day I had come home for lunch and my mother had cooked me some bacon and eggs. We all eat our eggs sunny side up. That is with the yolk on top. My mother was down stairs talking to our neighbor. I sat down at the table to eat my lunch. I took my fork to cut into my egg and I felt something hard in my egg. I pulled the top of my egg to the side and there were a big blue eye, which looked to be a human eye looking up at me. I scream and run out side where my mother was and told her. Again, she did not believe me. God knows that is what I seen I did not eat anything off my plate and see I loved food and by me not eating my lunch my mother should have known something was wrong. One summer I was out doors playing and a mosquito bit me on the arm and a week later sores was all over me I was taken to the doctor and a shot was given to me and that's all and the doctor said I had IMPETIGO and you talking about itching I was. I was not sick but itch like hell. One day our mother's husband met a blind man and he was selling this medication called itchy itch and he bought a small jar of it. It was a brown grease like medicine I tell you that done the job. That heal them sores up in no time as if they never been there. I do not remember how long we stayed up stairs and I cannot recall when we moved on Maple Street right across the alley in a big white house where somebody had died in. One day I, where in the rest room and I seen this big white rat the biggest rat I ever saw. I cannot say where it comes from because I never did know, but I remember it lowering its head and going through the wall. Now I do mean it went through the wall and it were not any hole in the wall. I asked my mother how a rat could go through a wall when there is no hole. She told me because it had no bones. Therefore, I believe that. I can recall our mother telling me after I was grown that late at night in the house where I seen the eye in my egg she would hear things like big tops hitting the floor and when she would get out the bed to see where it was there wouldn't be anything on the floor. Now I know this sound strange, even to me and I'm writing the book; however this is the truth so god help me. I can recall in the upstairs apartment we moved from which I was only six years old at the time but at times when I would use the restroom I would have a sexual experience and I mean it would feel so good I couldn't move, I don't know what it was because I was only six years old. We kids back then didn't even know the word sex and if we did we wouldn't know what it meant. However no sex on earth I know can feel like that ghost sex; that's what it was, I know now; there for, I gust the ghost use to be a child molester, there for I have to say my first sexual experience was with a ghost, the best sex I ever had was with a ghost, no matter how this may sound I'm telling the truth so god help me. Now it snowed there and it was cold in the winter but I do not recalled anybody ever getting sick I am sure they did but I just do not remember. However back in them days it was against the law in the wintertime for the gas company to cut anybody gas off. Then to the light and gas meters was in the house so there for nobody would let the gas people in anyway. However, come summer you talking about a high gas bill you had it. Now the hold time I went to school I never was picked on or called fat, I had so many friends I can recalled one valentine day I got more valentine cards then anybody in the classroom. We had kids that went to school that had deformity but we did not think anything about them. Kids back there in them days were different. In addition, kids never made fun of other kids who did not have things other kids had such as new clothes or toys at Christmas time. Other kids would make other kids who had nothing welcome to what they had. I had a little boy friend in my first grade classroom his name was Glean. He was the best-looking boy in our first grade classroom.

Chapter 23

when our class would go on walks

OUR CLASS WOULD go on little walks, Glean and I would hold hands I was the only girl hand he would hold, and he was the only boy hand I would hold. Glean and I were good friends and the kids were crazy about me it did not matter to them I was fat they all accepted me the way I was and so did the teachers. Now I was the biggest person in the classroom, in addition, another thing it is not true that all kids or a like because I learn their not. I stayed in the first grade another year because I was slow in learning, there for when we moved back to Bakersfield I was a grade behind the other kids my own age. It would be a while before we move back to Bakersfield. My baby sister Dana would be born now. Here it was August 15-1962, that night we went to the drive inn to see, walk on the wild side starring Sidney Poitier. We were in the middle of the show when my mother started having labor pains with my baby sister. Therefore, we took her to the hospital not long after our baby sister Dana Louise Green was born on August 15, 1962. She was a big fat pretty baby. Now there were three little girls. We stayed in Omaha for three years then my mother decides she wanted to move back to Bakersfield California and we did. The year was 1964. I am nine years old now. That same year we said good-bye Omaha and hello Bakersfield California Yes! Boy I was so happy to do so. Now we was moving back home I said to myself. Omaha was never home to me. Then to I missed my family in Bakersfield California. The last day of school in Omaha all the other kids was lined up at the door to go home for the summer expect me I was staying behind to get my papers I needed for school in California. The teacher had the kids to say good bye to me I said good bye also I was so chocked up I knew I would never see them again and they all left out the door and in a week we was moving back to Bakersfield California. When that day came we had a friend to take us to the bus station. No sooner we got to the bus station our bus was pulling in and we all got on board. Three days and nights we road I cannot remember the ride back to Bakersfield California and I was older now but for some unknown reason I cannot remember anything about the ride back to Bakersfield. All I know is again we take the greyhound back. It must been ok since I cannot remember anything about it. Anyway, after three days and nights I seen the gold and blue sign that read Bakersfield California on highway 99 headed north, which 99 has since been renamed Union Avenue. Now we pulling up to the greyhound bus station on Eighteen Street. Our family was already there waiting for us to pull in. Boy, I was so happy to see my family again. We had more cousins now since we move away yes the family had grown. When we made it to our family home there was our grandmother in the next room boy was she happy to see us. Nobody slept that night because we were so happy to see each other. We stayed with my mother sister Annette and her husband and kids. All together, it was thirteen kids and three adults but the house was always clean every room and the yard front and back with thirteen of us kids and some was so young that they was not in school yet. And some people house not clean with only two or three kids and everybody always had clean clothes and we always had food to eat little of much we had it. Our grandmother lived just up the street from us and sometimes she would come down to spend the night with the family. Now we would be moving up the street from her but that would be a while yet. Anyway while staying with my aunt I have to say I don't understand this till this day a lots of things happen I don't understand. One day I had washed me a dress out and I went out to the clothesline to hang it out. It was in the summer time and I did not have on any shoes while I was standing in the grass. In addition, I felt something bite me so I looked down and here was this little brown spider looking up at me grinning while it was going back down in the grass. I know this sounds funny but I am telling the truth that spider was grinning up at me. In that same house my cousin told us about that night he seen this woman floating by his bedroom without a head. He would be so sincere when he tells use this. I can remember when he was a little boy I will say around the age nine. He never seen his father that he can remember. One day he was in the house brushing his teeth In addition, his mother told use that he said he seen his father in the marrow. He told use this house came up out the floor and this man step out and introduces himself as my cousin father. He decried him to the tee, in addition, nobody had ever told my cousin about that big knot beside his father neck. The way my cousin had decried his father no dough at all he had seen his father that very same day and his father was still living in Arkansan. See my cousin was born with what the old people use to call a Vail over his face and all that is a part of the placenta on the baby face. A person that is born with a Vail over their face is said to be able to see ghosts. I never did know for sure I only can tell you what the old people would say and still to this day, what they say I believe. We stayed with my mother's sister and her husband and kids about nine months and we would be moving on Watts Diver in our own house. Our mother had the deposit for our house so she gives that to our rent man. However, in that same week she would have the rent. Anyway, before we moved in the house the rent man had to have the rest of the money. Now our family move us to our little place and who we thought was our rent man son was there when we pulled up. The only thing we had to move was two-day beds and our clothes believe it or not somebody had stolen most of them when we were on our way back to Bakersfield. In addition, what took the cake that day our mother called herself giving the rent man son the rest on the money for us to move in the house? Whom we thought was the rent man son told our mother his father was in the hospital and he was the rent man son and gives the money to him and that's what our mother done. He wrote out the receipt and hand it to our mother and the door was open so we thought nothing about a key because we thought it was inside our house which we later found out it was not. However, the next day our mother called the rent man and told him his son didn't give her the key to the house and will he please bring it over. The rent man asked my mother what son I have no son I have no kids at all our mother said oh my god! What have I done? He came right on over and told our mother you going to have to come up with my rent somehow because I need my rent so here we were left without any money. Our mother had worked so hard in the fields all summer long in the hot sun to get up the money for our house and now we was ripped off by a conman now what are we going to do our mother asked talking to herself. We had been ripped off and that was all it was to it, that man had ripped us off from our rent money and what in god's name or we going to do my mother said. Lord that day our mother had something in her eyes again and it was tears for sure. I cried also our poor mother sits down beside us and we all cried that day. That day I will never forget as long as I have my right mind. Looking back how can anybody do that to anybody? Not just somebody with kids but anybody. People thinks just because you don't have kids it's ok for people to take from you, but it's not a person with kids get all the help they can get but the one with no kids don't get any help that's the reason why women was having so many because the more kids they had the more money they would get. It was a time when a woman with kids was doing much better than the one that had no kids. In addition, a woman out working couldn't even buy food after she would pay her bills I know because I was one of them women. Now back to my story.

We did not have anything but I was happy just being back in Bakersfield. Home is where the heart is. I have seen people leave one place and go to another and they be doing better and making much more money than they did in the place they left. Nevertheless, they would not be happy. Other people would not understand why because they are doing so well all that does not matter. A person can have more money than they ever can spend and not be happy. They would give it all up just to be home again or have the person they love back in their life. Now days so much is based on money and how much a person have and material thing. Take a mother that trying to do the best she can taking care her children and giving them all the love she can give them and her children is happy and getting good grades in school. Now the lights and gas are cut off because she had to choose food over lights and gas. Somebody finds out that the family have no lights or gas so instead of people getting together to have the family lights and gas turned back on somebody reports the mother to child welfare and they comes and take her children away and put them in faster care until the mother can finds ways to better take care of her children. Now they put the children in homes where lights and gas is on and the people have money and a nice home and plenty of food they have everything the mother didn't have. But with all the food in the house the children hardly eats and they stays in dark rooms with no heat and get beating often and showed no love and they not happy at all some of the children stays in other towns far away from each other and none of them is showed any love and care. However, the welfare feels it's in the best interest of the children to be in foster homes at the time. However, it's not in the best interest of the children. The best interest of the children's is to be back with their mother where they showed love and a lot of it. A child may be surrounded in money and material things however that do not mean their happy. In addition, it does not mean money is spent on them and they being taking care of. A child grades starts dropping in school and they starts fighting and picking on other kids at school, which is something, they never did before. Just because a child is put, where there's money and material thing do not means that's in the best interest of the child. See I know firsthand what I'm talking about because I too been in a foster home and I know other kids who been in them and what I seen eighty percent of them is not in the best interest of the child. Some kids are rape and beating and some even killed. I know this can happen with the child biological parents. I understand that but it seems it happen more with foster parents. I know people going to disagree with me but that's ok I'm just going by what I seen and myself being in one. Some of the foster parents will put on a show when the people are trying to place a child in a home. In addition, they will make the child and the people that trying to place the child feel they are the best foster parents out there. In addition, if they get the child the real they will show. That's how I was done. The woman was ok but the man was hell, I leave it as that. Now I'm coming back to my story, on watts drive when we got our rent money ripped off god made a way for us out of nowhere for our rent. We do not know how to this day but we know our mother had given that man the rent money but our rent man never came back over for the rent again it was like we was all paid up we never called him to ask what was going on we just take it as god took care of it. The rent man came over with our house key and we never saw him again. What happen about our rent until this day we don't know? About two weeks from the date we moved in was when I start hearing this little girl crying. I would stand in the doorway of the first bedroom to my right and I could hear her crying, sometimes singing at times, and crying most of the time. She had a spooky sound about her. It was so long ago that I cannot recall everything about her, but I do remember that haunted sound she would make and it was so spooky. When I would stand in the doorway, the sound would sometimes stop but I could feel a cool breeze by her door. I would wonder who that little girl was and what had happen to her. I must tell you when I went to South High School Here In Bakersfield back in 1970 I was called shock and nobody knew how I got that name they just called me that now I will tell you why, it was due to this clock here the story. We had an electric stove that had this electric clock build inside it. This clock lay back in a hole on top of the stove. Now however I always have been the kind of person that always had to have things just right. Man I just could not rest with that clock laying back in that hole like that. It should be up just right I would tell myself. I would work with that clock every day trying to get it just right. One even my mother and my sisters had went out doors to set in our yard with some neighbors, but me I stayed in because I had a clock I had to get right. So here I was a lone just my clock and me. So I got to work. I pulled and pulled on this clock. Somehow, I pulled on some life wire and got the hell shocked out of me. That shock knocked my wind out, and I could not breathe! That is why a boy named me shock nobody knew the story expect my family and him and I. I came out side where everybody was and I told that this clock had shocked me and I could not breathe. One of the women who were over went to her house and got me a brown paper bag, and had me breath in it and my wind came back. Then my mother calls the doctor. He checked me out and told my mother the only thing that was wrong with me some of my fat had been scotch. After that day, I never mess with that clock again and I never heard that little girl crying anymore. Another thing we never could understand our electric was not on so how did I get shock? Does anybody have an idea what is our worst enemy is? Can you gust? It is no other then our mouth! Yes, it is our mouth. We talk too much! We tell all our business. Women tell their friend about their bedroom business you know you do. In addition, another thing people stop telling people about your troubles as they care because they do not. All the time you telling people about your trouble all the time they saying to themselves its better for you then it is for them. See people do not envy you when you is doing badly but they can envy the hell out of you when you are doing well. It's the same way with your man, now when a woman man is messing up on her nobody envy that but let a woman man love her and respect her and never mess up on her and another woman man is messing up on her she will envy the woman that's man not messing up on his woman. Another thing, some women will go as far to tell women how her man is in bed and guest what the woman be during? Now say you trying to sale a car now you will tell a person how well the car runs and it is good on gas you is going to say everything a person want to hear about the car even if you have to lie to sale the car. Now some body going to buy the car. The same thing about your man when you appetizing how good your man is in bed somebody going to answer your add. So start keeping your mouth close people and this goes for your friend. Do not be telling your friend your entire problem because even with a person you think is your friend can hold things over your head so the least a person knows about you the better off you is. You can let them tell you things about their self-but do not open up to them. In addition, another thing, some women will tell a man her life history why I do not know to save my life. Maybe she thinks that will make him feel sorry for her or love her I don't know what their reason can be. However, I do know this they should stop, because soon he gets mad at her he is going to bring it up to her. If you respected yourself, you would not tell him. Me I am telling my story to help others then to far as trying to get some man to feel sorry for me I wouldn't be telling him things I'm writing in my book. Another reason I say this is. Our mother went to apply for AFDC that's aide for dependent children. To receive it you had to be in California for one year. However, we only been back in Bakersfield for ten months I am not sure now but I know it were not a year yet and everything was off. Water, lights, and gas all was turn off. We had no food. Now we were having it hard. One day our mother went cross the street to visit with some Neighbors and they asked my mother had she applied for welfare yet and if so what happen. Our mother told them she had and she will be getting her check in three weeks, which would be the first of the month. Back then, the AFDC checks came out on the first and the sixteenth of each month. Oh boy! I said to my sister Louryette we would be getting some food. That's all I cared about it never inter my mind that the water and gas and lights wasn't on all I cared about was food. That was my life nothing else matter. I'm sure you notice how much I mention food. However, she told them we haven't been in California for a year yet but she told the neighbors she told her worker we had. However while waiting one day our little sister Dana was crying for water at the time she was two years old. I was nine and my sister Louryette next to me was four. Our mother was telling Dana all the little water we had was gone. However, there were some brown and clear milk bottles in the kitchen when we moved in the house. I got my sister Louryette and we got two milk bottles each and went next door to get our little sister some water. It was in the summer time we did not have our shoes on. We did not know there was sand bugs in the people back yard there for we got sand bugs all in our feet's. And while we was bent down getting our water we looked up to see two big boys which was brothers with their hands on their hips looking down at us getting their water. We never stop we were going to get our little sister that water no matter what and we did. We lived next door to some cows and the house we lived in had about two back windows out. So there for the flies would come in and what I did love to see was when night was falling' the flies would head for the ceiling. Man I loved to see that. I could be outside playing and when nigh was falling my mother did not have to call me in because I already was in so I could see them fly's heading for the ceiling. That little time we spent on watts drive when I was nine was the happiest time of my childhood. After we moved, I never was happy again. Now my mother had us three little girl's age nine and four and two years old. Now here comes the cold mess somebody did to us why God only knows. Well three weeks had pass. WE were so happy because water, gas and lights would be on. In addition, most of all we would have food in the house. Benign poor or not my mother never begged and she had her pride and self-respect because there was many of men liked her and most was married men and she never taken a dime from them because she did not want men over her girls. She had respect for herself and for us not like the ones my husband's would take up time with. See our mother is a lady it is a different between a woman and a lady. Any female is a woman but it takes a special woman to be a lady and our mother was and still is a lady. Now some women might say to feed my kids I would have taken them men up on their offered. However like I said it's a different between a woman and a lady, as you can see I'm still a life and I'm writing a book and my sisters or still a life and doing well. Therefore, we did not die and my mother is still a lady. In addition, every one of them men says the same thing about her. Then to we were happy because we had a house and our heath and family and each other. So we were blessed. See no money in the world can take the place of family. And another thing if them women didn't have kids they still would had taken them men's money they not fooling nobody they just use kids thinking nobody will say anything. Like you can't blame her for going to bed with men to feed her kids if you go to bed with men for money it's not for the kid you would do it if you didn't have kids. However our mother was asking us kids what we wanted to eat. We were saying this and that. In addition, latter she stopped and pulled me to the side and said Dorothy I have a feeling we want be getting our check. I said yes we would she said I do not think so. Therefore, I said nothing. So sure thing when the mail carrier runs he passes our house by. Oh what a sad day it was for us. Somebody had called our worker and told her we have not been in California for a year. What did eight weeks make anyway. How could they do us like that I do not know. We had not done anything to anybody for him or her to do us like he or she done. On the other hand, what did they get out of doing us like that? At a young age of nine, I had seen how cold people could be. Therefore, we did not have anything to eat that night there for it was another long and hungry night we had. A mother with small kids and didn't have much of anything what little we had such as our pop bottles people would steal them from us and we had nothing and I do mean nothing at all. I recall one Christmas our mother call herself going and getting us some toys from the welfare and by us being girls we gotten dolls. Now let me tell you about the dolls we got. They gave us black dolls with white arms and legs and no clothes on them one of each and a big box of puzzles that had parts missing out the box however we was thankful to get that. We didn't get Christmas basket the way they get to day. And stores weren't taking donation for needed children like they do today no store did that. It was everybody for themselves and god for us all that's how it was. Now days it's all about kids that were not the way it was back then. School kids didn't get free clothes for school and free lunches we didn't get anything free. And kids don't want to go to school now days when it was hell for most of us back then. Getting back to my story, when we didn't get our check the next day our family comes over with food and water for us. This is why I am telling you our mouth can be our worst enemy. We can talk our way in something and we can turn back around and talk our way out of it. That is what some people do in relationships. Now our mother was talking and thinking nothing about what she was saying at all yes but somebody was thinking about what she was saying because they told it and why until this day I don't know. However, we must check ourselves about our mouth because it's a time to talk and a time not to talk. Another thing in our relationship we can say things to turn a person on and then we will go right back around and start running our mouth and say things to turn a person off see what our mouth can do for us. It's a time to talk and a time to listen. Another thing take a person that runs his or her mouth all the time is a person who don't know much of anything because they too busy running his or her mouth to listen to something that makes any sense. Our mother wanted to go to the fields but nobody would keep us kids now we were not any trouble to anybody but people were not going to do anything to help us. Now they made it hard for us but they were not going to do anything to help us. We got our check two months later. Hard as we were having it, people still would steal what little we had. One day our mother had paid all our bills, she had bought me some school clothes, and what little money we had left over was for food. Lord somebody broke in our house and stole all our little money. We lived off beans every day until we got our next check. A woman knew about it because when she came over that what she would smell and she was laughing and telling her mother in-law about it. I can recall our mother would go over to other women house's and they would be showing off all their AVON to our mother and she would come home and look so sad telling me about it and I would say to myself when I'm grown I'm going to buy you all the AVON in the world. Well I am grown now however, I haven't bought her all the AVON in the world however I have bout her lost of it now she has AVON in her bathroom, bedroom and everywhere else in her house she want it. Some people will show off their things when they know you do not have anything. That is low down but some people will do that, not knowing or caring that God gives and he takes away. We moved from watts drive to a house where two twin sisters had died in by the name of Miss Pinky and Miss Tinky on Hayley Street with a big old tall Christmas tree in the center of the front yard and at times we kids would put our hands on the tree and we could feel the tree moving in side. Now in the house I must tell you would pop late at night and it would feel like somebody would come and sit down on my bed and I would try pulling the covers out under them but they was too heavy I was so little I just thought maybe my covers was stuck or something I would go to sleep. Now as I said the old house would pop however when my mother old man Michael would step up to the house no more popping. Our grandmother lived just up the street from this house the twin sisters had died in. I hated living there I just hated that house with everything in me. I loved the house on watts drive. I never loved any other house we lived in like I loved the one on watts drive. It was something about that house I don't know what but I loved that little blue house and even if we had nothing I still loved that house. Now here we were living in this white house I hated! Things change when we move there I was never happy any more. I never did feel the same I just wanted to move back to watts drive. Oh! Why! Oh why? Did our grandmother have to tell our mother about that dam house on Hayley Street that I hated? Seem like when you're a child and you love and enjoyed something or somebody it have to change every time. You move away or they move away and you have to try to cope with the changing which can be hard but that's part of growing up and it get to be part of life as an adult.

I never seen anything in the house but I would hear people singing hold that tiger! Hold that tiger! Every night, and until this day, I do not know what that meant. A week after we moved in our house one hot summer day our mother was hanging out clothes when a woman who lived next door to us welcomes us in the neighborhood. She tells our mother had not anybody lived in our house since the twins had died, our mother ask the woman what she mean by the twins had died in our house. The woman said yes I am so happy you moved there because I did not think anybody would move there. Thanks God you guys did. That house been vacant since the twins died. In addition, that has been two years ago she said to our mother. That is what the woman told our mother about two weeks after we moved in our house. I do think now that she had a good idea we was afraid of haunted houses because maybe she had heard most black people or afraid of haunted houses and she was so right we was and still is to this day. However, that same day our mother and my two sisters and I went up the street where our mother's mother lived because our grandmother never told our mother about the twins dying in our house. Our grandmother was in her house with the door open. She tells us to come on in before my mother could step up on the porch. Our mother asked her mother did she know about them twins dying in our house. Our grandmother told our mother yes she did know and our mother ask her mother why she didn't tell her that the people had died in our house before we moved in it. Our grandmother told our mother because she did not like for us being far out in the country as we were. Then to she says to our mother it is the living you had better worry about because the dead cannot harm you. With that, my grandmother tells my mother those people did not know you and you did not know them so there for you did not kill them so why would they bother you. So yes we done lived in some downright haunted houses in this world and nobody can tell our family and me there's no such thing as a ghost because we can tell you just some stories and I willing to bet you we can change your mind. I'm going to jump a head a little to N' street before I forget to tell you what my little brother told us keep reading I'll get to it. Now my family would tell me many more ghost stories, but through the years, I forgotten most of them, but I will share with you what I do remember I will tell you about two more that was on N street. Late one evening my little brother Michael was playing in the back yard. He said he heard a hard grunt and when he looked up he told us he seen the devil himself my brother was around eleven at the time and he stop whatever he was doing and run in the house and it was a while before he could bring himself to talk about it. Now still living on N" street my mother was in the living room looking out the window and for some reason she looked down just in time to see this round hairy thing with red eyes looking up at her. We were grown before she told us about it. Now I'll get back to my story. As I was saying earlier in Omaha NE I was put back in the first grade because of my learning disability and when we moved back to Bakersfield I was put back again so I would be two grades behind other students my own age. This is my story. When we moved back to Bakersfield I was one grade behind but nobody knew. See I stayed in the first grade for two years. Then still in Omaha I pass to the second grade In addition, here I was in the second grade when I should have been in the third grade. However the end on my third grade year I was put back again. Now I was two grades behind. Now my last day of school I was sick and could not go to school. So my mother had my so call friend May to pick up my report cord. She seen I had not passed. She showed my report cord to everybody. Everybody knew I had not passed before I did. Nobody ever said anything about it. She was so happy she had passed. Now she has a child that was born with a learning disability worst then I ever had. See that's what's can happen, now people can think kids in the clear that god will over look ever thing they do, but that's not true remember god don't like ugly that means with anybody. A person can think they getting away with something because nothing ever happen to them and they may tell people I did this and that nothing happen to me but you just did that and look what happen to you. Now what may happen in the long run it can come back on their kids. We can be the reason why our kids can have the worst life than ever because they may have to pay for our wrong doing. And our children don't know why their life is so bad and we don't know because we was only a child but we was older enough to know what we was doing to somebody was wrong. We don't have to be one hundred years old to know right from wrong. However parent will say when the child do wrong they only kids like they didn't know what they was doing was wrong. Kids have more sense then their parents give them credit for. They know when their doing somebody wrong that's why grown up should stop saying they just kids, a child knows right from wrong that's why when you see them doing things they shouldn't be doing they will run. If a person didn't know they were doing wrong they wouldn't run. When you just go out and hurt somebody for no reason at all your child will pay so check yourself. Now I know you remember that song if you happy and you know it clap your hands. Well the kids would sing that to me. However, they would sing if you're a dummy and you know it clap your hands if you're a dummy and you know it you can't help but show it if you're a dummy and you know it clap your hands! Now you clap them big fat round hands you go go pig the kids would say to me, and even the boy I liked would sing that song to me also and that is what really hurt. Nobody knew how dumb I really was. The only one knew I thought was god and I. Ever Friday at school, we had square dancing, and every girl would have a partner except yours truly. Didn't any boy want to hold my hand and oh, how I would cry. One particular boy the same one who was singing that song to me with the other kids I liked and if he did want to hold my hand, he would not let it be known. One day our teacher made me get up and she put me with a boy, the dance did not call for holding hands at this time. However, when it came time to hold hands the boy would not hold my hand. I was so hurt. I would try to hold his hand but he would tell me you let my hand go you fat pig you. The boys would run and jump on my back to ride me as I was a pig and they would hit me on my hip and say go girl go! In addition, one day I was on my way home and five boys, one girl jumped on me and one of the boys hit me in my chest and back. I went back to the classroom, and told the teacher and like always nothing was done about it. When a girl like a boy she wants to look her best act her best around the special boy she likes nothing got it for myself. Some girls' thinks they must be loud and dress like prostitutes to get boys to notice them. They so right they will notice them all right but not for the right reasons. With me it did not matter what I did no boy would liked me. I just stop trying. I tell you when you growing up them can be some hurtful years when you like somebody that does not like you back. Adults do not understand that a child feeling is real now you would think they would because they too were a child once up on a time. A child feeling can get hurt just as bad as an adult when it comes to liking somebody who does not like you back. And adults should be more consoling then they or and not take their child feeling as nothing because their feeling or real and adults should treat them as such. One day I was late getting to class and I always hated people to stare at me and walking in some were late you draw attentions to yourself. There for I stayed out doors. In addition, some reason the teacher come open the door and there I stood and she took me to the office and told them she think I would be happier with kids my own age. I never knew she knew I was two grades behind but she did. I was jumped two grades a head but I had to work like hell to stay there and people already were saying I couldn't do the work. Yes old dumb I couldn't do the work they were saying so I had to prove them wrong. I had to work like hell to prove I could do the work it was not easy no means was it. NOW after benign jumped two grads a head I was in the six grades. The kids were nice to me there. Four girls really took to me. It was not because the teacher had told them to be nice to me like I later found out and I will never forget how it happens. One day we were out for recess and one of my friends told me that the teacher had told them to try to be nice to me because I was fat and I would be the fattest person in the classroom, which my other teacher had expand to him. That hurt me so badly because I thought they all really liked me. Oh what a hurtful day that was. In addition, when we went in the classroom I could not help but cry. I cried for all the fat kids before me, and them after me. I cried until I had no more tears left. I never knew people had to be told to be nice to me. My friend did not try to hurt me that was not her intention at all she just wanted me to know that the other kids and the teacher did not mean me well. So that same day at lunch I did not want to go to lunch because I was so hurt and the teacher told me come on Dorothy everybody is trying to be nice to you, just as my friend had told me. So I got on up and went to lunch. I couldn't eat my lunch, I just did not want to be there; I did not want to be some were people had to be told to be nice to me. I was so sad, I thought the kids really did like me; and all the time it was just a put on, they never liked old fat me; and why they would? I am ugly, and fat; and no use for myself and nobody else, and out of shape, I am out of place wherever I go. So why would they like me? I remember this boy hitting me in my chest and the teacher did nothing about it. And a girl hit me with a bat and the teacher seen it and said nothing she didn't hit me hard she didn't want to hurt me but the boy didn't care he hit me so hard he almost stop my heart and no I didn't fight back. In addition, the hold time I wouldn't fight back the teacher never called my mother to tell her that kids could hit me and I would not hit them back. They do not tell your mother when you do not fight back only when you do. The teachers could see kids hitting me and kicking me and I wouldn't fight back never did they call my mother. Now let me hit a kid back which I think one time I did and calling my mother the teacher did. Now what a child to do when another child hit them? If they don't fight back that's a meant disability and that mean that child not normal and don't know how to take care their self. See that's way I tell people to let their kids fight back because as long as your child don't fight back not one person going to call you and let you know your child don't know how to take care of their self. If they do not fight back, kids or not going to let up off them and their not going to get help from anybody. In my case the teacher would stand there or sit there and smile when the kids was hitting me or talking about me. No child can learn anything under them conditions. In addition, when a child don't learn they will be held back. I would try telling the teacher all I was told was to go sat down and the kids would laugh at me and I would go sat down and cry. Sometimes the teacher would start the kids picking on me when the kids would not be picking on me. One day I went to the teacher on these kids, and the teacher told me Dorothy they just playing with you and she said I wonder why all the kids here at the school they would pick you to play with. Those kids were picking on me. Those kids were not playing with me. I know the Different between playing and not playing I was dumb not stupid. When the teacher would explain something, afterward she would ask do everybody understand. Any question? I would raise my hand the kids would say I knew dummy over there had her hand up. Put your hand down you old dumb thing you I knew you did not understand do you ever! However I can recall one day the teacher had expanded something and she said it's not over till the fat lady sing. This boy says out loud sing it Dorothy! Sing your song you fat pig you! Sing it girl. Everybody laugh including the teacher. One day we had a Christmas party when I was in the six grad and we had cake and ice cream and when the teacher asked anybody for seconds? A boy that sat in back of me hit me on my head not hard and told me put up your hand if you want to you big fat hog and I'll break it do you understand me? I mean you big fat round hog every time somebody ask who wants seconds your hand is the first to go up, now you put it up and I'm going to brake every bone in that big fat hand of yours you understand me? Now put that big fat round hand up he told me. I wanted more to eat but it was not worth getting knocked around over it so that day my hand didn't go up as it usually did. That year went by so slowly with all the picking and hitting on me I went through. Now here I was in the seventh grade, Junior high school and this when things or worst for me in school. However little did I know I would be going to Camarillo State hospital for the mentally ill patient doing this time. After all the hard work I went through to get my weight down and thought I was looking good and getting the boys I just knew I would be and I was not the biggest person in my classroom now and what a low blow that was for me in junior high school to find out l still would be picked on and now called ugly. Read my sad story. Now this would be the year I would be admitted to Camarillo State Hospital. This would be the year I would no longer be the biggest person in the classroom, yes this would be the year I would find out at a young age that true friends love you just the way you is this was the year of nineteen sixthly eight my first year of junior high school.

Chapter 24

my first year in Junior high school

I WAS AT THIS big old school. This school looked to be the biggest school in the world to me. Everybody looked so tall and it seems like I was so little. However it's funny when you're a child how things can look so big and when you're grown those same things can look so small. Anyway I did not like junior high school at all. The kids would use such bad language, I did not like mother this and mother that I want say the F word but you got the idea. I did not want to be there. I had gotten on me a diet doing the summer and I lost twenty pounds and I looked nice if I say so myself. Now thinking I was cool as everybody else and twenty pounds liter I thought I had it going on, the fat was gone my hair was much longer I just knew I wouldn't be picked on now. However, I was and even worst. I thought it was because of my weight the reason I was picked on back in grade school. Now I was twenty pounds smaller now but I was still called names. I went from being call fat to being call ugly. Therefore, I would stay to myself and not talk to anybody. There was a boy at school I like and he was crazy about me. However, everybody made me feel so ugly and out of place that I couldn't bring myself to talk to him. That boy is a man now and so successful. I done had opportunities that most women haven't had such as doctors with their own office wanted to date me lawyers with their own office, dentist that had offices all over town wanted to date me I mean rich men that wanted to dated me even singers. But I just was so down on myself I told them all no. I'm the kind of person that can let a man know I like him but if he comes to me that's a different story. I can talk so good as long as the man I like not with me oh I'm the best talker and I can even get downright mean but let him come to me he will think I'm not the same person. I'm not the same person I am over the phone or on the internet. I cannot say the same things I can say over the internet that I say in person to a man, because over the internet I can be who ever I want to be. Anyway, at school one day I got very lucky I thought because my homeroom teacher picks me out to be monitor and I wouldn't be in class for everybody to pick on me that day. I had to let my teachers of my other classes know I wouldn't be in class that day and why. Therefore, I had gone around to all my classes except for one and it was my sewing class. I went to tell my teacher I was monitor for that day. I open the door of my sewing class and the teacher came to the door and told me to come in, I tried to tell her I was picked to do monitor for that day. Nevertheless, before I could get the words out of my mouth she had slammed the door so hard in my face that she all but slammed my hand in the door. I know if I had not move my hand in time she would had broke my hand and nothing would had been done about it. Now that teacher was crazy and it's a blessing that she didn't hurt one of us student. However, most of the student would have beaten the hell out of her and she had a dam good idea I was not the one. Then again, she really didn't know that. I got so mad but I just went on all I was doing was letting her know I wouldn't be in class that day and why. I could hear the kids in the classroom laughing, and I heard while I was leaving the door that teacher telling a girl what you laughing at because you look like a frog my god I said to myself what a thing to tell a child. Now I could have open the door and laugh about that to the girl but even at a young age saying things to people to hurt their feeling never had been funny to me. One day in our art class this boy tried to steal my purse and the girl behind him which has pass away now was just smiling at him. For some reason I, turn around in time to see him going for my purse. I told the teacher but nothing was ever said or done to the boy. I told him he did not have to steal from me. I told him if he wanted something from me just ask me. Anyway, everybody was mad at me about telling on that boy. While I was telling our art teach what had happen the other kids and the boy was saying I was lying but still I could tell the teacher believe me. In addition, they say to the teacher it is all of us against her one and you believe her. The teacher says that is it! It is all of you against her one. It was time to go back to our homeroom. The kids told our homeroom teacher what happen in the art class. Instead of him saying if you see someone stealing from you or anybody tell it do not let it go. No way could he say that instead he told the kids to sic me. They would come up to me yelling like crazy people and he would say sit now sic her now sit this went on and on and on until I started vomiting and ran out the door crying and I had the worst anxiety attack you could imagine. However, at the time I did not know what was happen to me. I could not hardly breathe I was having respiratory problem. A yard teacher seen me and called after me but I just keep on running and she called after me again and this time I stopped I was gasping for breath. I told her no more! I was crying and trying to get my breath no more will I ever come here again nobody likes me here and nobody want me here not even the teachers because Mr. Child told the kids to sic me! In addition, I never wanted to be anywhere I was not wanted. I was crying and yelling. She said Dorothy I am so sorry come down it would be ok. I. told the teacher no it want no it want be ok I am not coming back to this school! I told her I did not want to go to school anymore and that I had enough I was crying. She told me to go to the office, and have some water and take a set. On my way to the office two boys run up behind me and knocked me down cutting my legs. There was kids out lined up and they all seen what them two boys done to me and all laughs. I was lying on the ground all bloody and all cut up. I went to the office and told the boy dean about them boys knocking me down. He told me to prove it. Now he knew everybody was afraid of them two boys. He told me to prove it as though I was lying and I lied all the time. I cried I could not believe it. I was in the nurse's office with cut up elbows and knees and blood running down my knees my white socks was red now with blood and I was in so much pain. However, that day I decided I would not attend that school another day. I was not learning anything and nobody liked me and why should I stay some place where nobody like me and I was benign abused every day and nothing was being done about it. So that was the beginning of me bumping in to the teachers to get kick out of school because I was so fed up with all the abused. In addition, I did not bump in to them long before I was kicked out of every school in the state of California. I would say about two weeks that is all it took. No child should have to go through what I went through to go to school because they want learn anything. And any teacher that do a child the way that teacher done me by telling those kids to sic me shouldn't teach not even a dog because a person like that is not good enough to teach a dog. However, before I did get kick out of school they called my mother in and myself to tell us why I was being kicked out of school. However, nobody ever told what really was going on. They would lie and say I only wanted attention. I didn't want attention from anybody I only wanted the abused to stop and to be able to go to school in peace. Now it's doing this time of my young life I would be sent to Camarillo State Hospital for the mentally ill, this would cause me to be called crazy for the rest of my life, this would be the reason why somebody will tell my husband and everybody else that come in contact with me I'm crazy, this would be the reason why I would write about Camarillo State Hospital in my book at the age of 56 telling the world I been to Hotel California. In addition, even some of the teacher was with the kid's abusing me. The girl dean god bless her sole she is dead and gone now but she did not go for anybody picking on me. In class I got to the place where I was afraid to say if I didn't understand something because I knew I was going to be laugh at and yes the teacher would stand there and laugh also. No way would I have gone for kids laughing at others kids when they didn't understand something. I would have told them look! This what you're in school for to learn and if you know it all you shouldn't be here and you bet not laugh at anybody because they don't understand something. Next time you laugh at them I will let you explained the question to them ok. I'm willing to bet you the one's that was laughing didn't understand and was afraid to say so because they didn't want to be laugh at and was happy that I said I didn't understand. Everybody knew how bad I was treated. However, nobody cared about me or how bad I was benign treated. I wanted to go to school in peace. In addition, I did not think that was asking too much. I did not want to be the most popular girl at the school nor the prettiest girl at the school. However, I had no help it was I against the world, a world I had no part in a world I never fitted in. I would feel like this world belong to everybody expect me. Now looking back, I know I had a mental problem but never knew it. I was kicked out of the seventh grade for about two months when I called the grade school I use to attend and told them it was a bomb on the schoolyard. This what I think that sent me to the nut house yes I will say nut house so nobody have to say it for me I know where I been. I was admitted to a mental institution for the mentally ill. So now, you hearing it first hand from me myself and I. Camarillo State Hospital were a mental hospital for crazy people. Even though not all the patients there were crazy, but once you went, you were branded as being crazy for the rest of your life. I want to be the first to tell you and if a man don't want me because I been in a mental institution that's fine with me because I never had any luck with men anyway so they can hit the road jack they don't mean that much to me now anyway. Just as I don't mean that much to men now I learn to feel the same way by them that they feel by me. I had to learn to feel this way. Through the years through all the hurt and pain I learn to love me more then I love men. The same person who wouldn't want me can in up in one also. I was getting abused everyday in school and they did not miss one day not abusing me. There weren't one person at the hold school I could tell. I done been in a mental institution, now I am out. It is over and it is behind me now, I am moving on with my life. I am going to tell you about Camarillo State Hospital for the mental ill patients back in 1968 and I am telling what the old people use to say and that is the way the cow ate the cabbage and that is the way it is. So you be hearing it from a person who has been there, who was a real life patient there, who done been in hotel California. So get the real story from a former Camarillo State hospital patient. I done been asked why I am not ashamed to tell people I been in Camarillo? Why should I? See the very thing you a shame of and do not want people to know about you will be told so why not tell it. If somebody knows your secret, it's not a secret anymore. In addition, if you been in one you hold your head up and don't let nobody make you feel bad. In addition, you remember where the sun don't shine if you know what I mean. I remember somebody calling our school and saying there was a bomb now that is where I get my idea. In addition, I think that's what sent me to Camarillo they never told me or my mother the reason why they was sending me away. I did not know they could trace the call and they came to my house and took me to juvenile hall. I never dream I would in up there. Therefore, after three weeks in juvenile hall I went on three B. Three B is a mental ward you go before you go to Camarillo and it's still here in Bakersfield on the 3rd ward at KMC, AKA Kern Medical Center.

Chapter 25

from Juvenile, to a mental word in Bakersfield, to Camarillo State Hospital

I WAS BORED IN that mental ward here in Bakersfield I was the only child there and had nobody my own age to talk to there. One day I found a lighter well the truth is a man gave me the lighter but I never told on him. In addition, I went to my room and was playing with the lighter when it got to hot and I dropped it on my bed and started a fire. I put the fire out but somebody seen the smoke and I had to come out my room. They gave me some kind of shot that twist my mouth to the side, my teeth would bite into my tongue, and there was not a thing I could do to stop it. I would go to the nurse's and try to tell them what was happen to me but those people wouldn't pay me any mind than I was not even there. This went on for some time. I could tell when it was going to happen. My face would start pulling to one side and it would not stop until my teeth were trying to bite my tongue off. The nurses never did a thing until they got ready. That was a painful time. I went through just some pain. Just imagine you biting your tongue until it bleed and not a thing you can do about it and blood be running down your mouth because a piece of your tongue done been bet off. Now you can see why I tried to put this behind me and move on and for somebody to tell my husband this. I was not trying to hide this from my husband it just that it was so emotional to think about it and I did not want to make myself sick by thinking about it. Talking about crying and I would try pulling my teeth out my tong but I could not. They knew what that shot would do to me. In addition, being in a nut house nobody pay you any mind when you tell what is being did to you. I knew what I was going through were not right. Nobody helped me; nobody I could tell about the shot. In addition, I would spit out blood and meat from my tong, I was a child a little girl left along being did like that. I had to go through that pain all alone. I remember the patients would try to tell the nurses to help me because I was just a child and I was in pain but nobody helps me until they got ready. I would cry when this was happening to me. I got to the place I could not eat nor sleep and I was so nerves all the time. Therefore, if anything good happen to me believes me I well done paid my debt to society many times over. In addition, I do mean many times over. I tell you nobody know what I been through expect God and me. See I am letting you know what been did to me when I was in the system being a child away from home from people whom cared about me. I was on that ward for eleven days, then one day a female police officer and her police officer husband came for me to take me away. I really enjoyed the long ride up to Camarillo State Hospital. However, little did I know what kind of place I really was going to. Little did I know I would be there for six month instead of three. Little did I know I was on my way to the most famous mental hospital in California. In addition, little did I know one day it would be me sitting here at my disk at age fifty-six writing my life story. No way could I have known one day my leg would be shot off and I would get my book title from a maintenance man in the hospital. However, here I sat writing a book and telling about my experience at Camarillo State Hospital and other things in the pass I could not bring myself to talk about. Now how could I have known this would be me writing this book years after leaving Camarillo State Hospital at the young age of thirteen? Now let me tell you about Camarillo state hospital. I know everybody want to hear about the most famous mental hospital in California and the biggest mental hospital they say in the world. Now I must tell you at Camarillo State Hospital I was told that I was not thinking clearly when I was talking as a twelve-year-old child. However, my thinking started changing and I never knew it. Camarillo State hospital was in Ventura County which is located approximately 49 miles north of Los Angeles California. That place looked so depressing with the sun-bleached building. I remember there were so many green trees there. When we pulled up at the white, pink Spanish style building, I got so depress and looking around was nothing but lonely looking mountains, and trees and buildings. It was enough to make you want to cry, it sure was lonely at Camarillo. In addition, for a while, I was the only black girl on the unit however, I was called Niger and my hair was talked about. The white boys would say, look at that Niger and her barbwire hair. I had no idea what barbwire was. I wanted to be white like everybody else. I did not like being black. I did not like my hair. I just got to the place I did not like me. I stopped caring about myself. I just let myself go. All the time I never knew depression I was suffering from. I never knew depression I was suffering from in school. One day a male nurse took me walking on the grounds because he said walking will make me feel better. It didn't but I said it did because I liked being out of the unit. He asked me how it felt to be black. I answer, it felt ok but it didn't. When the others went swimming they all could get their hair wet. But if I got my hair wet it went back home I heard older black people say and that meant it went back nappy. I would press and curl my hair and I would draw a crowd every time, because that was the first time they ever seen a black person press their hair. I was so happy when other black girls come there and had to press and curl their hair. About two weeks there, I was Gavin a brain waiver test. At this time, nothing too much was known about children depression. Since then things have come a long ways since I was a child. Now it is medications for children's with depression. Things or much better now days then it use to be. Now day's children do not have to be institutionalized because they suffering from depression. I just cannot tell you the way Camarillo really was. I thought I could, but I just cannot expand it to you. I do not think anybody can. I just tell you it is a place I do not think anybody would want to go. We kids were lock inside most of the time. Like any place, kids would lie on you for no reason at all. In addition, for some unknown reason you grow up fast in Camarillo State Hospital. You have to fight no way around that because there always somebody wanted to try you. I would try my best not to get in fights because I never have been the fighting kind. If I have a problem with somebody I like to try and talk it out and if that don't work I just stay my distance that work best for me. Everybody had clean clothes and lots of food. Sometimes, they would cut the kids hair even if they did not want it cut. They would give some of the girls who did not have clothes long out of style dresses that somebody donated because they did not want them. Talking about looking a mess, the girls did. I tell you they would look the part of being crazy. Once you were in the system nothing anybody on the outside could do for you to keep the people from doing whatever they wanted to do to you. I do not remember us having patient rights the way they have to day. Maybe being kids, we did not have any rights. Therefore, we had no control over what was done to us. I would cry at the drop of a hat. I was sad the hold six months I was there. I did not realize it until now since I have been writing my book that we did not have a TV. I was so depressed every day of my life. I had no energy I would feel weak all the time from depression and I never gotten over the depression and the doctor told me I never will now because I have been depress for so long. Even now, I do not feel like getting out of bed at times. This something I must deal with for the rest of my life. However, I do not care because dealing with something all your life comes to be a part of life. I never was told the reason why I was admitted to Camarillo state hospital. At that time, I think being a child they didn't have to tell you why. Then to if they had to that didn't mean they would tell you the truth. I never was told the truth. They just came after me and that was that. I was a twelve years old girl in Camarillo State Hospital. This was in ninth teen sixthly eight. I never did know why most of the girls were there I never asked to tell the truth I did not care. I tried to keep to myself but I found that to be a lonesome place and you had to have somebody to take up time with. Some of the workers there would hurt the children's feeling. However there you would get your feeling hurt and if you did not have somebody to make you feel better, you were left to deal with it on your own. In addition, being kids we had it hard. We who had sense enough to know it was hard and so depressing. Another thing I will tell you, once you been in that kind of hospital, you will be brand as benign crazy for the rest of your life and do not let anybody tell you different. You will always have that name, that name will go with you to your grave. There will be jobs you want be able to get. However, there were girls there that really were crazy.

As you may know where there's female, usually there will be some form of lesbian acts and Camarillo State Hospital was no different now hear the story from a former patient of Camarillo State Hospital. Late one night I had to go to the rest room and there in bed on my left were two girls in bed making out and they didn't care about us younger girls seeing

Them in the act and sometimes there would be more girls making out in one bed and I would be in bed with my head cover up pretending I was a sleep and I would hear some girl saying to another girl you kisses good. One night a meeting was called about the making out with each other, because somebody had told it however, the hold time the staff was talking she never told the girls to stop it. There for, they let us younger girls see all of that because we were there in the room with older girls. We kids were not shield from things like that. That never bothers me, I see and do not see. Nothing I seen the girls doing bothered me. I will say this about Camarillo State Hospital they did not shield us younger girl from anything we was in the dorm with girls up to seven teen years old because at age eight teen you were put with the adult. Now day's mothers try to shield their kids from the world and when the child gets out there, they do not know a thing about anything. In addition, I would see different things and when I left Camarillo, I never thought about it again. However, the older girls would do anything around us younger girls. However, I didn't want to do any of those things I would see the older girls doing not even smoking. And when mothers shield their kids from the world when they do get out there their going to be as dumb as they come and want know a thing about what's going on in the world. See there or worldly people out there and they looking for dumb people to use. I know because I run into them and I tell you they can use a dumb person up before the person even realized what happen. I'm going to let you know this about Camarillo on the children's ward. They did not put anybody in strata jackets and they did not have on white coats. We were behind bars but not like those that you see on TV that is just Hollywood and most of the people that was there looked like anybody else most didn't look crazy at all and if you seen them on the street you would never had known they was from Camarillo State Hospital. Now check this out will you, I remember a patient coming in the dorm where we girls all were with a gun. I cannot say where she found it at, I never did know for sure. Anyway, she came in the dorm where we all were, she pointed the gun at us, and everybody took cover. Some girls went under beds. Somebody went and got the nurse and two came in and took the gun from the girl and nothing else was ever said about it, it was no big deal to us. However, in them places nothing is a big deal as long as you didn't kill anybody or burn down the place. As long as you didn't do those two things nothing was a big deal. I was so depressed I had no energy I didn't want to get out of bed I didn't want anybody bothering me I just wanted to be left alone. I stop doing anything for myself. I stop bathing I stop combing or washing my hair, I start putting on weight as if I don't know what. A nurse came to me and told me Dorothy I know what's wrong with you I start crying, I didn't want to do anything for myself I just wanted to die at that time I felt life just was not worth living. You have to get yourself together girl. She told me after I had stayed in the bed all weekend that I had to get out of that bed go and take a shower and wash my hair and she said you will never get out of here the way you're going. I cried I wanted to die and was so down and was sick and didn't know it. My hair came out I didn't want to do anything but sleep all the time. All my energy was gone I was so weak oh why couldn't I just die I would say repeatedly. Why would god want me to stay here with me feeling this way what's wrong with me why can't I just die, why god want take my life and give it to somebody that want to live. Life didn't have anything for me I would say to myself. I don't have a life I don't have any reason to live. My monthly stop the hold six months I was at Camarillo. Before I come to Camarillo at age eleven, I came in womanhood, and then on it was right on time every month right on the twenty-eighth day of each month. I never missed; it came on time like clockwork. However after I come to Camarillo my monthly never came on the hold six months I was there. After I came home, it comes back on and right on time every month. I gust it was because I was so depressed. Depression can play a hell of a part on your body and mind. Depression can take over your life. After three months I went for my hearing to see if I was going home. Sure thing, just as the nurse told me I would not be getting out of Camarillo until I get myself to gather. I was so hurt. I couldn't cry I couldn't do anything; everything in me was gone. I just sat there, I couldn't talk. I didn't know until much later I had an emotional brake down. When I came back to the dorm, I went to my bed and got down on my knees and I prayed to god and this is how I prayed that day so many years ago. I asked god to tell me what to do, tell me god; how am I going to make it out of here? Tell me please, show me the way, please god don't leave me; not like this, you're all I got. I know I never called on you before, but I'm calling on you now please help me. Somebody pulled me up off the floor and told me, come on Dorothy; it's going to be ok. Time not long as it has been and you be gone before you know it, you will see. Who said that to me that day, to this day I don't know. I'll never know because I was there but my mind was gone. When I thought nobody cared for me and I had no friends and all hope was gone, a miracle happen, god sent me an angle for the time being. I can't remember now how long it had been before Don Come to Camarillo. However, I remember my angle came in the form of a fourteen year old blond haired Caucasian girl by the name of Don Le Little. I tell you she was heaven sent. I'll tell the story. One day we got a new girl and as I said, that was a lonely and bored place and you had to have somebody to hang with. I went over to her and I introduce myself to her I always tried to make friends. She told me her name was Don. We hit it off so well. We became best friend. She had big blue eyes and long blond hair. Most of the girls did not like her, but I did see she was pretty and many boys there liked her and so the other girls were jealous of her. I will say what little fun we could have we had it. We would go out in the back where the playground was and swing and sing our favorite songs. Don favorite song was if I had a hammer it went like this If I had a hammer I'd hammer in the morning I'd hammer in the evening all over this land I'd hammer out danger I'd ring out a warning I'd sing out love between my brothers and my sisters all over this land. My favorite song was Corina Corina. We song it like this. I love Corina, tell the world I do I love Corina tell the world I do just a little more loving let your heart be true. Oh little darling where you been so long oh little darling where you been so long boy how we laugh when we got to the part I had no loving since you been gone. I still laugh on that part. We always seemed to get in some kind of trouble. Not bad but what we could get in we got in it, not meaning to but we did and I was the one who got us into it I will tell the truth; it always were my idea. Whatever we got into my friend Don was down with whatever I wanted to do. Boy! That was my friend and what a friend she was. She was fourteen and I was twelve. I never had a friend like her since. One day we wanted to do something crazy why I do not know. Anyway, Don and I decided we go to the canteen nether one of us had any money to buy anything. We climb over the fence to go to the store on the adults' side. That is where the store was, we just wanted to get away. Somebody seen Don and me and called our unit, which at that time was unit 575. We took off running like the wind; and a man grabbed Don. Don was kicking and screaming let me go! She screamed at him. He finely let her go. We ran back toward the unit. When we made it back to the unit, we tried to get back over the fence but we did not make it in time. Therefore, Don and I were caught trying to get back over the fence and we could not go out with the others girls that night which we knew nothing about. Don told me Dorothy I am going to stay away from you. We always getting in trouble when we were together she told me. She did stay away from me for a day or so then, Don and I were at our old ways again. Don and I were sisters at heart one black and one white. Three months later Don told me she was going home about in one week. I got sick. That lonely feeling was starting to sit in. She looked sad because by now I was crying. That day came so fast. The day nurse told me I could stay in from school to see her off. I could not. I could not stand to see my best friend, my sister go around them old lonely looking mountains we had to go around leaving Camarillo in them days no, I couldn't stand to see that. Therefore I went on to school I cried the hold time I was at school. I already missed her and she was not even gone yet but I knew she would be soon and I had to get on without Don. When I came in from school one of the girls told me, Don said bye and good luck. We never heard from each other again. I would go outdoors and have a set on that same old merry go round Don and I had spent so much time on laughing and singing if I had a hammer as I said that was Don's favor song. I had to stop singing it because I would cry. I was so lonely and broken hearted with my friend gone. Some people you meet in life can have a lasting effect on you. In addition, you will always cheeriest the memories of them, as long as you live. In addition, that is my memories of Don. When I am alone, I wonder if she still living has she Married does she have kids and how many I always will love my friend and what a friend she was to me. She and Mrs. Robertson was the reason I made it because Camarillo State Hospital was something I cannot put in words to tell you. Well the time went by very slowly for me. I miss Don very much; I did not think I could get on without her. However I did. One day I was looking so sad and a nurse came and sits down beside me and told me Dorothy when you least Expect it you will be going home. It had been four months for me now. Time went so slowly for me and I would count the days on the calendar until one day a nurse seen me and she told me Dorothy don't count the days that only make time seem longer and she was right. I just did not think I could make it. I always heard God does not give us more then we can stand but I find myself questing God doing because I do not always understand it. In addition, I did not back then and still do not till this day, but I have learn it's not for us to understand, if god wanted us to understand we would. I am fifty-six years old now, and I just found out the staff at Camarillo state hospital that given us our medications were nurses. One was Mrs. Robertson Yes god sent me another angle and she was so nice to me. She became my best friend after Don left. I would try to throw her down to show her that I could. She would say girl you cannot throw me, I would say yes I could, she say let's see. She was right. See she was a little woman so I just knew I could. She would tell me never let size fool you. Dynamite comes in small packets, when she would be off, I would think of something we could do because I would have so much fun with Mrs. Robertson. She never did get mad with me I would pull her wig off she just say girl hand me back my hair she had pretty hair and I did not know why she would have on a wig. I would come up behind her and go boo! Because spooky things went on there, she would jump and say Dorothy your something else. I started back counting the days that was left for me to be going home. Mrs. Robertson would tell me Dorothy don't' count the days don't count nothing, Dorothy that only make time seem longer and she was right it would seem like time had stop. About two months later, I was in the day room when my mother, stepfather, and cousin walked in. I thought they were there to visit but the doctor was with them and he told me I was going home. When I was least expecting it I was going home just as that nurse had told me that day when my friend had left and I was so hurt and crying her words came back to me that day Dorothy when you least expect it you will be going home she weren't there that day so I could hug her and tell he she was right. I had big boils on my left leg one of the nurses had to take me to the doctor office, which was on the grounds. Our doctor was a little old woman who had gray hair. On the way to the doctor's office the nurse told me not to tell the doctor I was going home that same day because she would not let me go home. She did not have to tell me twice I knew what time it was. The doctor drains my boils and she covers them up. Therefore, we came back to the unit. I do not remember going in the dorm and packing my things, I know I did but I cannot remember. I just remember walking out the door when Mrs. Robertson called at me. I turn around and went back and we hugged and said our goodbyes. I broke down. Something I didn't think I would do. To my surprise, I got so emotional and started to cry. I wanted to say something like thank you Mrs. Robertson for benign there for me because when Don left I thought I couldn't go on. In addition, thank you for being a friend to me when I really needed a friend. Thank you Mrs. Robertson for crying with me when I was feeling down thanks you Mrs. Robertson for being you. All those things I waited for so long to say lone before I was released I couldn't say not one word of them. How can you not break down when a person been a friend to you in a place like that. How can you not say thank you. How can you forget about them? I don't think anybody can. That time when my teeth bitted in to my tongue, I had control over it. I went and got in the car. I looked back just in time to see Mrs. Robertson wiping her eyes, I knew she had something in her eyes like tears. In addition, we took off and I was on my way home now which seem like that day would never come. We were now going around them lonely looking mountains, but now they did not look so lonely to me. I looked back at that old tree I would sit and cry under when I was out for physical education at school. Yes I was taking that last look at old Camarillo State Hospital which operated from ninth teen thirty six and closes in ninth teen ninthly seven. Looking back I, can recall us girls singing where have all the flowers gone? I think back and thinking to myself so long ago we little girls were just flowers blooming now we all did bloom. So where have all the flowers gone long time passing? Where have all the flowers gone so long ago? Well after leaving Camarillo State Hospital I never heard from anybody again and still till this day I wonder how everybody doing and do they remember me? That been so many years ago from thirteen years old when I left Camarillo now I am fifty six years old now. I like to say wherever you may be Don I will always love you. In addition, here's to you Mrs. Robertson I love you more then you will ever know. I always heard when a door closes a window opens and it did, because when my friend Don left Camarillo State Hospital that day a door close however when Mrs. Robertson came in my life a window open I will never forget my two angles no matter where I may be in life as long as god bless me with my right mind I will never forget about my two angles that carried me over my bad hump god how could I.

Chapter 26

Just coming out of Camarillo State Hospital

JUST COMING OUT of Camarillo State Hospital I was in deep in depression from being in that hospital. I was in the 8th grade in junior high school at this time. I was picked on all the time and thank god, nobody knew my history because if they did I really would have caught hell. However, I got through that year. It had passed, now I was in high school. The year was ninth teen seventhly my first year at South high school. Now I was not feeling good about myself and I didn't think I was all that I didn't think I was anybody so it didn't surprise me at all when I was picked on again. The high school years or the worst, this when everybody trying to be his or her best and be all you can be. I was a freshman at South high school. I did not know in high school you had to take Showers in PE in front of everybody, and I had a problem with that. I like privacy that did not sit well with me. Most girls did not like that and we all talked about it. I did not mind PE at all but showering in front of everybody, no I just could not handle that. Therefore, what I did was try to beat everybody else to the shower and be out when everybody else came in. However, no matter what idea you have somebody else seem to have the same idea. I tried to make the best of high school. I even enrolled in the beginning girl's glee club. Now that same year the teacher let me sing with the other girls in the Christmas's program. At the end of the year ever girl in the glee club pass from beginning girl's glee to advance girl's glee expect for yours truly. I stayed in the beginning girl's glee club. Nevertheless, 1971 my sophomore year the teacher did not let me sing in the Christmas's program. He put me at the back door giving out welcoming forms. I do mean he moved me so far back that I could put my hand out the door. So far, back, if I tried to sing nobody could hear me. No one made fun of me about it because I could tell by the way the other girls looked at me they all felt sorry for me. I did not like that school, now some fine boys liked me, but I did not know until years later. Anyway, after Christmas that year I enrolled in Visit high school. Still a sophomore the year went by ok now I was in my junior year 1972. This was when that lie was told on me that I was having my stepfather and I ran away from home and went to Los Angeles. This sent me back to juvenile for three long months, And from there to a bad foster home so I am getting in to that bad foster home part now. Now you would think by all that had happen to me, people would give me a brake and not lie on me but they never gave me a break. Now I am going to tell you about me being in the foster home, now for a while I was in a foster home when I was sixteen I had run away from home, and went to Los Angeles California. However, I knew what L.A was about in them days, and that was about men's piping young girls no way was I dumb. In addition, no way did I accept anything from them. See with any man you just meet don't accept anything from him and even some you know and the reason I say don't accept anything from any man is because you don't know who just want to be nice to you and want nothing in return from the ones that does. See it's best to have your own money and if you don't just go without and make up in your mind that everything comes with a price and a price I'm sure you wouldn't want to pay, tell yourself nothing in the streets worth having is free you must work for it. However, I must say I was blessed I met good nice people in L.A. Now you know people lied and said this happen and that happen however nothing happen that I didn't want to happen and I was not going to lie and said it did just like people lied and said a man took me there which was a lie I went on the greyhound bus and no he didn't give me the money. I'm happy I don't believe in lying. No man rapes me, No man made me do things I did not want to do not anything like that. People was nice to me I do not have any complaints about anyone. I did not get beat up. Men took me around L.A. and showed me the town. I seen the hotel Sam Cook was killed in. I did meet some nice men's in L.A. who were starting up a band, and man could they sing. I had so much fun. I did not have to worry about food or a place to stay because motel was rented for me and no not for sex. I do not drink nor do drug but if I wanted it, it was there for me. People going to say what they want but I was the one there and I want tell lies on nobody, no man rape me nor did they beat me they showed me a nice time. God sent his angles to me. All I had to say was no to anything I did not want to do and that was it. Now school was starting back, it was now the end of August. I decided to go back home and enroll in school. My cousin got fighting mad when he found out I would be going to school with him. He didn't want me to go to the same school as he because he was so ashamed of me now I know you thinking because I been in Camarillo no that wasn't the reason and he let me know he didn't want to go to school with me.

You know what it didn't bother me at all. His brother said yes she's crazy and yes I'm saying it and I'm not biting my tong. We were over their mother house. It was my aunt and two cousins and my mother and me. I never in my life done anything to anybody and I don't bother anybody and I don't ask nobody for nothing. I stay to myself even at school. There for the next day I went to the office to change my classes around so I would only have one class with my cousin I didn't want that. However it would be a while before my classes come up. There for my cousin didn't have to worry about me attending school with him for a while because I knew I would go to juvenile hall. Sure thing I did for three months. But when I did get out I wouldn't say nothing to nobody I just stayed to myself.

I just tried to keep lies down but you know I learn that don't get it if people don't have nothing to say about you they will make up something so no matter what you do you can't keep people from talking about you. When I got out of juvenile that's when I went to a foster home. People were very nice to me in juvenile hall, well some of the girls would try to pick fights with me but I just tried to stay out their way. I can get a lone with almost anybody because I mind my own business. Now the foster home I was in was a bad one. These were church going people. The man was a deacon of the church and they would call people sinners and all. I'm going to tell you something I know people don't know and that is the lord gave Noah 60 commandment not just ten however over the years only ten out of sixty of the commandments survive. Nobody knows what the other fifty had on them. There for why should people be telling others their sinners? We're all sinners we're in a sinful world, there for depending on the kind of world we're living in; that's what kind of peoples we going to be. I'm going to tell you a short story about sin, One day I was on the street bus and here was this over weight woman on the bus telling this woman that was living with her boyfriend without being married which we all know is a sin, however this woman didn't know how to say what she said and let it go as that; which the way them people was living weren't none of her business in the first place. She just went on and on about the people was living in sin. Well the woman she was talking too had enough, she told the overweight woman don't you know over eating is a sin? There for the woman was right to tell her that to let her know she too was a sinner. We can look at a nice looking person and depending on what we thinking when we looking at that person can be a sin. There for stop judging others and do the best you can as long as you here on earth and when your time is up then it's over then god will judge us people don't have the authority to judge. Now back to me living in that bad foster home. They had three other foster girls living with them. Two of the younger girls were sister, and the other one was just a girl that her mother never wanted and I do not know why because she was a nice young woman she was thirteen years old at the time. Now another girl who was in juvenile hall with me named Tee was later sent to the same foster home as I. We had to go to church every Sunday which I did not mind that because I was rise up going to church. So anyway, this girl Tee was fifth teen and she always thought she was betters then me. She would tell those people every move I made and add to it because she wanted eyes off her, now she went to a motel with a man she had just met. She didn't know if the man had told her his real name or not then to the man was married. Well she was one of them women that a man being married didn't matter, she would come on. Now she would tell every moved I made to take eyes off her, the better way to put this she was the dog bringing the bone. She never told me but the man did, he told me she had paid for the motel. Now if she had heard that about me she would have told those people and everybody else that would listen. However, with me knowing this; I could have told those foster people on her but I never have been a vengeance kind of person, there for I never been a bone bringer just because she was that way didn't mean I had to be. This is why I will tell anybody to watch the dog that brings the bone. As I said that Tee girl would tell them foster people every move I made however, there weren't anything to tell the people. I was a teenager sixteen and I had teenager feeling such as liking boys and if she felt she had to tell that well I say to myself let her tell it. Now the woman was nice but her husband was hell on wheels. In addition, I could tell that man was the devil himself. This why I stated in my book you can't fake for very lone to be something you're not. If you're a devil you can't fake being an angle for to long because faking can get to be very depressing. The woman husband would tell me not in so many words that I would never amount to anything and not in so many words that I was dumb. Hearing this, coming from a church going man I believed it. He was a deacon in the church we attend so to me I believe what he was telling me. If he said I was dumb then I was dumb. Tee and I went to different school her school had a school bus mine didn't. I would have to take the city bus. I would get fifty cent per day to ride the street bus to school. In addition, my lunch was fifty cent per day. I had to decide on would I ride the bus to school and have no lunch or would I walk to school and have lunch. So I decided I would walk to school which was two mile one way and talking about cold here in Bakersfield in the wintertime. I would have to get up at 4: AM to make it to school by 8: AM but I went to school every day. If we were not at the house for dinner, we did not eat and they had a pad lock on the refrigerator so we could not get in it. One night I miss dinner I do not remember why now, but anyway there was this big can of punch on the kitchen floor, I was hungry, and I got a little glass of it. At the time the husband and wife was gone but I thought they would not mind since I missed dinner. Therefore, the rest of the girls got them some also. When the man and woman returned home one of the girls told it. Which I did not care, it was not anything to tell. In addition, she said it was my idea, which it was, and that man yells at me so loudly and he called me crazy all because I got a small glass of punch. I called the police to pick me up and take me away from there because I was sick of the mess; I was sick of Tee and that man. The police came and took me back to juvenile hall, which I was happy to be back and two weeks later I was home. That Tee girl called me once, but she could tell by the way I talked to her I didn't have much to say to her. She tried to talk about the foster people to me but as she could tell, I was not in the move for that so she says good-bye and I never heard from her again, which suited me just fine. She did me a number in that foster home. Some of them fosters homes or good don't get me wrong I'm not saying all them or bad I can't because I just been in one however that was enough for me. They like anything else there good and bad. That is why I will tell any child if you have caring parents you better stay yourself at home, because some of them foster homes do not care anything about the kids, some of them even beat them and some even go as far as to kill the kids. It's bad to say but everybody knows I'm telling the truth just watch the news. After that man in the foster home had said I was dumb I started feeling dumb. My mind started wondering in school. I did not know this until one day in math class my teacher seen me daydreaming in class one day and he asked me, Dorothy what is wrong. I have been noticing you. You look like your mind is miles away. I started crying and some of the students pat me on the back and said; don't cry Dorothy everything going to be ok. I said it wants! See I am dumb! I am a big fat nobody! I want graduate! My teacher told me Dorothy you will graduate; you will graduate with your class of 1973. You will Dorothy; however, you must forget what you been told you're not dumb your mind just wonders that's all. However you will be there when I announce the graduating class of 1973. This was 1972. I got myself to gather that day not the next day but that same day and I went on and finish the 11 grade that year. In addition, that next year was my last year in high school. Before I knew it, it is my senior year. However, you wouldn't believe this! Now I told you I wouldn't lie to you, there for believe me when I tell you it happen. I had one young man to give me his class ring and I mean a young man I liked since the 5th grade. A young man that wouldn't hold my hand when we had square dancing in grade school a young man that would call me ugly and fat. I looked around at all the young people that were once kids who had grown up before my every eyes. The boys had grown in to young men now and the girls were young women. I cannot believe how everyone had change and we will be eighteen, my where have the time gone I asked myself. This day use to seem so far away I was thinking as I was going home just think in two months it will be time to close books. However, before I knew it was May 6, 1973 my last day of high School, I am a senior, I finish three weeks early. My last day of school as I was approaching the gate I notices the girls that use to fight me and with all the others was all standing at the gate that day, I said oh no! Not again! GOD please god do not let them fight me again. Therefore, when I walked through the gate everybody started singing that old Bobby Vinton song I used to sing to myself so long ago, in case you do not know how the song goes I written a little of it out for you.

> A long, long time ago, on graduation day,
> You handed me your book, I signed this way.
> Roses or red, my love, violets or blue.
> Sugar is sweet, my love, but not as sweet as you.

I started crying and walked away than I turned and ran back and I hug every last one and they all hug me and told me Dorothy one day you going to do something good we don't know what or when however we always could see this in you. You always have been special, something about you always stood out from the rest of us, and we never liked that about you, and we thought you felt you was better than us. The boys told me Dorothy you or nice looking you not ugly like we use to call you the girls said no we all wanted to look like you. I said look like me? They said yes; look at your big brown pretty eyes and kissable lips. They all hug me again and wish me well. In addition somebody told me, Dorothy you have a gift; now it may not be singing or dancing but god have giving you a special gift Dorothy and someday you will find your gift and when you do Dorothy you will work on it. Now little did I know years later I would hear them same words? They all wish me well that day. Well a month later there we were at our graduation ceremony and we all in our blue caps and gowns and everybody were looking good. Most of us girls were crying including yours truly me now can you believe me of all people was crying, you know I never did cry. In addition, you know men they wanted to cry but no way, cry or you joking. Now one of the teacher was telling us to all get in two lines that way we would be by the person that name was in alphabetical Oder to ours. The graduation march starts playing, we comes in two at a time, walking and stopping till we got to our sets everybody was standing up for us as we was coming in, when all we graduate was at our sets then we and everybody sets down. Some families were crying by now. One of the teachers spoke about us and what a fine year it has been working with us all. Some of us were still crying such as me. They were calling our names now. Before they call mine, they said we have a young lady here never missed a day of school this year her first year in all two weeks last year two days this year not one day. All B's all through the years and on the honor roll all the years. Miss Dorothy Ann Darrough! I got a very long-standing ovation. In addition, the graduates were yelling aloud that's our Dorothy! That's our Dorothy! Moreover, they was clapping and jumping up and down. In addition, people were running up to the stand to take my picture and I was in the newspaper, I was the only one got a standing ovation and afterwards my math teacher proudly announce ladies and gentlemen this is the gradation class of 1973! In addition, I was there front roll center! I never missed a day of school that year but it was said I did to meet some man. See how the truth comes out. Well after words we had a big dance down town for all us graduates, I didn't know it but the boys from my school had roses or red playing when I walked through the door. I dance with mostly every guy from my school that night. The little fat girl who never could get any boy to dance with me or hold my hand in grade school had every guy wanting to dance with me that night. All the girls were handing over their boyfriends to dance with me. They would come up to me and put out their hands and ask Miss Dorothy may I have this dance I would take their hand and answer yes you may. Little old me dance the night away and gust what every one of the guys was proud to hold my hand. I was crying, not because any guy wouldn't hold my hand now it was because they were. I look back on them years now and I can say for sure they were hard but I learned that people treat you the way you let them treat you. In addition, if you have care, love, and respect for yourself you will not let people abuse you. In addition, I learn there or nice kids in school because I met some of them. Some of them or still around. Deep down inside I can't say I forgive the people that mistreated me because I am lying if I said I did. However I'll never hold it over anybody head because the pass is the pass. Maybe I let people abused me. However, no child should have to fight every day to get kids off their back. Not all kids or fighters I sure wasn't. I know I let people abused me. When I got out in the world, I still was the same way. Now I am standing up for myself a little better them I did before. Even if people hurt my feeling, I was careful not to hurt theirs. I did not fight back in school because I was so afraid of everybody. However, who knows I might could of bet up a lots of them however I was too afraid to fight back. Nevertheless, you know what through it all I made it! Through the worst place I ever been which was Camarillo state hospital and through all the hard times I went through, I still made it through high school. I went from Cs to B's and on the honor roll. In addition, on top of everything else I was abused by both teachers and students. So there is no reason, you cannot finish school. I am talking to the black student now. Our ancestors back in slavery died for us to have the opportunity to go to school when they could not go themselves. They had their fingers chapped off if they was caught writing. So why not take advantage of what they died for. Get all the learning you can. In addition, stop saying the man is keeping us down. The man was in slavery but no more. Back then the man did keep blacks people down. In addition, the man that keeping us down now is ourselves if we do not shoot for the starts. And young black ladies stop being loud and talking and acing like ladies of the night and stop going to school just to show off your clothes and going to school half dressed. It does not take that to get young men's to notices you. Remember your first impression is your last impression. Act and dress in ways that will make young men respect you, and when they notice you, it is for the right reasons and the right reasons only. In addition, young black men check the way you dress also. The way you dress says a lot about the person you or. In addition, remember nobody can keep you down if you do not want to be down. Look at myself I could have given up when I left Camarillo however, I had to get myself together and graduate out of high school. I have to tell you by no means were it easy. It was not easy walking that far in the winter with the wind blowing nothing but cold air on me but I made it. I would get up at 4:am on school days when I was in that foster home because all I was given was fifty cent per day and I had to make a choice if I wanted to ride the bus to school and back or have lunch. I would choose lunch so there for I would have to walk to school and back to the foster home. In addition, if I did not make it in time for dinner I did not eat until the next day before I went to school. Now you may ask why I did not carry a lunch to school and ride the bus. I did not because I did not feel welcome to ask for anything to make me a lunch. However, I am a funny kind of person if a person mistreats me I do not want anything they have. Therefore, with all that I went through if I made it I know you can also. See I did not finish collage but you finish collage that is what I did wrong. When you go to college, take reading, writing, and speech. Learn to speak well. Learn the meaning of different words so that way when you go looking for work when you fill out your application you can use them and that makes you look so well educated and that may inspire the boss to give you a second look. Another thing my mother did not have a lot of money and there was four of us in school so I couldn't go to school looking as if I was a rich mother child none of us did when we was all at home.

Sometimes not all my clothes match but they were clean. It was only one person that notices that my clothes didn't match out of the hold school only one person. Now the style is mix match. Our mother did the best she could with what little we had. One thing she had food on the table when we came home from school and we had a nice clean place to live clean clothes and she had to wash on her hands so I have no complaints. However as I stated take reading, writing and learn the meaning of words and learn to speak well. There for you or letting the bosses know you or up on top of things, you can make them think more of you. And never go on a job looking as you need one and please when the boss ask what kind of work or you looking for never say I'll take anything. That is sounding too desperate. You may be desperate for a job, however never let people know because when you do some people will work you harder than they will other people on the job and treat you with no respect, and speak up and speak out if you do not like something do not hold back and go through the pain of keeping your mouth close because take it from yours truly that do not make people like you and they dam sure want respect you and after all you do you will be the first they will let go if they have to let somebody go and even if not you will still be let go no matter what. Even if you living in your car do not let people know how desperate you or to work for them. In addition, with a good education, you want have to say you will take anything. Therefore, I say again play your cards right and stay in school if nothing else. Now speaking back on the foster homes, I do not mean for anybody to get me wrong I am not downing all foster homes just as I am not downing all churches.

PART TWO·

PART TWO

Chapter 27

talking about foster homes

THERE OR SOME nice foster homes out there, like there or some nice church-going people. However, do not think just because a person goes to church that they good old nice God fearing church people because some or not. Church starts in the heart. Your heart has to be right first. Looking back, I must say being a teenager we just learning what life is about. In addition it can be hard; it can be lonely with so many disappointments and it can be some hurtful years. See we all have a tenancy to want people that don't want us. That's human nature to want what you can't have. I know I still do all the time. When you want a person that don't want you it hurts like you wouldn't believe and seeing that person with somebody else even if you not with that person it kills you inside. That the reason why I tell mothers not to tell their daughters they can have any man she want because that's not true at all. The man she wants may be gay or may like fat woman when she's a little woman. It don't matter what you look like you can't have any person you want and if a mother tell her daughter that she is setting her daughter up for a big disappointment in life because that's not true, just like people want you that you don't want, you're going to want people that don't want you, but when this happen you have to move on. Let that person go and move on, it hurts but it hurts more to be in a relationship with a person you know don't love you back. Now I will get to the part of my book telling about me being out on my own for the first time without having the proper education. Now you will have an idea about what I been talking about when I was telling you about how hard times was for me without a proper education now I know they say it's not what you know but who you know. However don't rely on that's that may work for others however you get your education because it don't matter who some people may know they still want get any brakes. Because if you're a woman and you don't look like you will open up if the boss is a man you can forget it because in this world you don't get something for nothing it's always a price to pay. Another thing I have to tell you stop going out and getting them high ass loans for them short term programs because you want to hurry up and finish something because everybody seem to have the same idea as you however if you don't believe me just do it and see. All you going to have are a high bill to pay and no job. Now how you going to pay the money back with no job unless you have a rich uncle that love you because just because somebody in your family is rich don't mean they going to give you a dime. Now I'm at the first time I got out on my own. The year was 1974 I am eight-teen now and moving out to be on my own for the very first time. I was happy and saying to myself boy I am a woman now and having my own place and can do what I want to do and can have a man staying with me man oh man! The party going to be on! When I was in high school, I say in the tenth grade. I would pass by this little green upstairs apartment around the corner from my grandmother on Third Street. It by no means was the best-looking apartment I seen but it was clean with nice clean surrounding and the people who lived there was ok expect for the crazy woman on the right side of me you cannot win them all. Anyway, as I said when I was in high school I would stop and look in this little green apartment and say this going to be my very first apartment. Sure thing it was. I had saved enough money to get my very own place. I was a very young and naïve person and would let people take advantage of me. This was when I would trust people. Men I tell you it was no fun being out there with no Bachelor's or masters degree. Therefore, I had to take the lowest jobs out there such as babies sitting or fieldwork or cleaning houses. The tomato fieldwork was coming so I went and got hire with no problem at all. Now I was working nights in the tomato field. Bakersfield has just about every kind of field you can name. My old man was in jail for tickets. I thought when he got out and move in we was going to go half on the bills and food and other things in the house. I would work for sixteen or more hours six nights a week but I might as well say seven because we would get off Sunday morning and I would clean house and cook me something for lunch to last me for the week. That one day would go so fast. All I was doing was working to pay bills. We had a slum property owner that's another thing I didn't know nothing about renters rights you go to the library and learn something on renters rights learn all you can because people like young dumb people they see you coming older people will use the hell out of you. Anyway the rent man would up our rent ever six months because I didn't know the law or renting. However my old man got out of jail thirty days later. As I stated I just knew we would go half on the bills, well I tell you this, I was a lie if the truth was not in me. I had every dam thing to do myself. I could not depend on him for nothing. He would leave me and move in with other women. When I buy food, he would let anybody help his or herself to anything they wanted to eat or drank. My old man would let anybody take whatever they wanted of mine he even let somebody take my birth certificate. When I come home from work I would be so hurt seeing all my things and food gone I would cry. In addition, I thought he would do little things around the house to help me. Hell the fairytale life I thought I would have with my old man just was that, a fairytale. We had a little front lawn he wouldn't keep the grass cut. I would be so worked down till I just couldn't go anymore there for the grass was tall one day my mother came over and cut it. I was so dam ashamed. I had a man in the house and he couldn't even keep the grass cut and he was not working and didn't work. For as parting forget it I was too tired to do any kind of parting thing was not the way I dream it would be ant that usually the case. There for when you're moving out your parents house don't look for nobody to go half on anything with you, just look for people to use you and this means you're so call lover. I know this sounds mean but let's face it it's a mean low down world out there and like I told you that's all you getting from me and that's the truth like it or not because when you get out in the world nobody going to be easy on you so I'm telling you what's real you get your education and believe me when I tell you it's hard however it's hell without it. And when you get your education don't get it to take care anybody, it's too hard for that, when I first got out on my own I was a child only eight teen and people older than I would come over to live off me, when I had nothing. One time a man and his woman came over to live off me. People don't care they could come over and eat the last bite of food and when I come home from a hard day's work and think I'm going to take my bath and rest and then eat me something I had another thing coming. I find there would not be any food to eat when I ask about what happen to the little food, my old man would tell me his family or friend ate it, they did not care about me. My old man did not care so why should them. One thing my grandmother said and believes me it happens. One day I had come to visit my grandmother and I had my old man with me. My grandmother took one look at him and the next time I came to visit my grandmother, she says to me Dorothy that man is no friend to you, Dorothy that man is a snake in the grass and you need to let him go because he don't mean you any good. In addition, I found it out.

He would call himself buying me something and when we get into it, he would take it back. Now me I am the kind of person if I buy you something I do not care what happen between us that is yours. Now whatever you do with it is up to you, but I want take it back. If I take something back I given you that mean I did not give it to you in the first place. Another thing my old man and his family would do and that was give other women our phone number so they could call my old man I know they be looking for me to make a fuss but I just give him the phone. His sisters would bring his women over our house I never said a word as long as the woman stayed in the car. See they never knew I had my big daddy and no longer could my old man hurt me anymore because all the feeling I had for my old man was gone. His sister told me we was going to be back together well she couldn't hold her breath long enough to see that day come because that was in ninth teen seventh nine I gust he died waiting on that day to come if he listing to his sister. See when you're a fool people think you will always be other words they think once a fool always a fool. But see a wise man change but a fool change not. And see he would come home with blood on his underwear I act as if I did not see it. He wanted me to get upset but I could care less. Now he just knew he had me his good oh fool. However I just didn't give a dam any more. When the women would call and ask for my old man I never ask whose calling I just give him the phone and leave out the room are house. He would be over his woman house I knew where she stayed however you think I went looking for him what for? No love was there any more. The funny thing was when I left my old man and went my way the women did not want him anymore. One tried to hold on to him but he broke her arm I was happy about that because as long as I was with him the phone never got cold. Now the same way my grandmother was in seeing through my man and could tell me he was no friend to me was the same way my aunt was which was her daughter we call honey. The first time she seen my first husband she told me right in front of him and my mother that I didn't have myself nothing for a husband, she told me Dorothy I do mean you don't have nothing. I found out she was right I did not have myself nothing. Now when my sister Dana and I was out one night when I met my second husband seem just like somebody walked up to me when I looked at that man and told me that's a theft Dorothy don't have anything to do with him. However, did I listen? See most of the time we have warning when we be getting into something we should not be getting into but we do not pay any mind to our inter voice. In addition, when we do not we have hell to pay. As I stated earlier I had to take jobs I hated to pay my rent but I had it to do. I worked on jobs where I would make just enough to pay at my bills. Each check I had something to pay. My first check went for rent my next check went for bills and everything else. When your poor and on a low paying jobs, if you stay in your own place that's what happens. In addition, as I said people would try to move in own me. Looking back, one man did" because of my boyfriend. No job, no money, noting. They would not be moving in on me to help me it was only to use me. Now I had nothing and I do mean nothing. I did not have a bed of my own. What little furniture I had in my place was from the Salvation Army. Now take my boyfriend he's dead and gone now and may he rest in peace, but he were not any good and didn't help me, he got disability. I recall when I was—laid off my job for a while. My boy friend paid our rent once. Now I had paid it for five years every month. Now that one time he paid it, he jumped on me and told me he was sick of taking care of me. Now not only did I pay all the bills, I had to buy all the food which I would not have minded if I had been the only one eating which I was not. I did not have a car there for I had saved up and bought an old car from my old man cousin. I didn't think my old man would want to drive it because he liked new up to date cars and my car was an old little green dodge dart and I paid his cousin two hundred and fifty dollars for it. My old man took over my little car. He had gone and got him a set of car keys made to go to it. Now I never got keys made to his car because I never felt welcome to other people things because I know them not minds. I did not drive my own car that much. He had gotten new cars because his mother would help him. He would talk about taking a match to every car his mother would coast sign for him. See he never cared anything for those cars one reason was he did not have sense enough to appreciated anything his mother did for him then to as I said some things that comes easy to some people they do not appreciate them. On the other hand when some people go out and work like a dog for something that makes them appreciates it more. Like a woman that plays hard to get now a man that interested in her may ask to take her out now she may not have anything to do that weekend but she will tell the man she does. Not that she do not like him it is just that she will not make herself available for him by asking. She may want to go out with him but she will hold back and make him wait and work for her. Now some women will jump at the first call not knowing the first thing about him. In addition, some will give it up the first time he asks for it. Not known he is just trying to see how easy she is and wonder why he will not call back. Just because a man ask to go to bed with a woman do not mean he will call back most time they want and if he do it just may be for to get a easy laid because he want to realest that pressure because the woman he loves want give it up and he know you will. Other words easy come easy go. I did not know my old man had gone and had a set of keys made to my car. When I went some place and came out my car would be gone. In addition, when we went somewhere and he got mad at me for no reason at all because with some men a woman don't have to do anything to him for him to beat her or get mad at her. With this man he would get mad at me for something he seen on TV. Now as I was saying he would leave with me stranded anywhere no matter how late or how far. It did not matter where we were or how cold or how hot. My mother had told me not to buy that car from his people but like I thought, he would not drive that car because it was old and did not look good. My mother told me that man does not have a car In addition, there for he will drive that car or any other cars he gets his hands on keep from walking. I could be at work when I come out to go home the car would be gone. One night he hit a tree in my car, just mess it up, left it up the street, and told me he had some women in it and one bit him and he lost control and hit that tree. I ask him why he had women in my car and that I had more care and respect for him to have men in his car. That was it he did not have any care for me nor respect. He said not a word. He left and went to Los Angles I think because he could have been right here in Bakersfield the hold time. However, he did not give me a dime to get my car fix. It never did run the same again. He and the women got out my car and my old man just left it where it was. He never tried to help me get it fix. That was all on me. I had to work overtime and my days off to get the money to have it fix. In addition, when I got it fix he took over it again. Therefore, I just sold that old car and did not buy another one until I left him. Now this is a funny thing, check this out will you, when we was together, he had so many so call women. He even took everything in our house when I left him and him and some woman got a place together and he moved all my furniture I had worked so hard for. Now this happen to me twice however he did not have any luck because the woman moved out from him and she took everything from him. See there is so many people want something for nothing. Now me I did not think that furniture was worth fighting over but they did. See them people they would take anything they could long as it was free. That was free stuff and sure, they were willing to kill for it if it came down to it. In addition, when he went to get it back some man slap him in the face. See easy come easy go. I worked so hard on jobs trying to have nice things. In addition, what little I had men would take it and give it to other women. I would not fight for it back because I did not want to in up in jail over some house hold furniture it was not worth that to me. I had jobs where I would be so stress out and depress that I would cry and ask God to do something for me. God please make a way for me to be happy. Please make away so I do not have to work on jobs I just hate any more. I would be driving to work and I would cry and pull my car off the streets and park. I would pray to God to take the stress, anxiety and depression away.

I was on a job I just hated and with me knowing that I would get just enough money to pay at my bills and the work was so hard and back breaking today my back hurts, as you would not believe. People would come over to tell me I did not have anything and I was not anywhere. Now only eight-teen just leaving home for the first time looking back just out of high school and them people who was telling me this some was still living at home or been out on their own for years. To me if you're in your own place with little or much you have it going on and do not let anybody tell you, your or nowhere. Most people who were telling me that was staying at home with their parents and was much older then I. Now some people idea of being out on their own is laying up on somebody else with them footing those bills. Never let a person lay up on you, which is another thing I would do. When you let people lay up on you all your saying is that person is superior to you. Do not ever let yourself be use like that. Woman when you meet a man if he have no place to stay do not take him in your house. You let him stay where you found him. See he have friends out there in the street and when you take him in he's going to get all his friends together and let them know he has a place to stay and he going to bring them to your house. In addition, before you know it they done took over your house and you going to feel like you or a visitor in your own house. In addition, if you married him look out! Everybody going to need a place to stay you can count on somebody in his family. They coming to your house bag and baggage ready or not here they come. Now please do not look for any rent money because you just be looking. Do not let it inter your mind about them buying any food that is not in the deal. The deal is free room and board. Some men people will pull the oldest trick to be pull on you and this is if they have some kind of income and you know about it what they will do is tell you when they get their check they will pay you rent. Now let us say it's the tenth of the month, now it's a while before the first, now it's only three days before the first now they picking an argument with you now I am sure you know what it is for just in case you do not it's so they can move on see this is what you call squatters. They will pull this same old out dated trick everywhere they go. So let well enough do you and let mess stay out in the street please. Do not have an open house for nobody. Another thing I will tell you and this is you or not on your own until you move from home and have your own house and paying your own way. What little I did have peopled would steal it from me. I really had it hard and older people older than I would try to live off me. People do not care; you will meet all kind of leeches out in the world, and people who will try to take advantage of you even when you or at a young age. I would meet older women; you would think they would take me under their wings. Well they did, to teach me to have men for money, and tell me how to put them to sleep and take every dime they have. Yes, things to get me killed. On the other hand, I am an older woman now. Moreover, what I would tell younger women just getting out on her own is to first, get your education make that number one, then number two get you a career and work toward maintaining progress. Number three recognize opportunity and go for it. Number four. Make your own money and take care of yourself show a man you want him but do not need him. Number five do not take everybody for your friend, number six and seven let marriage and kids be last on your list. Those women would tell me, your nowhere anyway, why not its good money in it. I know some men who would pay well to have sex with you. I say no! They tell me I am a dam fool. Now lest say you out there prostituting and faith will have it you meet a nice man you likes and he thinks the world of you. In addition, one day you guys have went together long enough now and he wants his family to meet the woman of his life and you have an idea he will ask you one day for your hand in marriage. So here, you two or at his family house. Now he done told his family and friend about you. Now he wants you to meet his family. You have done put them street days behind you. When you walk in the man family house there sits his father you done turned a trick with, and over in the corner sets his uncle and friend you done turned a trick with. Man how in god's name will you explained that to your man. Now you know you're not a prostitute you was hungry or the rent had to be paid. Now you had sex with his father, uncle and friend and many other men they all know now was it worth it. Before you do something that may hurt you one day before you does it ask yourself would you want it known? I learn at a young age that older women will take young girls whom having it hard and make money off them. I am not the kind of woman who would do just anything for money and that's not the kind of person I want to be around. I like money but I cannot say I love money because I do not. See the love of money is the root of all-evil. If a person tells you, they love money stay as far away from them you can get, because that kind of person may do anything to get it and that might even mean killing for it. If you are blessed to meet a nice kind person treat them right don't misused them because they are a blessing because now days not too many people around that mean you well. In this world, it's mostly everybody for himself and GOD for us all. It is a blessing if you can find a true friend. People will use you, now I know people going to say if you let them. That's not always the case. Sometimes you do not know you being used until you had been used. Do not let nobody tell you, your dumb the reason you get used. See you learn from your mistakes. We all have been used one way or another. If you love somebody and you want to make him or her happy and they don't feel that way about you then sometimes they will used you. So that used to happen to me all the times I had to learn men's, now I am not saying all men is this way because they not. There are some good men out there but you have to take your time getting into relationships and not take the first thing come along because you're so afraid if you don't take them that's it for you, never in this life will you ever get another man. In addition, you will remain by yourself for the rest of your life. You will get a man. However, make sure he cares for you. Remember good things come to them who waits and something worth waiting for is worth having. I had to learn just because men do not tell you he love you as long as he shows it, it is much better because action speaks louder than words. Then again, it is hard for some men's to tell women's that they love them. There for if a man can't tell you that he love you that don't mean he don't, it's just that it's hard for some men to say it. Then to he may not want you to know, he just might be very afraid he will get hurt. Maybe he has been hurt before and he trying to make sure that want happen to him again. Men not strong no one is. Most men hide his feeling and this is something he learns to do when he is young by others men. Take a young boy that's trying to learn to ride a bike now he may fall and cry now some men will tell him stop that crying you're a man a man don't cry only a punk cries don't you want to be a punk? A man is strong be, a man. There for he remember what he been told about being a man and being strong so he learns not to cry not only he learn not to cry he learns to keep is pain inside. That is why women think men are strong, but they're not they're no stronger than women. Some people just don't care about some things there for it don't bother them and some people will take this as being strong sometimes it can be confusing. Everything a man knows he learns it. How to treat women he learns it how to mistreat women he learn it. Therefore good or bad he learns it. In addition, I learn how dirty some women can be when they can have babies and you cannot. Now I'm getting in to infertility a subject many women is going through and god be with you I feel for you. I will tell you this not being able to have kids when you have lived to see the day come you will be a mother and find out that is a dream that will never come true and me dying to give birth to my own baby was my dream. I will tell you my sad story. I always thought that someday I would be a mother because that's all I would see when I was a little girl mothers with their babies. I thought that every woman could be a mother. Never did I dream that one day I would not be a mother when I wanted to become one. Everything that's female seems to be able to give birth. I was hurt when I was ready for a family to find out it would never be. Now I could have children but it had to be through in vitro fertilization which all that means is a test tube baby and you talking about money you have to pay out your ears and it may not work at all no matter how many times you try. I tell you this it is not fair for some women to get pregnant without even trying and don't want to get pregnant and don't want the baby and other like me have to pay out our ears and never be a mother that's why I say life is not fair and it's not, never have been and I doubt it ever will be. I still today would love to have a child and no not adoption that do not do anything for me. I just don't want a child I want my child not another woman baby. I want to carry my own child. If adoption do it for other women fine I hope you happiness but if that's not what others women want don't try to make them feel guilty because they want their own child because we have the right to want what we want like others have the right to want what they want. And women that can't have children of your own don't try to make yourself take on a foster child if that not what you want to please other people. There's nothing wrong with wanting your own child. And Me I'm the kind of person if I don't want something I don't care what anybody think of me because I have to do what makes me happy and no matter if people tell me about all the unwanted kids out in the world that want make me change my mind. And if god don't see fit for me to have my own child then I do without. Nobody cared about how sad I was feeling about not being able to have a child if you think they did your dead wrong. Nobody cared I was dying inside when I would see them with something I would never have. Even my first husband went out and got a kid on me and would take it all-around Bakersfield because he knew I couldn't have kids. When people would ask him is that's you and Dorothy child he would answer no she can't have kids he would tell me and be smiling when he would be telling me. When I got shot he asked me could he bring that child to see me when I was in the hospital. I don't know why he even asked me that. I was too sick to go into it so I said yes then to I had nothing agents the child he was just a child but I felt I went through enough pain when my husband went out and got that child on me because I couldn't have kids. So why would I feel guilty about not wanting a foster child nobody felt guilty about having a child by my husband when they knew I couldn't have kids. That's a pain nobody understand unless you been there and I hope no woman ever have to experience that kind of pain. If a man has to have a child that badly and his wife cannot have kids just leave her and get with a woman that can. Don't do her the way my good for nothing husband did me and take the child to my family house in hops they tell me. No women deserve that. It's just not right, that some women have to go through hell to have a child when others don't even want then and have no problem having kids and just look what some women do to them. Women such as me would be the best mothers we could be and we must have millions to become mothers it's just not fare. But who ever said life is fare nobody told me it was. I always heard it was not. But I tell you when you want a child and can't have one there's no pain like it other than death. That's a pain that's worst than pain. And just to think your husband or man go out and get a child by another woman because he knew that would kill you and to take the kid around your family and friends in hops they tell you. God only knows how bad that killed me inside, however I wouldn't let the pain show. And when I see my family and friends pregnant I would be so envy. And I would be mad when I hear some woman say when she asked what she wants a boy or girl and she say a boy if it's a girl I don't want it. However I would have taken a cow if god had blessed me with it. However I never let my madness show and that woman was so happy she could give my husband a baby because I couldn't. That was a killing pain and you wonder why some women have to go through that kind of pain with something that comes so natural for most women other have to go through hell and back and still no baby. You go through so much pain because you can't have children and as I said no adoption for me.

However my husband never married that woman I just knew he would after I gave him his divorce which she was so happy for me doing so she just knew she would have my husband for her husband gust what it didn't happen. In the end, he wanted me back however, I didn't want him there for he went to somebody else and she still didn't have him and she died without him. This to show women don't have kids to get a man to marry you because nine times out of ten it want work and if it did he wouldn't stay with you. If men marry, you let it be because he loves you and you love him that's the only reason to marry. Now you may notices me talking about this many of time and the reason for this is that it hurts and I have to get it out later in my story I may say the same thing again because I can't say this enough.

Chapter 28

If you want your own child.

THIS LITTLE WRITE up is about me not being able to have children of my own and also I like to tell women like myself that want your own child adoption is something you might only do if all else fails. However, if you want your own child don't let anybody make you feel guilty for wanting your own child. If you don't want to adopt a child don't! You do what make you happy; you don't own anybody anything it's about you. The hold time you been unable to have your own child nobody cared about you and the way you feel when you see a pregnant woman or a newborns baby there for why let people make you feel guilty about wanting your own baby? You should want your own child nothing like your own. And no amount of money is too much to make your dream come true. Some women had kids now they hate they had them because some had them for the wrong reason. And some women tell you how hard it is to raise kids, if it's that hard why some women have so many and some women say how bad it hurts and again if it hurt that bad why some women have so many such as 10 to 13 they must really love hard times and pain. I know how bad it hurt I went into labor when I was pregnant the doctor told me I was. Don't let people tell you nothing about how it is to have kids. Never let other people tell you nothing about nothing when it comes to what make you happy. I been married twice both of my husbands were no dam good. However, I don't tell any young lady not to get married because my husband's played around on me and abused me. Just because I had bad luck with men that don't mean every woman will have the same luck. If you can't have kids your husband might not fool around on you and get another woman pregnant. Every man doesn't do his wife like my husband done me. I had good for nothing men, that's all I ever had. With some men if they wife can't have kids it's we can't have kids. That's what a husband is; somebody that's do whatever it takes to make his wife dream come true he will work day and night to get the money it takes to make his wife dream come true and his wife will do the same for him. Marriage is 50th 50th I never had it but I know how it should be and if it not that way, your home want be bless. I don't care how well the other party live if your marriage not 50th 50th god want bless your home. He wants set foot in your home. Even if I did have two bad marriages still I want tell nobody not to get married. Married life can be good and health and it can be a happy life. However, you have to keep others out of it and if necessary keep them away. Let everybody stay at their own house; if they don't have a house or no place to stay where would they stay if you didn't have any place to say? Don't start letting people move in on you. If people have respect for their self and for you they wouldn't want to stay with married people anyway. Whatever is said and done in your house they there to see it and hear it. Now I'll tell you about myself wanting a family of my own. I wanted me a family when I turned twenty-one. When most little girls are babies their given their first little doll and told this is your baby. In addition, a little girl around age five with her friend plays house and you both have your dolls as your babies and you feeding and drying your babies oh what fun it was. However a doll is the closest some of us women going to get to a baby. We grow up thinking we all will be wives, mothers and grandmother some day. However, we never told not every woman going to be a mother, not every woman can have children. There for we grow up thinking we will all be mothers and wives taking care kids. I never got my wish. The first time I got pregnant, it was an ectopic pregnancy. This where the fertilize egg keeps developing inside the fallopian tube or somewhere else outside the uterus. The first time they had to take my right tube. I went in to have a DNC this where they scrape the uterus and the doctor found a baby in my right tube. That liked to kill me, I end up on life support, and they had to take my baby. I never knew I was pregnant. But I would have server pain below my abdomen and it would feel so tender and each time the pain came back it would be more server then the time before and it would be very little blood on my bed sheet. I had a pregnancy test but it would come back negative. So I thought the doctors knew what they were talking about. But one thing with an ectopic pregnancy most will come back negative when you're really pregnancy. Now I am going to tell you older women and younger women when you have a pelvic infection it can cause scaring in your fallopian tube. See most women get pregnant in the fallopian tube. I will tell you how this works. See between women menstruate cycle like fourteen days after her first cycle she ovulates this mean an ripen egg discharges from her ovum and now this how the fallopian tubes works I'm going to go in stages to make it more simple to understand. Now starting with stage one. She discharges an egg or two. Stage two, one of the pair of fallopian tubes which conduct the egg from the ovary to the uterus there's fingers like parts outside the tubes that sweeps the egg inside the tubes now for two weeks or so the egg stays in the fallopian tube then inside the tubes there or cilia which or hair like processes capable of a vibratory or lashing movement which pushes the egg to the uterus where it attach itself in the uterus to grow and for nutriments for nine months. Now if there is scaring of the tubes the egg cannot be push to the uterus there for it will stay in the tubes and that is what called an ectopic pregnancy ectopic means outside the uterus. Now there is other ectopic pregnancy but benign in the tube is the most common one. Now VD, which means Venereal Disease sometimes can damages the tubes. Some women have to have a complete hysterectomy after an ectopic pregnancy. They or the lucky ones because some women die before they even know they or pregnant. That is why it pays to know your body and to know when something is not normal with it because don't anybody know your body better then you. Now usably when you done had one ectopic pregnancy you will have another one. Now not always but some women such as myself did. So sure thing with my second pregnancy it was another ectopic however again I had to have my remaining tube removed. Now at twenty nine was my last pregnancy with my remaining tube remove so that was it for me never would I be a mother now not in this life time. Women I am going to tell you something else. When you have a man out there, fooling around on you with different women and you go to bed with him it is like you going to bed with them women because all them germs going in you and it can cause you to have cancer at the uterus. Also I will tell you women if a man loves you he will not fool around on you. Hear me women? If a man loves you he wants have any other woman on you. If a man loves himself he want fool around with other women he will only have one woman. If he do fool around on you never believe it's a mistake no matter what he tells you and if he says it was a mistake please do not fall for that, that's the oldest lie in the book. Look that means his man hood mistakenly gotten ready and he mistakenly got on top of that woman and mistakenly had sex with her. Please do not be a fool thing such as that is no mistake. 1+1=3 now that's a mistake not having sex. Now how well I do know another old out dated lie women tells and that is if they have kids by them men they will hold on to them because here comes the out dated lie they want their kids to know their daddy's. Oh what a lie it is. Women be wanting them men for themselves and kids don't have anything to do with it and men not crazy they know what time it is they know women be lying and men not dumb they know how well they got it and a man know women going to come back to them again and again no matter what they do. That's why a women cannot put any demands on men because men knows most women are weak for them and some women will have a no good man just to have a man and she will say a no good man is better than no man at all. I heard a man say one day women are like buses if you miss one many more or coming. See what men thinks about women now why can't we feel that way about them? Something else I have to say women should stop using kids to try to hold on to a man I will say try because if a person don't want you no matter what you do they don't want you so you should move on. My mother and my aunt left our fathers and come to California and we're all just fine they didn't used us to try to hold on to our fathers. Other thing women should stop doing and that is having kids by men trying to get men and nine time out of ten it's not going to work and this when some women mistreat the child. Have a child because a child is what you want don't have a child to get a man or to break up somebody home. If a woman put her man out as you know nothing in the world is a grantee except death and taxes there for if a man do leave home it's no grantee he coming to you. I'm coming back to my ectopic pregnancy. Doing this time, I was twenty-one with my first ectopic pregnancy and I was twenty-nine with the second one. I just wanted to tell you this to show you how far apart my pregnancy was with one tube. Now I am not saying every woman is this way but I was. I had to go back to work before I was well enough to go back because bills had to be paid and like always I was the only one to pay them and it didn't matter if I had a husband or not in the house with me I had everything to do by myself. Now with my first ectopic pregnancy, I was working at the packing plant packing five and ten pounds boxes of potatoes for sixteen to eighteen hours per day. Not all my stitches were out of my stomach so one day they broke and my stomach start bleeding like hell. I went in the lunchroom, and got some newspapers and cover the wound up. In addition, I keep on working. See I had to do what I had to do to make it. Through it all I was not, going to give up so people can say I told you she could not make it on her own because people had said when I first left home I could not make it being out on my own and they just knew I was going to fall on my face. That is what made me work so hard to stay out on my own and god knows it was not easy. Other words what they were saying I did not have sense enough to make it out in the word on my own. There for they were going by me being in Camarillo State Hospital there for I am a nut case that's all it is to that. In addition, is not capable of being out on my own because I'm so crazy people were thinking that about me. There for I had to work like a dog to prove them wrong. I never ever asked anybody for anything no matter what begging never been my thing. People still holds Camarillo over my head and they will tell any man that likes me about it. Another reason I'm writing this book and I'm letting the world know I been in Camarillo State Hospital, now I'm telling it for whoever willing to get behind my back like they done before and told it for me for the mentally ill patient and I'm not ashamed about it and don't care who know it. Now I am the kind of person people would call strong but I know I am not nobody is. Therefore, they would have loved to have seen me fall on my face but I refused to give them the satisfaction of I told you so because I know people would had love to had said that about me. Through everything bad in my life I went through no man I ever had was ever there for me to lean on. Even when I lost both men babies the fathers was not there for me and that's when I needed them the most. What really hurt was with my first pregnancy when I lost the baby the father of my baby pass right by my place with me out doors hugged up with some other woman and with my second one I lost I was in the hospital for eight days my husband never knew I had lost the baby and was in the hospital until I came home eight days later which was when he came home. I knew men did not care about me but for a while, I went through a period of denial. That's what some people do when they don't want to face reality they will go into denial. When I first move out to be on my own not only was I taken advantage of by not knowing the renters law even some people much older than myself was taken advantage of because they had been living in the same family house all their live so when they decide to sale their family home and rent a place they did not know the renters law. However you have to pay for being dumb I found out. In addition, something else I found out when you're dumb and a person is using you up they don't want you around anybody to teach you any sense. Like when a man has a dumb woman for his advantage, he doesn't want her around any other women that may teach her some sense. If you're a dummy he want to keep you that way because when he tell her a dam lie that he caught VD from a stool the woman will believe it. He don't want anybody else to tell her any different. See it's hard to find a fool now days and when people do they want to hold on to them for dear life and they want to keep them that way as I stated early on in my book knowledge is power and when most people have a fool they don't want them with any knowledge. A man wants to keep his dumb woman away from other women. He don't want other women around his dumb woman to tell her look girlfriend, we done heard what your man told you girl, look girlfriend he played you girlfriend, you don't get VD by swimming in some dam pool ; you get it through sex girlfriend you had better check him, you put his ass in check and you can tell him I told you he told you a dam lie. My brother know he wasn't raises that way ; here girl friend I let you read this I got this from the health department it tells you all about VD. A man don't want to walk in his house one day and his woman standing at the door with her a baseball bat telling him, Billy you told me a dam lie Billy; you don't get VD by swimming in a dam pool Billy. you get it from sex Billy I know now Billy who is she Billy? No man wants that. However I have some sad stories to tell about working in them convalescents' hospitals. First I will tell you, people like I couldn't afford to buy ourselves lunch and wouldn't have food at home. Now the food that be left over they would have the cooks to pour it down the garbage disposal then let us eat it. And the boss would tell the cooks if they got caught giving the aides and housekeepers anything they will be fired. I'm telling this to show my young people what it means to stay in school. You working on a job and you not good enough to have a slice of bread when you hungry no food at home no money to buy you a lunch and you have to work all day without eating. However I will let you know what an education means. One thing it means you do not have to take a dog fair to stay on some low paying job that you not cared about nor respected on. It means just anybody cannot do your job. So kick your hills up and lest get back to my book. After the summer was over so was the fieldwork so I had to find something else to do. I found work at this convalescent's hospital right after the cotton season was over. At the time, I thought I was big stuff all in my white uniform. Soon I found out I was nowhere. In addition, the way it came about was, one day I overheard the administrator telling the Licensed Vocational Nurse what I thought was that more nurse's aides were needed. Therefore, I told him that I knew some women who were looking for aide work. That's when he told me he's looking for Licensed Vocational Nurses, not aides because he could get aides a dime a dozen and the LVN laughed and went in the nurses' station and told the other nurses what was told to me. The other aides asked me why I let him talk to me that way. In addition, why didn't I say something to that woman over there laughing because nothing was funny? By now I was in tears I was told I could be gotten a dime a dozen. No I said not a word about nothing that was said or did to me because I was trying to hold to a job where I was not cared about or respected. See when that's all you have to make your living some people would take most anything to hold on to it. However I didn't have a husband that had my back. If my husband had heard that man talking to me as he had the only thing he would had did would laughs and I knew that. One day two big women were going to beat me up and I had to stand my own ground with them. Why I was not respected because I didn't get people off my back by speaking up and speaking out and if I had to take something and cold cock the hell out of them some time it takes that to get people off your back. However I will tell anybody now letting people walk all over you don't get it because they will not respect you and nine time out of ten you will never get to be a leader of anything no where you go because first of all people want look at you as even being a person and believe me the more you take the more people will give. Even with men the more women take off them the more they give. And women know it don't take men much to not respect them and letting them walk all over you they sure want respect you. We have to demand most men to respect us. And after all the hard work I done and staying over time if they needed me and there for five years never missing a day and taking patients other aides didn't want didn't make me liked and cared for. After all I did on the job that is what I was told aides can be gotten a dime dozen and talking about bringing my but down it did. I felted as low as the titanic sunk when it struck that iceberg. As low as a person can get. Here I was feeling good about myself, which I did not ever feel. I was feeling smart, and just feeling good about my job. Yes, here I was working in a hospital and thinking I was somewhere and thinking I was somebody. Lord what a blow that was to be told I could be gotten a dime a dozen. What a low blow that was and I was standing there looking at this LVN laughing at me. All I could do was go back to work to a job where anybody off the street could do. My old man would tell me I had a nobody job. Now I will tell you there's no such job. That added to the pain. However, check this out will you. Before I got the job a woman whom was already working in the same hospital I would be working in was telling about her job and my old man told her who every works in a hospital should be saluted. He talked nice about her and her job he made her feel as if she was better than I was because I was in the field shopping cotton. And she had new things in her house and she was showing them off to my old man going to room to room because she knew I did not have new things in my apartment. Another thing I just found out not so long ago she had spent twenty years in the Air Force and had retired and was being paid good money from her retirement and then she had been working at the hospital for years before I ever came to work in it. She had a new bedroom set when all I had was a broken down old bed that was left in the apartment. She had a new car when all I had was a ten speed bike a friend had given me. Man she sure did show me up something big time. It made me feel badly. Therefore, after the summer was over I went and applied for an aide position on her job and got the job that same day and you talking about happy. Later my old man told me I was nowhere and why didn't I find a real job? I could not believe what he was saying, now when the woman told him she worked on the same job he said nice things about the job now me it's a toy job well when he ask me for money I would tell him if my job not real my money ant real and that would start a fight. I got to the place where I hated that dam job I hated the people I hated the smell I hated the name I hated everything about it I hated the patient I hated the dam call lights I hated the dam visitors' oh I just hated every dam convalescent hospital in the world. I hated that dam place so much that I cried I cried because that was all I had. I did not feel like a young ninth teen year old girl should feel. I was only ninth teen but I would feel weak and run down all the time. I would move slowly, and I did not feel like doing anything at home or on the job. I did not know what was wrong with me. All my hair came out and ball spots was in my head I looked a mess I put on weight as if I do not know what. I would find myself crying about what I do not know. I remember one day I gotten a little Chinese man patient, he wouldn't talk much because maybe he didn't have much to said like myself. I recall one day his son was coming to take him for the weekend. However my nurse says to me Dorothy Mr. Ways going to be gone all weekend his son coming for him for the weekend so will you give him a shower, I answers sure will be glad to. Well he was lying on the side of his bed when I walked in and called to him Mr. Ways your son coming to take you home for the weekend shower time. I was pulling at his shoes helping him to take them off when he stood up and went into a karate stance. I never knew that man was a 5th degree black belt in karate, I said well now! I left out his room, the nurse call at me Dorothy! he had his shower? I answer yes! He sure did a good one to! I happen to looked back and he was standing in the doorway looking at me smiling, I said to myself you dam old nutcase you, dam you; and that shower, your never kill me you dam nut you, if you never take a shower that's fine with me. I asked my nurse why they didn't tell me that man was a 5th degree black belt in karate. She told me they didn't know I said he sure is there was his 5th degree black belt in his closet with his black karate martial arts uniforms, they sent him away after he come back from his visit. That same day Mr. Ways went home for the weekend I gotten a young female patient and she was having her monthly. And somebody had put her on the potty she had in her room. Anyway when she was ready to get off her potty her mother puts on her call light. I came in the room to get her off her potty. Now I have a very weak stomach this I always had even as a little child. Anyway when I got her off the potty there was number two all mix in with blood now I didn't mind cleaning it up because that was my job but I got a little sick at the stomach. My patient mother told my nurse my heart was not in cleaning her daughter mess as if I should had been rejoicing over cleaning that mess and saying I'm so happy that I was picked to clean your daughter mess up thank you god I'm so bless please let me clean it again will you please it just make me so happy. One day this same lady gave her daughter a calling bell to ring when she needed something. At the time we only had black nurses' aides working at the hospital. Well my patient mother made a jet black Aunt Jemima doll to put over the bell there for when she ring it we come running. One day that bell takes legs and walked off. That was making fun of us black aides. Nobody in the big heads department cared about the way that made us aides feel. I was fed up I wanted to go to school and get away from that kind of work. Now wasn't nothing wrong with the work it just was nobody cared about the aides. Aides are needed in every hospital and aides are very important because they are the first ones to see the patients in convalescent hospital. Still the ones I worked in the aides was not respected. I went and got me a loan from the school because I decide I try going back to school. I could not keep up I would be so dam tired, I had to drop out. I did not want to but I was not passing my classes anyway. So I went and told the teacher I had to check out. She asked me way I told her I was working full time and going to school full time and I'm so tired. She told me Dorothy no please stay in school I started to cry because I did not know what to do I wanted to stay in school but I had to work and I knew I had no one to depend on because even being married when I would try to better myself I could tell my husband did not want me to do so. What I was trying to do was for the both of us. Any way with men I could be trying to do some home work and they would started bothering me and I would tell them please I am trying to study then they would get up and go to some woman who was not trying to better herself. My husband would go out and fool around on me with women and give me sexually transmitted diseases both of my husband's did. This why I never been the kind of woman that fool around on my man because I never wanted to give him anything. Then to if he gave me something I know where I got it. I would be so upset that I could not study. So I would drop out of school. I was having it hard. Also I had this Licensed Vocational Nurse on the job trying to get me faire and gust what she was black like me. Why she was trying to get me fired, I never knew. I had hell on the job hell at home with my husband fooling around on me and on top of this I was trying to have a baby and that's when he gave me pubic lice and Venereal Disease. With all this going on with me I had hell at school trying to pass my classes which I did not. Even with all the hardship I was having not making enough money to do the thing I wanted to do, the next thing I knew my check was garnish. I had taken out the loan and had no way to pay it back. Now my job could had told the people I no longer worked for them and my check would had never been garnish but no they was not going to help me. I knew they could have done that for me but I did not look for them to care about my problem. A crazy aide there would talk about me because I could not afford to buy people thing for their birthdays and Christmas. One sweet lady she's gone now but she was a sweet lady and I will never forget what she did for me one Christmas. One Christmas we was pulling name as we always did for Christmas. She knew that aide would talk about me not being able to buy anyone anything. When I pulled someone name she went and paid for the person a nice gift and put my name on it. When the person came to me and thanking me I did not know what they were talking about. My friend told the person Dorothy like that she just buy you something and never want it known it's her. Now this was the lady who bought the gift for me. She told everybody Dorothy been doing this all the time and telling us she couldn't afford to buy anyone a gift. I went in the restroom and cried god bless her she passed away now however I will never forget what she did for me that day. I always say a person shouldn't put others down because they can't afford to buy people anything are if they do they can't afford to buy a person an expensive gift. It shouldn't matter if the gift is expensive or not if a person can't afford to buy an expensive gift for you whatever they buy you or make for you it should be appreciated and if you do not appreciate it you should smile and say thank you anyway just make like you do and if you want when you out of the person eyesight you can give it away or throw it away or whatever but don't hurt a person feeling by letting them know you don't appreciate they gift.

Chapter 29

A job that was too good to be true

NOW WE ALL know that old saying if its sounds too good to be true it usually not true. Now I will tell you about this job I got from the unemployment office after I left the job at the convalescent hospital because I gotten so sick of the mess that went on there. It was not that long before I was called to come in about a job. I said about a week after I had applied for the job. I was called to come in for this restaurant job. Now that job wasn't worth getting that's why it was so easy to get. Remember usually anything worthwhile doesn't come easy and this can mean jobs and anything else. The person told me a little about the job and where it was located which was on a not so good side of town. However I needed to work, there for I went on. I notice when I got there it was hardly anybody there and it was doing my lunch brake lunch time when I made it because I was told it didn't matter what time I came in so I went at lunch time that way I could see how busy the restaurant would be because I know I have trouble with counting large sums of money and I know how nervous I am and I know I would had made many mistakes. I could get so nervous and mad that I would give all the people money away I know me and I know how mad and nervous I can get and I say the hell with it and get the hell out of there. Anyway when I got there I soon notices nobody was there except for one man sipping on a cup of coffee which I learn he was the lady husband and his face was all burned up and even when it was just him and I there I never asked him what had happen to him no way would I asked anybody what had happen to them first of all it it's not my business and a person have the right to tell me that. I met the woman and I could tell she was not my cup of tea right away but I needed a job there for I knew I couldn't leave every job I got because I didn't care for the people so I made up my mind I would stick it out long as I could and I found out fast that wouldn't be long. She told me my first day there that she was call Candy and her restaurant was called candies place even if the name was not on the place. And she told me she liked me the first day she met me and she wouldn't pay me by the hour instead she would give me half of what comes in the restaurant. Well that sounds good don't it? That's what I thought. The problem was she didn't make anything so there for I could work day and night and nothing came in because nobody would come there and I found out why and it didn't take me long. One day I had come to work and she was not there yet and a man came in and he told me young lady you get yourself out of here that woman is no good and you notice nobody comes here I said yes and he told me why. He told me when that woman lived on little street I'll call it. She was going with some man and her and the man got into a fight in her front yard of her house and she took out her gun and put it to the man head and made him get on his knees and beg for his life and she blows his brains out. People knew about it and told others who didn't know about it and nobody went to her place of business. She didn't like for men to come in and talk to me. Most men like to set and talk with me they didn't say anything to her. And one day a woman told me Candy husband use to be a very good looking young man and many women liked him. However that Candy was crazy, one night while her husband was in bed asleep. Candy got some lye and poured it in her husband face. That man never talked about it everybody thought he was ok with it and oh crazy Candy just knew she had her husband wrapped around her finger but little did she know what her husband had planned for her bad but. We found out he had something heavy on his mind such as getting her back and I tell you he did to. I had left that place as that man told me to do and thanks god I did. I was told the night I didn't come back to work was the night that man pull his gun out and killed that woman right there in her place. She always went for bad but there's a place in the grave yard for everybody on the planet. That place is no more and nobody would buy it because of its reputation and all the things had happen there and everybody knew that woman had demons and many of them. You know god didn't have a thing to do with that man and woman getting together. Not every time you go out and get yourselves in some mess god have anything to do with it. Not only did I have a job that was too good to be true I had a man that was too good to be true however I knew this man was not for real but this woman didn't know it she thought I had found myself a rich man however that man was not rich that's why I don't want a man just for his money and only what he can do for me and when I really did find out the man didn't have any money that never bother me then to we would buy for each other and that's how it should be not just one person doing all the buying and the other person just enjoying it. In a relationship it should be 50 50 that way nobody won't feel used. Anyway as I was saying the woman thought I had found myself a rich man but I knew I didn't. He was good to me and I knew something was wrong because no man is good to me they misused me and I knew this man was too good to be true. He would be going up town and call me and ask me what I wanted him to bring me back and buy me things for my birthday I just knew something had to be wrong with this man no man every buy me anything not me I'm the one do the buying and never receiving anything that's my story. One day he called me up and ask me why was I trying to kill him good as he was to me and why when he turn on his TV there I was in living color having the FBI how could I do that to him he asked me crying and why did I try to blow him up why baby he asked me good as I been to you. The next thing I knew the police was taking him away to a mental hospital he was bipolar see what I mean I knew something had to be wrong with that man to be nice to me; I just knew it, I couldn't let myself think god had sent me a good man. I know men not good to me, if they or look out, something not right about him and I know that.

Chapter 30

here's the lie people tells on god

I KNOW THE PREACHER says what God has joined to gather let no man put asunder. Now 70% of that mess God does not have anything to do with and they should stop lying on the lord. He did not give me them no good men I want lie on him I went out and got them no good men on my own without the lord help and I will tell you I paid a hell of a prize for it.

When God give you a husband or wife no man can put asunder and there will be no other or nothing that will come between you two. Now this I learn the hard way. When god gives you a spouse you want have to worry about them mistreating you and if you're a woman that cannot have children he want go out and get a child on you because he want a child. Because god only knows that is a killer no way around it. That's as low as a man can go and to put the kid up in your family face. I know that made the woman feel good about she could give my husband something I could not. But you know what I am so happy I did not have kids by my husbands. At the time I thought I would die when that woman got pregnant by my husband now I am so happy god did not see fit for me to have them kids by my husband's because they would had use them kids to hold on to me. Lord I did not know it at the time but my greatest blessing came in the form of an unanswered prayer and I would be mad at god because he would not answer my prayer and all I wanted was a child of my own. And I will tell anybody no matter what your dream may be you hold on to your dream. I know my dream was to have children and I never did. I gave up on it. But I still wish I had children of my own that is a dream I'll never gotten over.

Now I will be telling you about this psychic that written me one summer day after my 39th birthday which is June twenty first this was June the 30th back in ninth teen ninety three. I do not believe in psychics but something happen in my life that made me think twice and here my story. One summer day I went to my mailbox here was a letter from some psychic that I do not believe in however I open the letter and this what it read, Dear Ms. Dorothy Johnson I don't know you and never met you, but I thought about you and when I thought about you a black cloud came over me this means dangers, now the danger is so servers I want charge you a dime to tell you what to do to avoid the danger. Just read on and I will tell you how to avoid the danger. As I said I didn't believe in that kind of stuff. I just tore the letter up and throw it away. Two weeks later, after my 39th birthday, which was June 21 of 1993 I went out in the country again. It was June 29 of 1993. I was sitting and talking with some people, later that night I seen this white car in the driveway besides the building

96

we were sitting at. Two men's was in side, the older man was driving, the younger man got out the car and walked pass me, he had a long knife in his hand he stopped and look both ways left then right. He walked pass me again going to the car. I asked one lady did you see that man with that long knife in his hand, she answer no, I got up and went to my car to go home, for some reason I got back out and sat back down on the porch. This was around 11: pm. One mind told me go home Dorothy please go home. I didn't then something said get up Dorothy just as a person was talking to me. I did not get up something pulled me up and soon as it did, I got shot beside my right knee. I did not know it at the time but the hold side of my right knee was a big hold. I heard a man say they shot her leg off. I laid back I thought my eyes was open but I know now they was not. It looked like the place was lit up with the most beautiful clear light I ever seen. No light on earth is that beautiful, it was so clear to me. I was peaceful as I thought I was sitting up and looking around at all the people that were standing around me all dressed in long white gowns. However, one thing I did not understand they was just bodies no men or women and they all looked alike with long black hair. I never believed in psychic but I tell you what, this made me think twice.

Chapter 31

the psychic that wrote me

I REMEMBER HAVING A dream before I gotten shot I dream my grandmother and I had went to heaven and we both was standing on clouds I was standing in front and she was standing around the corner from me. There were not anything but clouds, we had nothing at all. No comb no water no food not even a house not nothing. I asked but nobody where there but I got an answer when I asked why we don't have anything? My answer was the more you do on earth the more you get rewarded in heaven. That meant you had to earn a toothbrush, comb, soap all your personals. So everybody goes to heaven but the more good you do on earth, the more you be rewarded when you get to heaven. Now when I said heaven I'm telling things the way I dreamed it, so people won't be saying she said there's no heaven or hell I wish she make up her mind which one is it so I thought I explained that. Other words there or no hell or heaven only the sprit life. In addition, you had to earn people to be around you. If not you will be a lone, just you by yourself. We could eat the clouds they tested like lemon pudding. Now here I lay in the dirt in a pool of my blood. That light was gone. And someone was asking me what day was it, and what's my name, I found out it was that policeman the same one who came to my mother house, and broth my ID and asked about me. The ambulance came and took me to the hospital. I was near death I was told later. The doctor took one look at my leg and said the rest of it has to come off. I scream and said no! No! Please GOD not my leg, I prayed as I never prayed before. My sister Dana was there with me. My mother just could not come. My sister Dana like to had fainted when she seen me cover in all that blood. My mother and brother and stepfather and my sister Louryette and her husband and kids and my first husband came two days later. The only reason my ex-husband Williams came he knew it would take a lone time for me to be release from the hospital and he wanted to stay in my apartment and drive my car was the only reason he came not in good faith, he wanted to use my tragedy to his advantage he's that dam sorry bad as I was and in critical conduction and for a while they didn't think I would live. I recall I would let him use my car to go to work because my car had a heater and his did not and his job was much farther than my job. Then to I worked inside where it was nice and worm and he worked outside where it was cold. I being a nice person told him to drive my car. Well one night I went out and I run up on him with a woman in my car I told him about it and he told me I could take my car and stick it you know where. One night he went out and got with some woman and left my car on a bad side of town in a field so somebody could take it or do whatever they wanted to. I had to go to work so I called a cab and went to work. A woman that works with my mother told her she had seen my car abandoned in a field. See when a person does things like that, that person don't care nothing about you. If a person doesn't have care and respect for your belonging, they don't have care and respect for you. However, my family told my ex-husband no he couldn't stay in my place and drive my car. I did not owe him anything even when I got the divorce he said he will pay half I told him no. I would not take anything from him. He was taking care of another woman and her kids but I did not ask for noting the only time I ask for a little something was when I had to go to the doctor and the only reason I did was that I had Paid two hundred dollars for his doctor visits each time and I paid two hundred dollars for his medications which he wouldn't take because he was an alcoholic and he couldn't drink on his medication because it could give him a heart attack so he loved that alcoholic more then he loved himself. Therefore, he still did not have anything because other people used the hell out of him. He did not have any luck see if the left one want get you the right one will. So now, I am having my operation. They had me sign some papers for my leg to be taken off I went on and sign them. They could not stand to take my leg off they sent me to Visalia California because they had something new they wanted to try on me, they put this bar in my leg that grows the bone I never learn what it was I stayed there for one week. Then they sent me to San Francisco California. There I stayed for three months. It was so hard I had crying spells. I thought I wanted to die; peoples would come in and tell me GOD loves me I did not want to hear anything about GOD and I knew he didn't love me not now not ever. I had this bar in my leg it was so heavy I had to call in my nurse to lift it for me. So one day I decided I would try lifting it myself because my nurse aide didn't have much patient for us patients. However the first time I lift my leg it went ok, then I lift it again this time the vine popped I panic like hell my angle was passing by, he was a RN I call at him and told him something was happening to me then I pass out. The next thing I knew I was back in my room from my operation, they had removed that bar. Therefore, I told them to take the leg off. I had a bad experience, and I did not want to go through that again. However, before they took my leg off they had about ten different doctors from different states to come and see me? They all looked at my leg to see if they all recommend amputation, and they said if one says there is something that can be done they wouldn't amputate, but not one said something could be done so amputation take place about a week later. My family came up there to see me through it all. Now my right leg was amputated through the knee. One day about two weeks later, I start having pain like I didn't believe. My hold body was hot, as I don't know what. It's cold up there in San Francisco California but I was hot, they put me on a cooling air mattress. That helped some I told them my stomp hurts, they thought I didn't know what I was talking about I told them something was wrong with my leg I told my doctor take a look and see, he did to shut me up, sure thing I had two infections. They told me they were sorry and that from now on, they would listen to me, and they did. They had to take me back to sugary and make a hold in my stamp and put a tube in it and a jar attach to the tube and would inserted medications in my stump with a needle and let the medication stand in it for a while and let it run out in the jar. Sometimes the medication would be cold and you talking about hurting. They had to take blood so much from my arm that all my vines was used up, I have sunken vines they have to go so deep to try to find one, so they had to put a line in my neck. That hurt like hell I scream and scream lord it seems like it took hours for them to get through. However, it was worth all the pain, because they did not have to pick my arms any more. I stayed depressed all the time and I would cry, I had to be on bed rest for two weeks with that tube in my leg. One day they took it out, man I tell you I was so happy. I was sitting up in my room on my bed crying and a janitor came in moping the floor he ask me what was wrong I told him I do not know why GOD let this happen to me. He told me to look to the mountain look to the sky but don't look back and don't ask why. That stayed with me. After that day, I will say a month later I was laying in my bed crying late one night when this nurse comes in my room and takes a set at the foot of my bed now I was at the head of my bed when she came in but now I never got up to move to the foot of my bed but still here I was at the foot of my bed and the nurse picks my head up and laid my head in her lap and rocks me very gently like I was a baby and she says to me, my little Dorothy god has a plan for you, now you don't know what the plan is but one day you will know and when you do you will work on it. She told me Dorothy it is a reason why this happen to you. I said yes because I did not go home as I was going to, I said if only I had gone home this would not have happen to me. This when she told me about our life book which is here when we come to the world. It even has the date and time we were conceived. Now this I'm telling you for some reason I can recall it so well many thing that happen to me I cannot recall however I can tell you how that nurse looked now she never told me her name and I did not recalled even seeing a name tag however I'm not saying this weren't a real person all I'm saying is when I asked about the nurse I was told there weren't a nurse on the floor that resemble the nurse I asked about. However I'm getting back to the story.

Chapter 32

our life book

THAT NURSE TOLD me that night Dorothy if this weren't in our life book Then Dorothy this wouldn't have happen to you. Dorothy, god has a planned for you, but you do not know what's god planed is, but one day you will know Dorothy one day you will know. In addition, when he let you know Dorothy you will work on it she told me again. I do not remember when she left I went to sleep never knowing who she was. Now as I said when she comes in my room I was at the head of the bed when she taken my head in her lap I was at the foot of the bed. Until this day, I do not know how I got there but when I open my eyes, I was again at the head of the bed. In addition, I never seen that nurse again and every time I asked about her I was told they did not have any nurse there that walked with her left feet turned inward. One night I was so sad I put my face in my hands and was crying and asked GOD if you have a plan for me what could it be for you to take my leg dear GOD please tell me. I heard a voice say when its time you will know and not until then my child not until then. Also we have a BIBLE life and our bible life is our BASIC INSTRUCTION BEFORE LEAVING EARTH. There for we're just learning the basic instruction of life. However the first letter in basic instruction before leaving earth spells BIBLE. One day I was looking through my nightstand and I run up on this poem called footprints in the sand. I cried on the part that read the Lord replied, "My precious, precious child, I love you and I would never leave you. During the times of your trials and sufferings when you saw only one set of footprints—that is when I carried you. I said the lord been with me all this time I know god loves me and he would never turn his back on me. Well I stop feeling sorry for myself, I started working out more, and feeling good about myself, which is something I never did. I would go down to the piano room and play the piano even though I do not know how. See all my life I never felt good about myself, I always felt other people was better than me and nothing good ever was going to come my way, and I felt I just did not belong nowhere but on low paid jobs, and never could be a leader of nothing. I guessed that is why I always gotten in bad relationships. I felt I could not do any better than I was doing. That is why I stayed on hard low paying jobs. When others did not want to do something here, come the yes woman. They know I would do it. One woman told me I will get something out of it yes she was right. I sure did pain, and all broken down that is all I got out of it. Well now I was counting the days, I know I would soon be fitted for my practice leg. I did not think that time would ever come. Therefore, one day the doctor came in and I was taken down to the exercised room. They rap my stump in the stuff that looked like flour water. In addition, it was so cold.

In addition, when it dried he pulled it down and it came off. That was called the mole. So in the mean time I would go to the exercised room with the therapy and he or she would have me lifting weights to build my body up for my prosthesis leg. The work was so hard and very painful. However, as if they said no pain no gain. Therefore, I would work out hard every day and it was well worth all the pain because finely I was ready to meet my prosthesis and I was ready to get to work. Therefore, one day it was ready and they brought it to me. It came with a big thick ship skin sock, the leg looked so ugly to me, I never seen anything like it. However, I put it on and was ready to go. I took my first step in my new leg; all the patents came to see me walk for the first time with my new leg. A month later, I was going home I take the gray hound bus. About thirteen hours later we were in Bakersfield. My family picked me up from the bust station I went over my mother's for a little while then I went home. I had to get use to being home. Now I could see how I would manage at home without anybody helping me when I fall. I wanted to see how well I could take care of myself.

Chapter 33

Coming home

YOU NEVER KNOW how well you really are until you come home and have to do everything for yourself. When you fall you have to get up yourself with no help. That's why it's good for you to learn to get off the floor on your own because someday you want have anybody there to help you get up so that's why you should learn to do things on your own then to you will start feeling better about yourself because the more you can do for yourself the better you feel. It was nice benign home. I would fall and it would hurt so badly. However, I would get up the best I could, no one there to help me. Really, I did not want anybody there. I had to learn to do things different now. I did not feel like going out doors I was not ready for all them question, and the stares. My stump would hurt like hell. I just had been home for two weeks and one even a knock came to my door I open it, and there stood my crazy ex husband Johnson smiling now not so much to see me. I was all dope upon my painkillers and I told him to come in why I do not know until this day. As Soon as he came in, he tried to take him some. I push him off me, and tell him to leave. That same might, he calls me and asked me to take him back. I told him hell no and hung up the phone. He calls me back and said you know what bitch you think you was hurt but you have not seen nothing yet bitch I'm going to kill you. I called the police, went over one of my neighbor's apartment, and told her what had happen, and she looked over to my apartment and he was at my door, the police came but by this time, he had left. The police told me to do whatever it take to protect myself. I did not want to kill him I just wanted him to leave me alone and go to them women that he uses to tell me that wanted him. He called until I had to unplug my phone. He steals all the time so he soon went back to jail. He would send me

Pictures of him with the chest out, and write on the back of it I am one of the kinds that shock your mind, now a grown man writing stuff like that. I am a grown woman that does not do anything for me. I think a man is crazy if he write stuff like that to me, he have to be, no grown man in his right mind writes that kind of stuff to a woman. So anyway, as I said I was not ready for the questions and the stares. As soon as I came home, there came the questions and the stares. One day I was on my way to the store and this man was delivering something at the store, and he smile and told me your in bad shape. In addition, some would tell me you were so pretty before you lost your leg. In addition, some would ask me do you still have the need for sex. Do you have to take that leg off to have sex? In addition, you are half a woman, no man wants half a woman, he wants a hold woman. If I had only one leg I would want to die. Believe me I done heard it all. I mean these people did not even know me. One day I was going to the doctors on the bus, I did not feel well this was one of my bad days. In addition, people started staring at my leg when I stepped up on the bus. I stop and raise my dress so they could see my prosthesis leg and told them see everybody I have a prosthesis see do not stop looking you see this bitch I said to one woman who was staring the most look everybody this leg was made for me it's called a prosthesis. Then I sat down. They still do the same thing I don't believe it will ever stop. I never have been the kind of person like the people I meets out. Now I have to tell you about my grandmother last days it still hurt till this day to talk about it. As the old phrase goes time heals all wounds I'm sure you familiar with the phrase, how untrue it is time don't heal all wounds never have and never will here's my story. About five months later, I started having dreams that my grandmother had pass away every other night. One night I dream we all was at my grandmother's funeral, and we all was in this big white church, and two undertakers came by us walking really fast with my grandmothers in her caskets, and she was dressed in a long dark red robe with very long sleeve and they turn to the right going down this hall. My grandmother raises her right arm up as if she was shouting and the people in the church shouted. Six months later, my aunt called my mother I was there at my motherhouse at the time. She told me her sister told my mother my grandmother was in the hospital and she was not doing well. I got my brother wife to take me up there to see her. I would go ever day she was 95 at this time. She got to the place she would not eat. Her heart was so weak; my mother had to sign the doctors to put a pacemaker in her. We all prayed all through her operation. Soon it was over. I just could not except she was dying. For the last time I went to see her and I thought she was doing better, I told my family she was. One day a neighbor and I were sitting outside when this woman came by and ask how my grandmother was doing I said with a smile she doing better. Then an hour later my mother came out and told me she had pass a way I just sit there it came back to me what she had told me so many years before. In addition, that is just what I had said she is doing better, and all the time, she had closed her eyes and went to sleep. I just thought I could not make it I knew some day this day would come but I did not want to live to see it. However, I did. The last thing she said to me was I see my angles I can see her face in my mind now. That is the reason I try to be right with people. I have something some people do not have and that is a conscious. In addition, when I have done somebody wrong my conscious bothers me. There is some cold blooded no caring peoples in this mean world. Not everybody has a conscious. Therefore, like I said before if you or blessed to find somebody that cares about you do not mistreat him or her and abuse him or her because they want care about you along. That is what happens to me with my husbands. I loved and cared about them they did not have sense enough to appreciate me. Men thought I was crazy just because I used to be right by them. They would go to jail for a year or more, and I never mess up on them. Like my husband, I sent him money and I went to visit him every Sunday but when he got out, he treated me as if I was nothing. Men had told me that is what he was going to do. So next time he went to jail I had my fun then on the men did not have to tell me twice. I had to tell you that so I could show you what happens to some people when they try to do right by some people. Now with good men's who tries to give his woman anything she wants some women use them kind of men's now the next woman going to pay for what the other woman done. Now he want do anything for the next woman who mean him all the good in the world. See we all going to be use one way or the other, and it's nothing funny about a person being use and that don't make that person dumb, so if you're being use don't feel you're crazy because you're not. As I stated earlier on in my book when you love somebody you plays the fool we all do and there's no exception to the rule no matter who you are and how smart you think you is because there's always somebody smarter then you and it goes on and on. Now getting back to my grandmothers funereal, she was laid out in her casket dressed in pink and white. She had a wig on and God made her look like that woman I used to work for who I didn't care for and the men called her a whore one day and told me to go home. That is how I made it through her funeral.

Chapter 34

Now I'm going to tell you
some true ghost stories

I HOPE YOU'RE NOT frighten of ghost stories because I'm getting ready to tell you some more ghost stories so kick back and get ready to read my true ghost stories and GOD knows their true from the bottom of my heart.

Now I am going to tell you about five dead brothers that died back in may of 1955. Now check this out will you please. I was not born until June 21 1955 they died a month before I was even born. In addition, why they come to me I do not know but this a true story please believe me GOD knows I am not lying to you. So please read this story because maybe somebody out there knew these boys.

The Montgomery Brothers

I was just sitting on the side of my bed just thinking over things one day when these five boys come to me in spirants I gust that's the way to tell you because I never seen them they was talking in my head. They told me to take notes because they had something to tell me. They said they were the Montgomery brothers; Billy and Bobby and Tony and Freddy and Charles Montgomery. They told me the reason why they had come to me. And the reason was that they want people to know how they were killed back in May of 1955. Now they never told me who was the people they wanted to let know how they all died and I never asked. But anyway they said back in the 50's they lived in this big old green brick house on the corner on 4th and Virginia in Bakersfield California. In addition, that it was just five boys and their mother and father. They said they always dressed alike in short black leather jackets and levies. They told me four of them went to Bakersfield high school at the time. In addition, their older brother Billy was married and living with his wife and little girl. However, they laugh and told me that it did not seem like he ever left home because he was always there. They said they were all singer and dancers and they would compete in talent shows at school and they always won. They told me they had a song the four of them made up about their brother Charles. They said they would sing using all their names, which went like this. Billy, Bobby, Tony, Freddy, and Charles he is never ready. They said that every time they got ready to go somewhere Charles was always the last one to get ready In addition that they always had to wait on him. I wasn't writing this down and they got furious with me and in the other room something hit my bedroom window hard and I got up and got a ink pen and some paper and started writing down everything they was telling me. They said that one of them was graduating out of high school. In addition, the school was giving a graduation party at Kern River Park for the graduates and this was May of 1955 they never told me what date I gust that didn't matter. They told me all five of them were going because they always went every place together. They told me only one of them had a car and it was Billy, the oldest of the five. Tony said laughing; that old car was ugly as hell but man could it run. They said they went up there and had a nice time but the weather for some unknown reason turned cold here in Bakersfield California in May and the sky turned black and the wind started to blow and it started raining cats and dogs. They left early. Tony told me he was in the backset bouncing up and down because he was the baby of the five and he felt he was entitle to act a fool. They told me while they was driving around the crave leaving the park a big new looking white truck came around the corner on the wrong side of the road on their side. They told me they tried to get over but it was this gray car on the other side of the road where it should have been and they could not do anything. They told me they just stopped on the road and the truck run in to them pushing them over the cannon. All five died that night. Tony told me he was the last to die. One of them told me they all went to heaven. In addition, Billy was the first to get his wings and halo. They told me while they were lined up going through the golden gate they all was saying their name. In addition, singing their song. Billy, Bobby, Tony, Freddy, and Charles he is finely ready.This is their story: They just used me to tell it for them. In Loving Memory: The Montgomery Brothers R.I.P. Now as I said this is a true story I'm telling it just the way they told me to tell it. I have asked people about these young men and everyone says they remember when this happen. So if their family out there anywhere here's the story and here is the way they told me they died and this is the truth nothing but the truth so help me god.

The Doll

The year was 1966 doing this time we was all young and stayed on the same street my aunt Annette stayed on which was Haley Street. We lived just a few houses up the street from my aunt Annette and her family. One day my mother and aunt had went to the goodwill, while they were there my aunt found this old doll that had teeth she both the doll for her baby daughter. That same night around 3.AM the dogs start barking and running around in the yard. We had never heard them dogs carry on like that before. The next day my aunt comes down to our house and tells my mother what had happen that night which had never happen before. She told my mother that early that morning the kids ran out they bedroom saying something come in the room and went under their bed and was shaking the hell out of it, they said whatever that was under the bed they could hear it talking but couldn't understand what it was saying. Nobody could. However the next day my aunt and mother went back to the store taking the doll with them. My aunt told the lady at the front desk what had happen and that she thinks there's something with the doll and she believe it use to belong to a child that passed away my mother told me later that same day. The lady didn't say a word for a while then she told my mother and aunt that the doll use to belong to her mother when she was a little girl and her mother never parted with the doll. She ask my aunt did she want to return the doll my aunt said yes the lady gives my aunt her money back and nothing ever happen in their house again.

The ghost of Mark Luther King Jr.

When we lived on N street here in Bakersfield California a man told us about a friend of his who had went hunting back in Stair City Ark. He told us this man was rabbit hunting all that day and never had any luck. Then here come this pig he tried his best to shoot this pig he just couldn't seem to shoot anything all that day and he knew everybody back home was praying that he had something to bring back home to cook. Night was falling and he was far off in the woods. He had been on his feet all day so he was tired and set down in some leaves that was pile on the ground. He heard a sound of somebody walking; he could hear the sound of leaves they was walking on. He grabbed his hunting rifle and stood up just in time to see Mark Luther King Jr walking with his head down carrying a lantern looking very disappointed. He said his friend told him whatever Mark Luther King would point at he would hit it. He wound just point anywhere and he would hit it. He hit so many rabbit that night and even the pig. He never told anybody except his fried what had happen and it was years before he told him, the man told us. Now Mark Luther King Jr. had died before his friend was born however he would read about him at school. He knew it was DR. Mark Luther King Jr. Now you know it had been a time if a person told a story such as this one that could had sent them where? To the nut house that's way he had better kept it to himself.

Ghosts stories: On N' street

A lady that use to live in the house we moved in on N' street had told my mother about a baby she would see in front of her bedroom door playing on the floor at night and she said when she went to pick the baby up it would disappear, however our mother never told us the story until years later here's the N' street ghost story. Now on N' street the old house we lived in was over one hundred years old so you know from that people use to lived there had long ago pass away. We know of one man had stayed in our house had been killed but not in the house but at his girl friend house and she was the one killed him. This is how the story went. We were told something like this. The family whom stayed in the house before we moved in the woman had a cheating husband and his woman lived next door to the neighborhood store we would all go to. He had been going with this woman for a while. As usually, she wanted him to leave his family which he did not. However, one day he told his wife he was going to the store. Next thing she knew the police was knocking at her door to tell her that her husband been killed over this woman house. The wife knew the woman and she knew she had been fooling around with her husband. There for maybe the big man that sat on my sister Dana chest was this man we never knew for sure but maybe he was. However, for as the baby the lady would see on the floor we don't know nor do we know who the devil was or the ghost that was looking up at my mother that day. I will tell you the ghost stories on N" street. Like I told you about the woman who use to live in our house. She told my mother she would see a baby on the floor crowing and she would go to it and try to pick it up, but it would vanish, my baby sister had her baby a little girl name Marquita. Her little girl was sick, my sister, and her baby where in my mother's bedroom; I was married to my first husband at the time. She said this big tall man came out the living room to where she and her baby was sleeping and sits down on my sister chest she said she reach for her baby and he told her don't touch that baby. She was looking face to face at that man. She said she don't remember when the man got off her chest because she said she passed out from not being able to breathe. When she seen the man was off her she got her baby and went in the other room where our mother was sleeping and told her about it.

My mother said one night she looked out our window and on the ground, something hairy looked up at her with blood shot eyes. That is all she said. Another time our mother told us late one night she seen this black and white cat walking across the floor now we all was home doing this time. She said she laugh and said to herself them kids sure would be afraid if they seen this cat. She said the cat walked up to the cooler and rise up and jumped out the window. Now the next day our cousin came over and our mother was telling him about it. He looked at the window were the cooler was and he asked our mother to show him where the cat jumped out. She looked at the window and said no way he could because boards was around the window and the cooler had the window blocked and there was no way the cat could had gotten out so there for she knew it was a ghost. My grandmother stayed overnight one day and she slept in the living room, and my sister next to I name Louryette, told our mother that she could hear many people talking around my grandmother and she said when she would get up and look in on our grandmother they would stop. She said they were all talking at once. Now I never seen or heard anything in that house and I would stay there sometimes by myself. Now my little brother saw a ghost when he was around seven. One day he was in the back yard playing when he heard something grunt he looked up and here stood the devil himself and was grown before he could bring himself to talk about it. Our house was not the only house on that block was hunted. Let me tell you about the people next-door who were on our left-hand side. Now the people that lived next door to us were one of the men from the group I will call Bobby. His kin who lived on our left in the front house was his aunt and cousins. In addition, in the back of them in the back house lived his mother and father his family lived here in Bakersfield during the 70s we know most of them. His aunt and one cousin and mother and father who use to stay by us have passed away now. However, when his aunt was living, she told us when her baby daughter would get sick she would see her father in the bed beside them, which he had pass away long ago. In addition, the oldest daughter done pass away now but when she was living she said one night she was in her bed she liked a dark house to. She said she seen the devil. And another woman told me since my leg been amputate that she and her daughter were a around the corner from N" street getting ready to go some place when they heard this young lady call out to them and they turned around and she was standing six feet off the ground and she told them I'm going your way, Then she vanishes. On N" street we rented from that same teacher of mined when I was in the 7th grade who told the kids to sic me. He died and my mother told me that night he died she was in the room I used to sleep in and the closet door was close and it open and the cable wire swung. He was a mean old man at one time. And if you acted up in class he would tell you look punk didn't matter if you were a girl you were a punk, he said look I got my education and good God he did to he was a school teacher and a foot doctor and many others and he didn't mind letting you know it. He worked hard to get where he was by no means did he have it easy and he was proud of his self and he had a right to be.

Now I cannot recall what year this was. But I do know it was in the 1970's and my grandmother had moved up the street from us on N" street and she would complain about hearing things in her apartment and we never paid her any mind because she had gotten older now so we just thought that it was all in her mind. She would keep on about it. Therefore, my mother and my stepfather had decided to have her spend the night at our house and they stayed in her apartment. They just knew they would not hear or see anything. So that night my mother decided she wanted to watch TV late like she usually did so she told her husband to go on to bed and she would be in there later. So she had watch TV until she had gotten sleepy so she had fallen to sleep when she heard the heavy breathing and she looked up and here stood this big black thing with a hold in the middle of its body growing from the grown up until it reach about six feet tall. In addition, she called for her husband and this thing disappeared just like that. She told her husband about what had happen, they left that night, and my grandmother stayed with her daughter Annette until we could find her another house up the street from Annette.

The Dead Man's Car

My stepfather bought this red car from somebody. Now he never knew this was a dead person car. However, it would rain inside that car when it would not be raining here in Bakersfield and that car had a life of its own. For some reason that car would not start on Sundays. We did not know way. In addition, you could turn the music up in the car, the music would stop, and you could not turn it back on. In addition, we would see blood on the floor of the car and when we went to clean it, it would not be there anymore. My stepfather sold the car and one night we were watching the nightly news and we heard a man was found dead in a red pinto and the cause of death was under investigations. They tried to show the man body in the car but every time they would try, the TV would mess up. Well sometime TV's does that.

My Grandmothers Gown

I do not remember how long it had been since we had buried my grandmother. However, I had both this stationary bike. In addition, I was in the bedroom putting it together. For some unknown reason I looked up just in time to witness this old short badge gown, which was in the air dash by. I knew it was my grandmother's gown and I keep working. All though she never wore a short gown, they do not always appear as they were in life. I seen her again when I was in the hospital one night. My room was up on the fifth floor. I had my operation on my stomp, I happen to look out the window, and there on the grown was my grandmother looking the same way she did when she was in her early sixths. However, for arms there were two long skinny sticks for arms. She did not move she just stood there looking strata. She stayed in that same position until I went home. I know something I done right in her life for me to be seeing her. Therefore, I know she were not disappointed with me. In addition, she told me one day since she been gone not to worry about putting flowers on her grave because I been good to her. In addition, the way it comes about was one day I wanted to go and visit her grave and put flower on it. However, I just could not make up my mind to go back to her grave. I knew I would cry and be depressed for days to come. However, I knew I had never went to visit her grave or put flowers on it and I thought to myself that was wrong of me not to had visit her grave. Then as though she sit down next to me and said Dorothy don't worry about visiting my grave or putting flowers on it. See you were good to momma. That is what we all called her momma. I do not really know if all the family knew her real name or not. I really do not think everyone does. Then I felt better. I am happy I do not have any regrets in the way I treated my grandmother all her life. I just do not understand how anybody can mistreat somebody without feeling sorry afterward and when that person never done a thing in the world to him or her I just cannot, see it. People or passing away so fast these days. In addition, as fast as their passing away now days you do not always be granted the time to make up with them and that would worry me to death. That is why I try to do right by people. In addition, when I do I am called silly every time. However, I do have a clear conscious and that's what counts.

The day my cousin Diane passes away

When my cousins Diane pass away due to breast cancer the day of her funeral after I got home, I was crying I undress and got in the tub for some unknown reason I looked in the living room and I seen this big ball of light shoot out from the bar that divided the kitchen from the living room. It then bounces but never hit the floor, and it shot out toward my cooler and outdoors, I am sure. I told my mother about what I had seen and she told me that was my cousin Diane letting me know that she was ok, and I know she was right. The same thing happens after my grandmother's funeral. I came home and I lay down on the sofa, and it was warm that day so I had the cooler on and I could smell snuff coming through my cooler, which my grandmother use to dip snuff from the age five till ninety-five years old. I knew she had passed by on her way to heaven and I just smile and said the way to go momma! The way to go.

The ghost in my stepfather's house

When I was first married my husband and I and an old man friend of ours moved in my stepfather old house that him and his family all lived in when they was just kids. Many family members had died in this old house. Therefore, the first night we moved in I was sitting in a chair next to a picture of my stepfathers' father. Now he had died many years before. I looked at the picture and it looked just like the eyes would move. A cold feeling come over me I turned the picture away from me. Well one day I had gotten off work, I was in the kitchen cooking, and I was by myself in that big old house. In addition, I could hear something in the wall hitting it inside and later sound as if something come out the wall, and was running through the kitchen I stop cooking and I left there. However late one night my husband and I and the old man had gone to bed my husband and I was a sleep and the old man called out loudly, oh guys! I see somebody walking through the kitchen! We never said a word. The next day I asked the old man what was that he said he seen. He did not say because it got to him so badly. Now after that night the old man went to live with his girl friend. I would be left in that big old spooky house alone because my husband would smell some outside c.k and the way he go. Now I was working in a convalescent hospital and anybody that done aide work in a convalescent hospital can tell you how hard and back breaking that work is and when he had smelled something and he wanted to get to it he would accuse me of having some man now at first I didn't understand where he was coming from. I was only twenty-three and he was fourth. We both worked and even the day we gotten married we went back to work the next day. With him it was nothing but work, work; work, all the dam time and never had a dam thing to show for it because he would give money away and I had all the bills to pay by myself. He didn't pay no bills, see he didn't mind staying with anybody didn't matter how many was in the house are how nasty the people was. Check this out he had left me for the old homeless woman she was getting dam good money but she was another that didn't pay bill. There for he moved her and her kids in these people house and bout of these people got good money from SSI but they was the kind of people that cared about nothing. However he was going with the woman while I am at work. Now this what he would do when he wanted to get to a piece of filth. And I do mean filth I can't tell you how that house was because ant no words for it. I just put it this way no way in hell would I had stayed there I would live out doors first, I would be homeless first and what I mean them people had dam good money coming in that filth. Anyway my husband moved that woman and her kids over all that dam filth and he had to go in that filth so here he come with some crazy mess, telling me I was having some man; now it didn't take all that to get to that filth. The toilet wouldn't flush and if it did nobody would buy toilet paper. Anyway he moved in that filth with that woman. However since the toilet wouldn't flush and the people wouldn't buy toilet paper they would wrap with newspaper and throw the piss and sh.t out the bathroom window. Now they would bath over that, and cook over that. However that's what my husband would be looking crazy and acting the same and be lying on me to get to that filth. They would cook and eat over all that filth; I didn't know the man I had marred was that dam filth. I said hell no! When he wanted to moved back in my clean house, hell no! He was to dam filthy for me. Divorce time, I file for a divorce I didn't want that filth in my house nor my family houses and didn't want his hands on my family babies hell no. It made me sick at my stomach just to thank about I was having sex with a filthy man like that and kissing that kind of filth no wonder I had VD no telling what else he would had giving me. Now fools had envy me with that filth they can have it because it's too much dam filth for me. We all come up poor but one thing about it ever thing was clean, our mother would wish on her hands but she kept everything in our house clean. The floors was so clean you could eat on them we was nice and clean, she didn't have clothes to put on her back but what she had she kept it clean. There for all of us are the same way we can't stand filth of any kind, even my brother the same way he can cook and clean like a woman. I have one leg but that don't stop me from keeping myself and my house clean, I bath twice a day every day no if and's buts about it, for as filth hell no. And another thing my husband didn't mind being put out a place for not paying rent. Unlike me I love my own everything, my own place; my own car, I don't like anything that's not my own. And I don't like even spending the night at nobody house and I sure in the hell don't like people staying with me. That's why I'll never marry again for them reason. Because I know when you marry somebody, here come the dam in-laws ready or not here they come that you can count on. Somebody going to need a place to stay and it just might be more than one and with kids that have not been rise. Because when you marry somebody in some families they feel you own they for having the person in the family and it don't matter in you have one bedroom house six people will live there with you and don't care that you have no privacy that's what kind of mess I been in, not with my first husband but the second one. Now back to my first husband, he would leave me and go to the other woman and if it don't work out here he come back this went on for some time. However everything comes to an end. The last time he left me that was that. I went and file for a divorce I gave him his walking papers. From then own he got women like himself that didn't mind being put out in the street. He didn't pay bills and they didn't ether. See the women thought they be getting a man to pay the bills however, little did they know he wasn't the paying bill kind of man. They would tell him you're the man you pay the bills I'm not. Well my husband was used to me doing everything that had to be done. That's why I tell any woman that going with a married man, if a man is any good ant no woman in her right mind going to walk away from a good man. That's the way it is. And when a woman husband fooling around on her with you, please believe me when I tell you ; if he fool around on his wife, he going to fool around on you if she put him out. Because don't think you be taking him from her because you can count on it if a woman put her husband out and he comes to you nine times out of ten he will be down on binned keens begging her back that you can count on. Now by both my husband and woman didn't pay any bills they both be looking like two bowl weaver looking for a home. Now when we was married he would leave me by myself in the spooky house and just about every night I could hear people walking and talking in that house when there would be nobody there but me that's why I moved from there later.

111

The Ghost in the rest room

I can recall my brother telling our mother and me about the night he went over one of friends house when he had to used the rest room and he just open the door and went in and there sat a man on the stool and my brother excuse his self but before he could close the door to the rest room, the man asked or there any tissues paper? My brother asked his friend was there any tissues paper his friend answered yes man you do not see it. My brother answerers the man in the rest room asks for it. His friend asks what man? Ant nobody here expects for you and I said my brother friend. My brother said man come here and look he open the rest room door and sure thing there were not no man in the rest room. My brother left his friend house that nigh without another word about what he had seen he never told us about it until a year later.

The ghosts at the kitchen sink

One nice summer day I went over my grandmother's house and she was sitting on her front porch. In addition, I was about sixteen I say. I had a set on the porch beside her. For some reason I turn back and looked in the house; she had the fount door open. I seen this old man bent down with a long gray over coat on coming from the sink and going to the stove. Then he was not there anymore. I know I seen this man I will never forget how he looked. I never said a word to my grandmother about it then to she never was afraid of ghost's anyway it wouldn't have matter anyway but I just never told her. Later we came in, and for some reason She said Dorothy one day I'm going to get sick, and you all going to say one day momma getting better, and all the time I'm going to have close my eyes and went to glory, then she smile. That hurt me; god only knows how that hurt me.

Chapter 35

an unanswered prayer

HAVE YOU EVER prayed for something repeatedly and your prayer was never answered? I do know that sometimes it do happen in our life and we do not know why our prayer weren't answered because we did not ask for much. Well I am going to tell you something; sometimes our most greatest blessing can come in the form of an unanswered prayer now we want see it at the time because god works in mysterious ways, but first and most importantly you will be happy that your most greatest blessing came in the form of an unanswered prayer.

You can be the reason why your prayers not answer

I'm going to tell you a story about two men I know I'll call the oldest one Ray and the youngest one bobby. Now Ray had a wife I'll call Jan now Ray and Bobby had been married I'm just gusting I say two years. Now Ray wife was in Ray's corner one hundred and ten percent. Now Ray had been on a job he just hated and he wanted a job in a mental hospital working as an aide but he had already said if he gets the job he was going to leave his wife soon as he get on his feet's he prayed and he prayed for this job but his prayers weren't answered and do you wonder why Now the younger man I will call him Bobby. Now bobby in collage now he plays basketball in college and he gets help from his sister whenever he needs it and he came in to some money now he did not think about paying his sister back her money. Now bobby has said if he goes pro he's not going to help nobody now do you think he will make it? Therefore, before you pray have goodness in your heart. And when you pray always put other people first never yourself, never pray just for you because you must always put yourself last, always.

Chapter 36

Let it go

THERE COMES A time when you have to come to the point where you have to let what people say go in one ear and out the other. There is always going to be somebody who thinks they know what best for you Instead of minding their own business and leaving yours and everyone else alone. They put their two cents in other people business. If a person have time to mind your business and everyone else business his or her own business is not been taking care of. If you take, care your house that is a full time job. Like when I was marriage my husband used to let his family and friends but in to our business and come down any time they got good and ready and no I didn't like that. I felt we were married and what business they had invading in on married people and laying up on me. What they should have been doing was taking care of their stuff. See when you get marriage things is hard enough trying to make thing work and keep your marriage together it is a full time job. Another thing when we got ready to go some place his please would go and jump in the back set of my car without even asking me could they come alone. I wanted just my husband and me not them. They did not have any respect for our marriage. Nobody do not need any outside interfering because it takes two people to make a marriage not three or four are more. Everybody else should keep their two cents out of it and if you have any pried about yourself you wouldn't want to be going places with married people uninvited and showing up at their house unannounced. In addition, for as wanting to stay with married people get your own place so they can have their privacy. I will tell you this, just because one party invites you to stay the night if the other party do not do not stay. I had men family who would lay up on me and I tell you by me they was not welcome in my house not at all but I had their brother and they felt since I had their brother they had the right to my house and my food and my things just the run of the house. If you or in a family like that, you had better get out of it because your happiness and health should mean more to you than any relationship. However on other hands if you're going in to my kids this and my kids the other just stay in it sister.

If you like a person leaves them a lone

Now I know this sound funny but the reason I say this is sometimes we can and not meaning to but we can be a pest to a person we like. What I mean by this is a person can give a person their phone number and that person who calls can make a person hate they ever gave it to them because every time they pick their phone up that person on it. Some people you can't let them know where you stay because you can be getting ready to stash a pot of piss out the door and you will hit that person in the face with it; so don't make a person hate you because you don't know when to hold up let the person call you some times.

One+1=3 is a mistake

Now I wish people did not tell their kids I do not want you to make the mistake I made talking about having a baby. See how can you mistakenly take off your clothes and mistakenly lay down or whatever position you get into to make a baby that's no mistake not at all so stop telling children's their a mistake because 1+1=3 now that's a mistake not a baby always make a child feel good about themselves and telling them their a mistake sure not making them feel good about themselves and if a child don't feel good about themselves they usually don't do well in adulthood. So depending on what kind of upbringing a child had it has a lost to do with the kind of person he or she will turn out to be and anybody should want their child to be all they can be. However, you most tell them positive thing so they can grow to be a positive person. See positive in positive out.

If it sounds too good to be true

Like I always said if it sound too good to be true usually it's not true

Now I am going to tell you about this man I will call him Lee now Lee is the kind of man that loves to lay up on anybody him and his family. They do not work. They or freeloaders, now check this out. I will call the woman Betty. Now Betty was dying of AIDS. Now Betty would call this cub outdoors pay phone. Now whatever man answers it that is the man who can come over and have sex with her. Now most all the men's here in Bakersfield knew this woman was dying of AIDS. This Lee man was out of town. Now Betty called the pay phone and Lee was there to get his death call. Therefore, he answers it. In addition, Betty talked to him and asks him to come over. Therefore, Lee did. She let him move in that same night. So one day I seen Lee at this woman house and I called him to me and asked him how did he meet her. He told me and I said you fooling around with her? He told me yes this a good woman she took me in and didn't even know me you sound like she's a bad person mind your own business he told me. So see he may have AIDS now but he thought this was a GOD-fearing woman that out of the kindness of her little heart was doing GOD work and taking in a freeloader that she did not know. In addition, all the time she wanted sex because she knew she was dying of AIDS. Now she is dead. The man I was telling you about he's dead. You see a person not going to let you move in with them just like that and don't know you unless something wrong with them one way or the other so I knew that woman was too good to be true.

Chapter 37

remembering what
my grandmother said

NOW YOU CAN learn a lot from older people if you just listen. I use to listen to everything my grandmother use to say. I can recall her telling me one day Dorothy when I was a little girl my mother told me a story about these people who was trying to fill this can up with water. What they were trying to do was to run it over. Now everybody was working hard getting the water out the well. I mean everybody was sweating as if I do not know what. They almost had it, but by this time they just couldn't go any more everybody just was to tired they had worked so hard trying to run that can over all they need was a drop more but everybody had just given out. They all looked down at the can one lady was holding a baby the baby had a cup of water in his hand he drunk all the water in his cup and he started playing with the cup through the baby playing with the cup a drop of water fail from the cup and the can ran over. Therefore, she said see Dorothy every little bet is a help. I knew what she meant and I am passing it down to you.

Some men love their wives

I know it is rare, and I do mean very rare; I mean so rare that I didn't believe it myself, I had to go around asking was it true because I didn't want to write something that wasn't true. However, believe it or not; there or some men who really do love their wife and will not mess up on them. Now those the ones outside women call gay however, they know they would love to have a man that wouldn't fool around on them. My husband use to tell me when he tell women he was married they would say oh no! And his friends tell him, man you act like you're afraid of women, now here he was married to a woman and somebody telling him he acting likes he's afraid of women. I could tell he was upset over it. I said to myself, his friend won't have to ever tell him again he's afraid of women, he will be a free man because, I never been the kind of woman that wanted a man to feel he was missing out on something. I didn't want no man missing nothing because of me, whatever it was he wanted I wanted him to have it.

Every job is important

Now I want people to understand no matter what kind of job you may have every job is important and if you do not believe it now lest say if the sanitation people stop working just think how your city would look if you did not have them to pick up the trash. The field workers put food on the table and they provide other things we needs. The word needs the entire worker to make our world a good place to live. However there's some good workers out in the world and they cannot be gotten a dime a dozen and it takes a dam fool to say they can and who every tells their worker this is the dumbest no class good for nothing person around and I do say person lightly.

Another thing the administrator use to tell us aides he could get use a dime a dozen. In addition, that we were not in any position to voice our opinion about anything. That meant we was uneducated and I do mean very much uneducated and dumb on top of it. I'm going to show you something. Now I recalled we had a man who was a RN, he was very smart and good in doing his job. But one day he stop giving out his medications and was looking all around the hospital and he did not know his name or where he was and he did not remember he was a RN. Come to find out he had a brain tumor and once it was removed he still couldn't work anymore because his mind was not right anymore. Now just that fist his life had change for the worst. Now he never told us he could get us a dime a dozen but that happen to that nice man. In addition, another thing I want people to know it don't matter what your position is on a job, it is just important than anybody job. No matter if, you or a dogcatcher, milkman housekeeper, aide, or janitor, garbage man, or you may work in the field. Your making a honesty living. In reality an aide and a housekeepers and the janitor and the RN's and LVN's at the hospital is more important than the Administrator because they sees the patient first if the janitor or housekeeper in the patients room and something happen to the patient, they there to get help because they goes in the patient room through the day. The aides are the most important people in the hospital no matter if the administrator knows it or not. They should get the up most respect from everybody. Your employer should make sure every employee is respected on the job no matter who you or are what your title may be.

Your human and you have feeling and emotional. Even a car it is a machine and if you mistreat it long enough it to will fail you when you need it the most. If you have anything agents people do not get into the business of working with people. People come in all shapes and sizes, and colors, and male and female. Why mistreat somebody when they have not done a thing to you. Would you like to be treated or your child be treated the way you treat people. If you can answers, yes then your treating people right. If you cannot then stop and check yourself, remember what goes around come around. It may not happen to you, but it wills somebody close to you. In addition, that hurts even more. So employer: please tell your employee thank you, and that they done a good job. In addition, they will feel good about themselves and will do even better. You cannot make it without them.

In addition, always remember God hears everything you say and he sees everything you do without making a list and checking it twice because he knows when you or knotty or nice.

Chapter 38

some of us must work harder than others

And never get a head.

I KNOW IT IS not fair but it's true that some of us if we want to get somewhere in life we must work harder than some people and never get as far and I know it's make us feel bad and at times it makes you want to give up and say the hell with it all. In addition, I know that on some jobs the harder you work the last you will get respect, appreciated, and never be told thank you for a job well done. In addition, somebody else do not do as much and is making more then you or and always being prays and gets the up most respect. That is the way it was for myself the person who done the most work and I done work that were not mine and never did I get a thank you. And the same thing it was when I was married I tried to be a good wife each time I was married and I paid all the bills and would buy all the food but I see now that's not a good wife that's just a good fool. I recall when my second husband whom made jail his first home had made it to the halfway house. He calls me one day to bring him some candy and cookies and other things he wanted. Therefore, like a fool I did. when I came up there people was looking from him to me and laughing. He told me people was lying on him and saying he was caught having sex with some woman there. In addition, later the woman came out and sat with her legs open right in front of my husband. A woman whom worked there saw what the girl was doing and called her back in. About a month after my husband got out of the halfway house, I overheard him telling a friend of his that some woman caught him my husband having sex with some girl. I was standing in the restroom combing my hair, I came out the restroom and I knocked the hell out of him and told him to put my dam phone down! In addition, I do mean now! I told him I am divorcing your crazy no good ass! Just wait and see! By this time, I was crying! You not giving me VD ever again I said through all the tears and I meant every dam word of it. Therefore, as always, he went back to jail and I started on me working on my divorce. See it is easier to get a divorce when the person in jail, because they cannot stop it. He told his mother about it and his mother tried to get his sister to talk me against it. However, I just look this way they thought they had themselves the biggest fool that ever walked the earth. I had all them fool. As I said, I just look this way.

Chapter 39

IN GODS WORDS

GOD SAID IF your faith is the size of a muster seed, and you say move the mountain the mountain shell be moved. First, you must believe that the mountain will be move. No used in asking God to move the mountain when you have no faith that he will move it. He said asked in my name and you will receive. Now this does not mean if you asked him for a million dollars you would receive it. He may not see where you need that million dollars but he sees where you needs a job. Now he may bless you with a good paying job where you can work and save up to have those million dollars. See God do not give you something you can very well get yourself. Now I know sometime a person can buy a winning lottery ticket and win millions when someone else cannot seem to win a dollar. However, someone else already has money and wins the lottery and the homeless poor person do not even have a home to live in. Well just like us women who want children and cannot have them and women who do not want them can. See the person who has all the money just might not be happy at all. They may have health problems or they may have lost their hold family to cancer you just never know. That don't mean that person is happy, sometimes big money can bring so much problem to a person house hold but I'm like everybody else I still would love to have big money, I know it can bring problem but so does not having it. Not having it seem like to me can bring on bad heath problem because you have no way in paying the bills and you worried about how you're going to pay rent and other bills, how well I know how fast the months goes by when you have no ways to pay bill

Something, so if you asked them what would they rather have the money or their family back? If they loved their family, they would say their family without even thinking about it.

Yesterday was September the 11. Now if God had them people love ones that was killed in the twin tower or in them two airplanes in one hand and a million dollars in the other I'm willing to bet you they would pick the hand with their love ones in it. So friends you just might be the richest person in the world but just haven't taken the time out to count your blessing. Start counting now one two three keep on now stop you just might have something around your house might be worth that millions.

Organizing yourself for success

You must organize yourself for success: What I mean by this is you must move yourself where you can be successful and this means in successful environment and around positivists and keep out of nativities. Look successful, ask the part; dress successful, talk successful, have a positive personality, and be around positive people because being around negativity has a way of rubbing off on you and then t, you or judge by the company you keep.

After the storm, the birds sing

In the summer when there is a storm afterwards, the birds will sing. In addition, what a pretty sound they make. That is our life. No matter what it may be, things do get better. That is the birds singing. Everything comes to a pass. Somehow we make it through it. We have to believe things happen for reasons. However, we may not always know what the reason is. However, we must believe it to will pass. Life is our learning tree and the bible is our basic instructions before leaving earth. We or here to learn we come to the world not known a thing. Learning does not come easy for some people. However, some teachers do not have patients for students like this.

Getting into relationships
for all the wrong reasons

There is a person who gets into relationships for all the wrong reason and that is for money and fame. That is the wrong reason to get into relationships. When you get into a relationship, it should be for the right reasons and the right reasons only. Don't get into relationships for what you can get out of a person. Love them for them because when all the money and fame is gone what is left? Just remember what goes around come around. Just as you used somebody someone is waiting around the corner to use you and some body is waiting around the corner to use them and the using goes on and on so if you don't start it there's want be nothing to stop. Do equally for each other that way nobody will feel used

Because nobody want to be used it's such a bad feeling to know that the person you love is only using you, I been there and I tell you it hurts.

Benign in abusive relationships

I'm going to tell women, just because a man may not put his hands on you he still can abused you with words, playing around on you, not taking you any place because I gust he don't want to be seen with you, I don't know. Take myself, I had men that didn't want to be seen with me out in public because I have one leg, do you think I care? The hell with them however, it takes time to come to this conclusion and you can't come to it over night. It had been times I would had cried, this why I tell people we heal at your own pace and never think about how well other people doing with their healing and you not doing just as good., just considerate on yourself in a positivity way. Another thing I will tell you, people lies about how well they feel about different things. They will say they feel just fine with their leg off to the hip, known they telling a lie. I'm sure they can't wait to come home and fall out on their bed and cry like hell when nobody there. I'm not going to lie to you, I feel better some days then I do others. I still cry, and asks why me god? What did I do for this to happen? Why lie, and say I'm over with all that crying? I'll never be over with all the crying. I want lie and said I'm so happy now, don't know why I was crying in the first place; this nothing to cry about it's so easy for me to get around. If I told you that, I be lying and why lie? We're only human and things get next to us. This not easy, I still fall, it hurts when I fall, and clothes I use to wear I can't wear anymore. Now coming back to abusive relationship, I'm telling you about my relationship with my first husband, now when we went some place together he be laughing and talking to his male friends, if women was around I would talk to them if not I sat there and say nothing because I don't like to talk around men like that, than to I would feel out of place around all men. When they come over the house I would get up and go in the bedroom, that's the way I always have been because I just feel out of place. Now as I said I just sat there and say nothing when the men or talking it was like I wasn't there and that was the way I liked it. Now when I be talking to women he would be listening and voice his opinion and we didn't want him in our compensation it was for us women then to he didn't know anything to talk about that made any sense. I don't care what he be talking about I never would speak on nothing because I was not ask anything than to nobody be talking to me, he be talking to men, I'm a woman; I stayed in my place and then to that would be disrespecting my husband, men be talking; why would I get in it. And I could see he was enjoying himself with his friends. I would talk with the ladies. Now when I am talking about something he would but in and if I looked happy he is ready to bring me back home. This abused, anytime a person don't want to see you happy; and enjoying yourself, and bring you back home, knowing that its good for you to get out that's abused. I was working hard every day. And if I wanted to buy something for the house like one day I decided I wanted to buy a new bedroom set. He told people, Dorothy buying a new bedroom set; I'm not helping her. Dorothy putting up wall paper I'm not helping her. Now what is that to go out and tell people, that's why I will tell anybody I don't look to lean on anybody and I don't ask anybody for nothing. I make it on my own. Going through hard times and making it out of them can be good for you because this how you get strong. Life not supposes to be easy, we suppose to learn from life and if it was easy we wouldn't learn anything. There for life is the way it supposes to be, hard, difficult; mysteries, unpleasant; depressing, unbearable just the way it is. Now I hope you see how you can be abused without a man laying his hand on you. I know there or so many women in abusive relationships and way? The number one reason women use is they want their kids to know their father. Now any fool knows this a lie and that lie is so out dated till it's time for it to have a face lift. That lie was being told when my grate, grate grandmother was a girl now it's time for a new lie now. Everybody knows the real reason women stay in that relationship has nothing to do with the kids knowing their fathers. And women should stop using that same old out dated lie and find another one to use because everybody knows the number one reason is they love that man. Why would any woman stay in an abusive relationship for the kids if that lie was true anyway? What good is that doing the kids? That doing the kids more harm than good for them to see their father beating their mother. In addition, they will start hating their father. Because the average child loves their mother more than they do their father anyway. Most fathers done left the homes and the mothers or the only one the child has. Mothers or not doing their kids any justice by staying in them abusive relationships. In addition, the child grades will start dropping from A's to D's. And they will develop behavior problems that's recognizable in a problem child coping with a mental disability such as bed wetting and not wanting to come home or problem with their speech or not wanting to eat and can't sleep or have problem with their peers at school when they use to be a kind and happy child now they starts fights at school. In addition, usually when a boy sees his father beating his mother sometimes now I will say sometimes a boy will grow up to be a woman beater himself. The reason why I say sometime the boy will become a woman beater is the chain have been broken we do not have to be any way we do not want to be we or and always have been our own person. Now I am getting back to the woman beater.

The child will become very depress and withdrawn. Now see this used to send a child to a mental hospital see how easy it use to be. This is depression a mental problem but in the 60's if you stayed depress for some time you was consider a nut for sure. Now things done change most everyone you see is dealing with some form of depression.

It's so common now that when you tell somebody they can tell you about the kind of medication their own and tell you the name of their doctor. So if you're in an abusive relation I'm going to give you a number to call to get help. In addition, you call it and get out of it. Love yourself enough to move on there is better thing in life for you. Women do not ever feel that you need a man to be a woman. You were a woman that day you turned 21. The best thing you could ever do for yourself is to move on. Staying in that relationship will beat you down and take all your pride and yourself-worth and your motivation. You will start looking older than you or and you will stop keeping yourself-up remember that was the way I was when I was in Camarillo remember what I told you about me not wanting to get out of bed and bath and wash my hair and put on clean clothes I want lie to you, I stop bathing and keeping myself up that depression is nothing nice I tell you it can make people kill themselves. You will start putting on weight or losing weight. And the strangest thing or you won't even realize how bad you look until somebody tells you. However, you will be lucky because you will still be alive.

Chapter 40

for everything, there is a reason

THERE IS A reason for everything g that is happen in our life good or bad. There is a reason why some people have all the best luck without even trying. In addition, there is others that have to work their self to death for little of much. Some people are born in richness when some people are born in the poorest of families. Now what could that reason be? Theirs are people who live to be one hundred and five. When theirs others who do not make it till five. Well life not fair, which is just the way things are. There is nothing we can do about it. However, one thing for sure, when you go out and work hard for something that makes you appreciated it. Take the person who gets everything hand down to them they do not appreciate it as much as the person does that have to work hard for it. In addition, when a person does not care for you they want appreciate what you do for them. The more you do the more they want you to do. That is way when a person see that another person do not care for them and do not mean them any good they should find the pride in their self to get up and get out of the relationship. There's reasons why that person treats you badly and the reason not because they love you the reason is they don't love you nor do they have respect for you nor will they ever love you. I had to except that and move on. It is not easy and you do not find the strength over night. It comes with time and lots of it. With some people, it may take longer for them to find the strength to move on and if it does, that is ok. Everybody is different. You may have loved your person more than the next person loved theirs if that is the case that is all right also. Whenever you do fall out of love with that person you will be out of love. In addition, that person can never hurt you again. No, matter what they does. All the love you had for them will be gone. In addition, it never will come back. A person can only hurt you really only once because deep down no matter what you may think, after the hurt you will never feel the same for that person and that person could do the same thing to you again and it want hurt like the first time because you want feel the same. They cannot hurt you repeatedly. In addition, the love is lesser and soon it will be none at all. That's why at times it's good to be alone that way you will have time to think about what you want or what you don't want. It's good to give your heart a long rest and not get in another relationship for some time. You're not lest then human if you don't have a person in your life sometimes you're better off being alone in life then being mistreated in an unhealthy relationship. It has been said it is unhealthy to be a lone well I feel it is just as unhealthy to be in an abusive relationship physically or mentally. I hear some women say it's best to have a no good man then not to have a man at all that's what I call a nut I would rather have no man then to have a no good one, but then again, everyone too they own opinion.

There is no dumb child

That is one thing I hope I never hear and this a parent calling their child dumb. There is no dumb child. Some children just has a learning disability And when the teacher asks, does every one understand the assignments?

The child not going to raise he's or her hand to say no I do not understand. They know them teachers can be impatient and most are very impatient with a child that is harder to learn. See I been one of them kids myself. In addition, I remember how I was treated for it. I would be afraid to raise my hand to say no I do not understand in case someone would say I knew old dummy did not understand. Do she ever? I would get beat up after school for being dumb they would call me. If I told the teacher, I would be told to sit down. Kids would not go for that to day. I do not blame them at all. Now I do not say kill anybody are take a gun to school. I do not blame them if they calls hell by suing the hell out of the school for the teacher letting the child be miss treated by others kids and doing nothing about it. Another thing I can remember the teacher telling us that old saying, when the fat lady sings. One day when the teacher said when the fat lady sings one kid says to me sing it Dorothy! You fat pigs you sing it girl! Sing your song! The kids and teacher all laugh. I went through school never raising my hand and admitting that I did not understand the assignment, which is why I have problems in everything such as reading and spelling and so on. I am sure there were other kids like myself that didn't understand the assignment but they didn't want to be called names as I was. However, at the time it seemed that I was the only one in the hold school that never understood the assignment. At the time, it seems as if I was a loser, I just never feel as I fit in anywhere. This girl would invite me to parties just to make fun of me to other kids, which was no friend. I would get so nerviest when I had to get up and go to the front of the room to speak that I would stutter. However, to my surprise nobody ever made fun of me. Swat would break out on my face. However, I just learn not to long ago just before my father pass away that I got a brother on my father side of the family that stutter also. Just as I still do at times. So just have patient for your child. Do not think their just at school playing around and not trying to learn. That may not be the case at all. In addition, do not let anybody compare his or her child with your child. That is not fair to your child. Their child may be younger than your child is and maybe they can spell words your child cant. That do not mean anything, someday your child may grow up to be something special and the child that could spell may grow up to be a bum, because they did not have the get up and go it takes to be something. So you never know how a child going to turn out. We just never know. Kids or laughed at in school when they have a learning disability. It may take some kids longer to learn something. However, once they do learn it they want forget it, and they're going to be good at whatever they learn. Therefore, a learning disability may not be very bad. It just makes you better at something once you learn it. In addition, some people just cannot learn at all. That still does not make them dumb. That just makes them disable to learn. We all have some somewhat of a handicapped some people or more noticeable than others.

The devil has his life book

Remember when I said that before I almost got fatally shot, that I seen a car pulled up in the drive way; and there were two men in the car, and the younger man got out with a knives in his hands; and looked left, then right; like he was looking for someone and nobody didn't see this but me, and my first mind told me to leave. Now I don't know for sure if this was just for me to see, or if these were real people; because I can't always tell if they real people or not, because I see so many ghosts all the time; so I don't know. However this might had been my warning. Other words the devil has his life book for us also, remember when I said whatever god has the devil has also. Now as I said, if it is not in your life book it wants happen. No matter how things may look; believe me when I tell you if it's not in our life book it want happen. Let's say if your mind lead you not to go somewhere and you go anyway and something happen to you, now it's so easy to blame yourself for it happing. I will tell you don't, don't ever do that; because it can, and will; slow your healing process down. However, as I said; it's in your life book for it to happen. And something else I will tell you. Sometimes a person can do wrong to others and maybe the person who did the wrong, nothing ever happen to them; however one of their love ones will have to pay the price for them. That way it will hurt you the most. That's the reason why you can do something to some people and they want do anything to you. There for, you think you have gotten away with it and all the time they going to kill some child of yours because they know that will kill you anyway and they want you to live to see it. there for, that's why god let some people have kids and then take them; there for, if you don't want something like this to happen, don't do anything to have this to happen to you because believe me it will happen. Now I will tell you how our blessing can come in the form of an unanswered prayer. Like my two children's were taken away from me. I question God, I wanted to know why did this had to happen and why do women who will be good mothers and want children's can't have them and women who just using kids to try to break up a marriage or to get a man will have good luck in having a baby. This not fair to me at all. However, I am happy that I did not have my second husband baby. This was the last baby I lost. Well my first child I would have loved to have had, but however with my second child god did know what was best for me. I prayed to have my child and cried when I did not. However, to day I praise God he didn't see fit for me to. See sometimes our greatest blessing can come in the form of an unanswered prayer mind did.

Chapter 41

Just because your daughter
may mature early don't mean a thing.

I LIKE TO TELL mothers just because their daughters may mature earlier then most girls their own age don't mean they fooling around with boys. Some girls may have a full chest of breasts that don't mean boys are playing with them every silly thing other women may tell you about your child not true. Take a look at some of the married women with small breasts you know they have husband and they husbands you know feels on them so let your little girl be a little girl she will look young for her age as she get older.

Chapter 42

let us take reasonability
for our own mistakes and failure

I T IS SO easy to blame somebody else for our mistakes and failure. It is about time that we start taking reasonability for our own mistakes and failure. In addition, let us stop blaming other people for other people mistakes and failure and wrongdoing. What I mean by this is let's say if we have a man ladies, and his friend comes over and the friend say man come ride with me some place. Now deep down in your heart you know that friend coming to take him to another woman, nine time out of ten that is what he comes for. In addition, your man leaves with his friend. Now you may not see your man no more until the next day.

Now you hate the friend because he came over to take your man to that woman. Now check this out did the friend have a gun and made your man go with him? Is your man retarded and don't have a mind of his own? Don't you blame the friend blame your man. If your man love and respect you he want get up and leave you alone and go with his friend. He would tell his friend man I am where I want to be and that is with you. Depending on what kind of man you have, he does not have much love for himself so you should know he could not have it for you. See if people love their self they want spread their self around.

Some men will take
advantage of the situation

Women the worst thing any of us women can do after we done gotten in a fight with our man and we're hurt and in tears over it is to go out to a club by ourselves. See there or men waiting around to find women who or venerable. In addition, when we or hurt we or temporary insane. We have a tenancy to do and say things we would not say or do if we were not in this state of mind. In addition, the green-eyed devil is the number one reason that makes us that way. Jalousie! It will do it every time. No matter how many times we go through it, it does not go away. Now there is not a thing in the world wrong with being jealous. Because if you have a person you're in love with you don't want anybody messing with them and hands off. But some people don't respect your feeling not even your lover. There for, if that's the case you will forever be hurt as long as you with them and love shouldn't hurt always, that's not a health relationship and you should get out of it, it's not worth being hurt all the time. Now you go to the club alone, now here where the other man come in; he's already there at the club and he dam sure going to be looking good and he might look better than your man remember I said whatever the devil have he going to make sure it looks better then gods and why is this? Yes to excite you. He sees you, he can tell yours hurt. In addition, he has a dam good idea what's you hurt over. So he going to come over to your table and ask you in a nice and sweet low voice; is you out with any one like your man knowing to he never seen a man with you all night and he know you didn't come in with a man but that's braking the ice and you tell him no he says to you sweet and low if you was his woman I wouldn't let you come out alone then to I wouldn't hurt you baby like your man did. I can tell you're a dam good woman a good woman needs to be treated well. Baby what you like to drank, please say nothing never let them buy you anything whatever you eat or drank buy it yourself. Men can put stuff in your drank or food to knock you out and you won't know what happen and sometimes depending on what they put in your food or drank it can kill you. Just be careful please see that's the devils son and he's out to get you and if you don't be careful he will get you. See the devils kids or like their father they always working and they work twenty-four hours a day, seven days a week; three hundred and sixth five days per year.

Sinful World

Now as I state earlier there or some GOD fearing church people. However, they or all sinners. We cannot but help be sinners because we or all born in a sinful world. That is why I say don't tell a person their sinners because as GOD said he who with sin let them cast the first stone. And don't act like you better than a person who doesn't go to church because GOD don't like ugly and he's not crazy about pretty.

You are rich

We think that it takes money to make us rich. However, in some ways that is not true. You can have a rich mind free from worry and free from wrong doing and feeling bless that you and your love ones and friends or well and doing well. That is what richness means to some people. As long as there's love in their life and they have a way to pay their bills and a house to live in and food to eat and clothes on their back and shoes on their feet's they happy. However, not everybody is happy with just that until it is gone. What little bit you have that can be taken from you. Everything you had is gone and money cannot replace it. Family pictures and little things you never thought about until now. Your first little doll you had since you was a little girl. Your first birthday card your grandmother sent you. Your baby hair your grandmother cut from your head after your birth. Just little things like that. Not all the money in the world can replace the things you lost. Little things you never think about until their gone and never coming back. Think about how bless you or now since that haven't happen.

Chapter 43

the day my sister put out the fair

You know it's so easy to forget about the good thing people do.

Here is a short story about my sister at the early age of four.

I RECALL WE HAD just move back to Bakersfield from Omaha and we was staying with my mother sister and her family, and one day we kids was in the back yard playing and somebody had been burning something in the trash can in the back yard and it still was burning a little. Therefore, my baby sister Dana who was two year old got a stick and was playing in the can with it. In addition, her hair caught on fair and Louryette my sister next

To me that was four years old; she took her hands and beat the fair out.

Now us older kids was so shocked we just stood there while that four year old child took her little hands and beats the fire out of our sisters hair what a pearl of a girl.

The day my mother stop breathing

We had just moved from watts drive and now we were staying on Haley Street in this little white house were the two twins' sister Miss Pinky and Miss Tinky had dead.

And we was still the same ages we were on watts drive I'm nine and my sister Louryette was four and my baby sister Dana was two. At this time my mother was sick in bed. My cousin and I wanted to go out and play ball. However, my mother told me not to go out. I went any way because we just be outdoors by the house and I will say about an hour she called me and I went inside. This is when she told me she had stop breathing and my sister Louryette was standing over her fanning her so it's fair to say that little four year old child save our mother life that day. Now looking back, I do not know how she knew how to do that ate age four. I have to give prays where it belongs. She saved our mother's life and our sister's life both times at age four. What a girl.

So from the old days to the new Miss Louryette Green this page is dedicated to you.

Life can change fast

Yes I know firsthand how fast your life can change believe me. In addition, it happens when you or lest suspect it. Like me, I left home with two legs and when I left in the ambulance, you can truly say I left with one.

That is why I can tell anybody don't make fun of handicap people. In addition, do not go up to people you do not even know and ask them what happen and tell your kids not to do it. Handicap people or like everyone else we have our good days and our bad days. In addition, at time when we feeling ok we will see you looking at us and we will come on out and tell you what happen. However, let us do that on our own free will. See people act just as if we do not have any feeling at all. In addition, when we crossing the street driver really drive fast like they going to run us over so we can hurry and get out the way and sometimes they will run us over. I am so happy when I see a police officer because I know people going to drive as they should. In addition, drivers have killed so many people with their fast driving. Now if something happen to one of them and they become handicap they will understand where we handicap people coming from. The same way they driving on streets while some handicap person trying to get a crossed they going to have the chance to see firsthand how we handicap people feel. In addition, when things happen like that you have to find away to cope with it and I tell you it is not easy. Not only your hold life changes, Your clothes have to change to fit your life style. Take your shoes now women may love to wear high heels shoes. Well if they have they leg amputee above the knee the high heels shoes have to go. You may love to wear flats with the toes out they most go. You must cut back on eating because you can get too big for your prosthesis and you have to have another one made. In addition, in the mean time you do not have any leg to wear. So now you cannot get around you, have to do the best you can for yourself. If you live, a lone and you can be living with somebody but that do not mean they will help you. You be in pain to. Take myself my leg cuts in to my skin and makes blusters one time I got a bluster that was so bad that when it burst it was so bad that now it looks like I had a big part of skin pull off my leg and my back hurts all the time. No pain pills helps so I have to live with pain every day of my life but so do other people, if they can live with pain so can I, I am no better. People can change on you when you need them the most. Now they do not have time for you. They feel like you putting their life on hold and they have their own life to live. See doing this time in your life you will see if you really have friends and do they mean you all the good in the world. I never ask anybody to do anything for me and I do not ask them to take my anywhere because I know how people or and how fast they can get sick of you. See people want you up not down. So don't think you going to have friends coming out of your ears to help you because if you think that you're going to get highly disappointed my friend because that's not the way it is.

Chapter 44

You must teach your children's about the up's and down's in life when they trying to be successful.

IF YOU WANT your child to be successful in life, you have to start when they young teaching them that they want always do well in something but do not give up. Just because they did not make it the first time they go to do something does not mean they never make it. Teach them that the best of people did not make it the very first time they went out for something. Teach them no matter how good they or in something, always remember there always going to be somebody better than they in the same thing but that don't mean nothing that's life.

Do not ever prays somebody else child and not your own. Don't ever do that, even if your child get a bad report card and the other child got all A's still don't make your child feel the other child is better than your child. Don't let any other parent prays their child and you not prays your child, if the other parent say this is one smart child I have here; you say your child is just as smart, no matter what grads they get in school, that still don't mean your child is not smart. In addition, don't let the other child feel them any better than your child. That is the reason why so many people have low self-esteem. See you must be very careful of what you say around your child. Words can hurt worsted then a hit. In addition, the burse inside the heart takes the longest to heal and some never do. Teach your child to have respect for themselves and other. In addition, teach your child to work for what they want and not to beg because a person that begs has no self-respect and other want respect them. In addition, teach them to stand up for what they feel is right even though not everybody going to agree with them tell them that is ok. And also teach them to speak up and speak out for themselves even though some people will not like them for it but that's fine because they want be their friends anyway and teach the girls not to be afraid to tell a boy no about sex, because he will have more respect for them and tell the girls just because a boy ask them for sex they don't always mean it, they just seeing if the girl is easy and if she is he don't want an easy girl because he feel if she give it up to him the first time he ask just how many other boys has she given it up to? Other words play hard to get, that will make boys respect you and he will feel a lady that hard to get is worth getting. However no matter how many times I tell women this; it don't do any good, the leg fly open all the time and they wonders' why men give them the four F which mean find them fool them and f—k them and forget them. In addition, teach the boy to have respect for women that is why a mother must teach her daughters to be respectable of herself. I stated once before men's will try you to see how easy you or. If we women want our men's to respect us, first we must respect our self and stop acting like whores. I do not like our men's acting the way they does with us women. Sometimes it seems that they hate us women and maybe some does. But I hope one day their stop and realize we have feeling to and most of us want them to go back to the way they us to be as in opening doors for us and helping us with our coat and pulling out our chair and I like to be call Miss Johnson. I liked the old ways men use to be. And another thing ladies when you have a man don't act like you need that man some women act like they just have to have a man don't act that way. In addition, don't act needed all the time, have your own money be independent take care of yourself and kids. If you have kids don't make them go in rooms all the time when your man come over, don't act like you don't have kids for no man, you always put them ahead of men and you know what you may not believe it but a man have more respect for you when you remember you have kids. Don't put your kids off on other people so you can be alone with your man because you're not alone you have kids remember. Don't go out looking for a father for your kids. In addition, do not have your kids calling every man you meet daddy and when you get mad at the man then you tell the kids he is not your daddy that confusing to a child. In addition, do not tell a man everything about yourself hold some things back because believe me he is not going to tell you everything about himself. As I stated early on in my book our mouth is our worst enemy that is true. In addition, women pick up the check sometime that is what I mean when I say don't acts needed like you just hard up for money and you will do anything for it.

Inferior and Superior

Do not ever feel as if you or inferior to anybody no matter who they may be or what they may have. You or just as good as anybody else is, and don't you ever forget it. Not even Kings and Queens or superior to anybody they only man made kings and queens god have no kings and queens we all or somebody special in this world no matter who you may be. So let us say it loud I am special and I am proud!

The heart

I will tell you something about the heart; the heart is the strongest muscle in our body and it's an involuntary muscle, which means we have no control over it like we do other parts on the body such as our eyes our mouth our hands our feet's, we can move them we can open and close our hands we can wiggle our toes but we can't do anything with the heart. It beats on its own and it will stop on its own. Now I look at it this way since we have no control over the heart we have no control over who we fall in love with. We can know we falling for the wrong person but still our heart is falling for that person and sometimes a person comes our way that mean us all the good in the world but we don't care anything for that person but love the hell out the person that don't mean us a world of good. We have no control who we fall in love with the only thing we have control of sometimes is our action and the reason why I say sometimes is we can be temporary insane and if that's the case we have no control over our action.

Let well enough do

I can remember when my grandmother was living she had many old saying she would use. In addition, one was let well enough do you. Now I know so well, what she meant.

Like when we blessed in life we should let well enough do us. When we have something good such as a good kind decent lover why test the water. I know some of us have our own saying such as there is more fish in the sea. Yes your right there may be more fish in the sea. However, let me tell you this. Now I have known people to go fishing and catch their self a big nice fish and come home and cook it up and eat it and that fish make them so sick they wish they could die. Therefore, my saying is what looks good to you is not always good for you.

Thinking success

Dream success

Crave success

Be hungry for success

Ware success

Talk success

Walk success

Your mind is a powerful thing we can heal ourselves with our mind and we can make ourselves sick with our mind and we can let our mind control us in to failing in life there for why we cannot gain success by thinking about it and getting up and working on it. Now like I said early in my book we have to pray for what we want then work on it because god help them that help themselves. If we tell our mind we can't do something then we may never be successful in anything we take to do. Other words we must think positive and be around positive people and move yourself to positive environment. Positive people want to do positive things and be around other positive people. A positive thinking person do not want to be around a negative thinking person if they trying to do positive things for themselves because it's like one is gas and the other water they don't mix.

Chapter 45

older men v/s Viagra

TELL ME SOMETHING older men, is five minutes worth of sheer pleasure of sex worth you having a stroke are heart attack, are even going blind for a temporary feeling? Now ask yourself is it worth all that? Now if you have a woman that want you to forth nature back

So she can get her freak on there's other ways and if that don't satisfied your woman and she want the real thing and you can't give it to her and you afraid she might go out and get somebody that can do the do, maybe she's not the woman for you. If it's your wife and you can't get it up any more because we know a woman is different from a man she can at any age, maybe it's time to depart, because age not the only thing that can effect a man sex drive, he can get sick are have an accident and he can't have sex and would the woman leave?

Falsely put away

I have to come back to Camarillo State Hospital for a while more because there has been people falsely put away there for never think because a person is in a mental hospital their crazy just as an innocent person can be jailed a sane person can be put in a mental hospital. Please believe me. Back when I went to Camarillo kids was there for running away from home, this right just for that I know firsthand what I am talking about. That is the reason why I tell you just because a person has been put away in a mental hospital do not mean that person is crazy. Also once you been in one it all ways will be agents you. Take the Kobe case now I do not know and it is not my businesses anyway if he raped that young woman or not. However, they said she had been put away so she just might be confused about getting rape. A person who been in a mental hospital done lost his or her capability and their not looked up on again as a responsible person. Now their reputation is ruined. Some jobs they can never have. They cannot get in to the army. In addition, some people do not want to be around them now, which that would not bother me at all because I don't care about being around people anyway I prefer to be alone I'm a loner and always have been.

I am going to get into men using women because it is going around. I know some women use men also but I am just talking about men.

Now women other women may laugh at you if they finds out that your man used you, which it is nothing funny about it. They laugh because to them you or dumb. In addition, they think their smarter then you or. Don't feel you're dumb because you're not. It is just that you did not see that your man was using you because loving eyes can never see. While they laughing at you if only if they knew what they operates was doing to them they would be crying. See If you have a man that's nice to you just enjoy it while it last but don't laugh at the next woman and put her down because her man not doing nothing for her and tell her you're a fool if my man weren't doing this for me or that for me I would put him out. You might would, but do not call her crazy are dumb because some women do not feel their hold unless they have a man. You may not be that kind of woman. Therefore, in that case, they will take more than you would take. Then to, there are some women just afraid of their men to tell them to get out. So do not call other women dumb and crazy because their putting up with something because you really do not know their business.

They know you vulnerable

Women you that suffering from infertility and want an adorable little bundle of joy and will do anything it take to make your dream come true I tell you other women that can have kids will take advantage of your situation. It is a very sad thing but they will. They knows you vulnerable because you done tried everything there is to be done to have your own baby but nothing have work. You done been to doctor after doctor after doctor and they can't find anything wrong with you or they have found something wrong and have told you that you will never be able to have children. What a sad thing to tell a woman that want children its hurts more than anybody can tell you.

So now, the doctor tells you that you can adopt and he knows a young woman who is putting her baby up for adoption but what he does not know is that young woman is telling him a lie. Now she has told ten different couple that they can have her baby. Now all those people or taking care of that woman. They paying all of her doctor bills, paying her rent, and buying her clothes, food, and anything else she need now the caseworker only thinking about the mother needs and not the woman who cannot have children. See when you look at it all they doing is punishing you and you punishing yourself for not being able to have children. In addition, I tell you do not do it do not put yourself out there to be used like that. I did not I was told I could adopt also. No not I if I couldn't have my own baby then I just went on without a baby and for as foster care they will give them sick babies to you to nurse and get them healthy and they take them from you and give them back to the mother. They tell you that they going to take them back.

Again you're being use when you get the baby looking well and all good they take the baby back and give it back to the mother it's not about you and your feeling at all only the mother's. There for if it's not for you to have a child go get yourself a little puppy that want be taking from you after you fall in love with it and let that be your baby a puppy needs love. I will say again do not let yourself be used. However, if you do not care about people getting over on you in the name of a baby you're not going to get nor anybody else than put yourself out there, because liar and user out there looking for people like you. However, I have been used by men and dam if I going to let a woman used me to take care of her for her baby I am not going to get and then to I never wanted some other woman baby. No somebody else baby would not do it for me anyway. Now all the things that I thought I just had to have mean nothing to me anymore and I am happy for that. If men meet me now and I acts cool it is because I do not have the felling I used to have for men. I am not that same Dorothy I use to be. Men did not appreciate that good caring nice Dorothy they did not respect me. Now the same way they used to feel about me I feel that way by them.

Sticks and Stones

Now we all know saying sticks and stones may break my bones but words do not ever hurt me is a lie. Telling a child who's over weight to tell other kids this when kids call the child fat just doesn't get it because words does hurt and depending on who's the words coming from they can make some people kill them self or give a person a nerves brake down. Therefore, who ever came up with that, one should have kept it to them self because it is a lie. In addition, the person who said it knew they was lying to themselves because words can hurt worsted then being hit. Now I know most of us do get over it but to lie and say they do not hurt is a lie. In addition, that is why people say them because they know they hurt their not trying to make you feel good by saying them. So if they hurt us grown up just think what they do to a child. In addition, when a child is likening the opposite sex or the same sex depending on what they prefer and words or spoken about the person around the person they likes, it can be devastated. When you have feeling for someone, you want to be at your best around him or her but when certain words is said around them about you that is negative can hurt like hell. So yes words does hurt so there for please use words that make people feel good just little kind words spoken to a person can mean so much to that person more then you will ever know. And if a person like you and you don't like them back please be kind letting them down because with some people you just have to let them know you don't want them because they just don't get it, but with most people they understand you don't want them and you don't have to just come out and tell them you don't want nothing to do with them. And if you don't want a person don't take anything from them and don't let them buy you anything don't let yourself open for them to think there may be a chance for them.

Who to pray to

When you pray, you should pray to our father God, not his son Jesus. The only time you should go to Jesus is when you want to see the father because then you have to go in through by the son.

Some people pray out loudly and some pray to themselves. Any way you pray to GOD as long as you pray for others first is

The right way, and he hears us so there no wrong way to pray as long as you praying to God and it is from the heart.

Well friends I'm just about at the end of my book there for I just thought about something I have to tell one of my ex teacher something.

To the teacher that never had patient for me because I had a learning disability, I would put my head down on my disk, and many times I would cry. If you should ever wonder what become of me, the little girl who would never hold her head up and would never smile and the little girl who everybody made cry well I must tell you all, that little girl is all grown up now and is the author of her very first book look to the sky

Chapter 46

Learn to be thankful

WE MUST FACE facts we all or not going to be rich and we all not going to have a big nice home. Most of us going to rent a house or an apartment. However, lest be thankful that we have a house or an apartment to rent. In addition, lest stop worrying about the Joneses and what they got and appreciated what we have. When you learn to be thankful for what GOD has given you, he will give us more. First, little of much we must be thankful. No matter what GOD does for us, we or not thankful. If GOD bless us with a dollar we say now what can I do with a dollar? Now see if you had been thankful for that dollar maybe GOD would had bless you to take that dollar and buy a winning lotto ticket. That is how GOD works. So let us be thankful for what we have.

It is ok to be different

You do not have to be a monkey see monkey do kind of person It's ok to be different we don't have to be like everybody else and do the thing they do we can have our own mind. That is why it is so good to live here in America we can be our self. We can dress the way we want to as long as it is in a respectably, we can all be our own person

Stop using excuses:

Now I am talking to some people and you know whom you or. Now when you stop going to school or just don't try to do anything for yourself, stop using that old excuses that the man is keeping us down because see I done been in a mental hospital and I know if I can go out there and get a job and get my own place and work and keep it nothing stopping you but you. You can make it if you try and can't anybody keep you down if you do not want to be down. See now check this out. I know the door is close in black people face but you do not give up if you have an education you can knock some of them doors down. It is hard with an education but it is harder without it. And it's ok to get a job you don't want, to make ends meet; but don't stay there if you have to work days and go to school at nigh do that but please stay in school it will pay off one day.

Chapter 47

you do not have to pay for your blessing

People or too eager to give their money away on some scams.

I DONE HAD PEOPLE write me and tell me that they done seen not one but two new cars and me in a big nice house. Yes, Dorothy it is your time to be happy. God has a blessing for you all for your Dorothy. Your will be living the kind of life you always hope for. All you have to do is send me just $300.00 dollars. As if I am, some dam nut. Sending some body my money to do what? Some people will give them their money for a blessing. Look people blessings or free. Anything god gives us is free. Nobody can do anything to make you have a blessing' do not believe that. If you want to give your money away, you can send it to me. In care of Dorothy Johnson, I need your money. I can lie to you just as good as other people watch me now I see a blessing for John Doe. I see you in a big six-bed room house and not one but six new cars and five million dollars in the bank in your name, I see you with two pretty girls on each arm Mr. John Doe this can be all yours. All I ask you to do is send me every dime you have and live in a card board box for me while I live it up on all your money you crazy thing you however you should know I could not give you any blessing. That is what I will be saying to myself about you. So stop sending your money like that.

IF IT IS IN GOD's WILL

Parent before I end here something I want you to always tell your child and please start when they or very young telling them. Always tell him or her no one is better than they no matter who that person may be or what they may have. In addition, never tell your child what they cannot do. If your child tells, you that he or she going to be the next person to walk on the moon do not laugh. Tell them if it is God's will then you will walk on the moon. If your child tells you, he or she is going to make a star, name it, and send it to the sky. Tell them honey GOD has more than he needs and at this time he do not need anymore. Never and I do mean never tell your child what they cannot do. That is wrong to do anybody like that. Away make your child feel as they can do anything. In addition, do not never put your child down or talk down to them and call them names expect for loving names. Don't wait till your child is grown before you start telling your child loving things it's too late then you should start when they young because after the child is grown whatever you done told the child or didn't tell the child is the only thing that matters in the child's life now. In addition, listen to what your child have to say. They may not always make sense to you but pretend they do. In addition, they may clean house or try to cook a meal you know it is not right but do not make fun of it because they did try. Tell them honey you done a good job but let me show you some tricks to make it even better. Say see you done it the hard way but there is an easy way to do it and that way you or showing them that you appreciate what they do for you. Prays your child to others with your child hearing it see what your child take in when they or young will stay with them for the rest of their life.

Chapter 48

What we wear

WE MAY NOT think about it, but what we wear specks loud about the kind of person we or In addition, the place we go and the people we or around. Now if we not whores women why dress as such. See you may attract some men but its negative attractions. Sure men going to look at you with your but hanging all out and you have on a see through blouse with no bare on. However, all you or to him is a lay. In addition, some men do not want you for that. They want you to go out and make him some money and you know what I am talking about. Ladies you may not know it but men's like for women to dress conservative. That is the way men like for a real woman to dress. If he is looking for a striper that is what turns him on then he will go to a strip joint. In addition, if he is looking for a church going woman he will go to church not a club. See ladies this why when we go to clubs looking for a man then usually that's what we gets a club man. In addition, for men that is looking for a downright stay at home woman want go to a club looking for her. See a real man wants a real woman. In addition, a real woman wants a real man. What you two have is only for each other to see not the hold word. I am the same way I do not want my man showing too much ether. Leave something for the imagination. I am a careful woman See you do not put a hungry dog in a house with a stake and think he want eat it and that is all it is too it. So no I don't want my man showing off what suppose to be mine and that's not so much of been jealous it's just been cartful that's more like it and also it's about having respect for yourself and your lover. In addition, if you or jealousy so what if you love somebody you want him or her for yourself and yourself only. You do not want nobody else touching it and felling all over it you want to be the only one doing that. Only a fool wants to share their lover and if you're not that fool then let other know look but do not touch!

The devil's grass

He is going to make sure the sun going to shine brighter on his side. You know whatever God has the devil has also. In addition, whatever the devil has it will look better then Gods. In addition, whatever god gives us the devil can give also. However, what give us comes with a price and a price you would not want to pay. See the reason why whatever has going to look better then god's is to entice you. See you can be married to one

141

of god's children and you two can be happy and doing well. Now the devil will get the weakest one on you away from the other, now he will send one of his children to you, and he will make sure that his child will look better then gods child, that's the bate the devil use to break up your home. However, if you both know you want and love each other and have god in your heart the devil cannot move in on you. In addition, you will turn your head from his children's, the devil cannot do no more then you let him. You have to know whom you want and what you want, if you do not; do not even bother anybody about getting into a relationship with you. Why go out to brake somebody heart. People have feeling and never do to somebody that you don't want do to you. I will say again, what goes around come around.

Failure

It is ok to fail really it is. You do not always have to be perfect at everything you do. Really, you do not. The smartest person fails at times. That is what makes them smart. They learn from the mistakes. You know mistakes have made the best inventions. In addition, do not be ashamed because you fail just see where you made your mistake and work on it. In addition, do not feel that you or a failure because you fail at something. You know some times we or just not cut out to be different things. Just words to live by.

Chapter 49

God don't like ugly
and he's not crazy about pretty

GOD DO NOT like ugly and he is not crazy about pretty. Now this means that no matter if you try to live right he is not crazy about you. I am happy about that because again I will say women who think their save and think just them going to heaven that is not so. I will say women because we the main one or who talks about other people I am no better so I am not leaving myself out. However, when I do go to church I do not think I am any better than the people who do not. See you don't have to go to church to know God or have him in your life church is just a building where you go to worship God, church first starts in the heart and your heart have to be right which some people or not. Some people play with God and God knows when he's being played with and he will play back but you want like his playing. In addition when you go to church please go for the right reasons and the right reasons only. Don't go to church trying to find a lover because the devil is everywhere.

And if that's the only reason you going to church nine time out of ten you're going to get disappointed because all your going to find is the devil kids because their even in church. Never go out looking for love because love will come to you when you're not looking. Take when you done miss place something in your house you can look and look for it and want find it then one day you have forgotten all about it just done made up in your mind somebody must have taken it. Then one day while you weren't looking you find it. That's how love works, if it meant for you, you don't have to go out your door it will find you. When love does come your way if god sends that person to you, you will know. However no matter what your mother may have told you about you can get any man you want that's not true and here why. What may look good to one man may not look good to the next man. The main man you may want if your black he don't have to like black women or he don't have to like women at all he may be gay if he is then what? Your mother told you, you can have any man you want. I'm going to tell you about fearing your man will leave you for another woman and you want have any women friends fearing he might leave you for one. If a woman must fear that her man will leave her for another woman she should not be with that man so no use in been jealous of other women because if a man loves you then he loves you and that is that. Then to depending on what kind of women a man like he might like them that you feel you have no need in being jealous of. You may be jealous of a woman that is twenty-one 5 feet six and weight 105 and 36-24-36. But all the time he likes women who or seventy and weight 350 pounds and five feet two every man is different like every woman is different. Now take me, I like older men because older men been there and done that and knows how to do it and knows when not to do it and knows when to stop. I do not have to teacher him anything he might be able to teach me a thing or two. I do not want no man I have to teach things to no more, because I done been there to and do not want to go back. When a man comes to me, I want him already school and if he is not too bad because I am no schoolteacher. Some older men feels they don't have it anymore I like to show them that they do because nothing gets old but money even old clothes is coming back.

Men will try you ladies yes they will

Ladies I must tell you this, ladies just because a man may asked to go to bed with you soon after he meets you don't mean that he want to. See women men will try you to see how easy you or and see how far he can get with you. Now he may have in his mind to make you his lady which he have made up in his mind there's no decent young ladies around anymore but he meets you and feel god has bless him with a nice young lady. Now he has known you about a month, now he has a test for you before he can say for sure if he wants you for his lady. Now he will see if he can go to bed with you and hoping you want let him and you want! You tell him no you just want to be friends at this time you're not looking for a man to go to bed with and then to you tell him you two don't even know each other. Then you tell him you're not that kind of woman to go to bed with a man you hardly know. One day he ask you one too many times and you feel if you don't give in to him he will leave you, not knowing if you give in to him you have a better chance in him leaving you anyway. See women, no man want an easy woman to call his woman. Not if he's in his right mind he doesn't. Men will try you. He knows if you give it to him just by asking you that mean you have no class; you're too easy. Make him work for you, play hard to get then he will feel a woman that's hard to get is worth getting. So if a man going to leave you if you don't give it up he was going to leave you anyway. It hurts worst when you give it up then he leaves you then it does when you don't give it up and he leaves you. You want feel used.

Misery loves company

Misery Loves Company is true: because when I hear that somebody else lost their leg above the knee like me due to an accident makes me feel better. Now I said due to an accident because diabetics and poor circulation do not count because that is a medical reason. Now I do not wish this up on nobody. However, if it happens it does make me feel better to know that I and somebody else or rocking in the same old boat. Now I am not the only one who feels that way I just happen to be the one to be truthful about it. But then again I am wishing them the best recovery. I went through just some pain both physical and mental. I was in so much pain that I could not stand for anybody to move me. In addition, when the nurse would come in to change my bandage on my leg before they had to amputate it completely when they would hold my leg up all I could see was a big hold I could see right through. Some of the nurses could not stand to look at my leg without crying. They would try to hide their faces so I would not see them but I knew they were crying. One doctor told me child I been a doctor for ten years and I done seen all kinds of gunshot wounds but honey yours is the worst I ever seen. In addition, the reason they was trying to save what little bit was left of my leg was that I did not want it amputated. However, they told me if it set up infection, they would have to amputate to save my life. What a life I am going to have I said to myself. What a dam life I going to have. Just because some dam fool took a gun and went out that night shooting. They did not know me from Adam house cat. People asked me was I paid for this. When I tell people I did not get any money for my accident, they cannot believe me. Everyone thought I was paid. No, I was not. I was on the intensive care heart unit in Bakersfield before I got transfer to Visalia from there to San Francesco California were my leg was amputated. Until this day, I have to take medication to make it through the day and I must see my doctors for pain medication often. However, other than that I think I am doing fine. I just wish people would mind their own business and stop thinking they know what is best for me and leave me alone.

Do not forget

Now don't forget what I said about not letting it get you down if you and somebody else has an accident at the same time as yourself or if your accident was before theirs and it seem like they doing better then you or because you don't know how their really feeling inside. We all heal in our own time and you can't rush it In addition, like I stated early on in my book religions plays a big part in our life and it plays a big part in our healing process. However we must take our healing process one day at a time.

They're going to be days were we feel better than others, but that's ok that is the way it is with everybody whether they had an accident or not.

Don't think about how well the other person doing because that can be a setback for you just think about how well your doing and what you can do to get better because it's all about you now and nobody else.

Make yourself-happy

I hear people saying all the time I need somebody in my life to make me happy, well I tell you what, sitting around and waiting for somebody to come alone and make you happy you be like a duck sitting on rotten eggs. We must make our self-happy and do not wait on others to make you happy. That is what wrong with some people they depends on others to much. You should depend on the LORD and yourself. Ladies you do not need a man to make you happy. Because most of the time they do not make you happy anyway. And if they did what little time it would be you would know not to get too happy because you know about the open legs. You know you wouldn't be happy for long because there's too many legs open and very flew men won't go there. That's why I said early on in my book that women shouldn't laugh at other women that man is messing up on her because if only you knew what your man was doing you would be crying, unless you don't care and that's only if you don't love your man because if you love a person you cares about what they do. Like when I loved my husbands, it would hurt me when they would stay gone for mouths at a time for no reason. However, one day I did not care about nothing they done any more. That was because all the love I had for them was gone. I am saying this to say that. Just because John Doe's wife does not care about where he goes and how long he stays doesn't mean that his wife understanding is better than your wife. That is not so John Doe's wife do not love him and your wife loves you that is the only different. In addition, one day your wife may feel the same way John Doe wife feels about him and I wonder will you think that your wife understanding is good.

Now I know why

Now I know God let this happen to me because through it all something positive came out of it like my book and my inventions. Now I can pass God's word on to others and let them know that GOD is real and his word is real. In addition, God do not always give us what we want but what we need. In addition, trust in him and everything will be all right. However, when you pray you have to believe in him. Therefore, God done made a believer out of me. God done showed me that the bright light people say they see just before death is read because I have seen it. In addition, God showed me that death is nothing to be afraid of because it is just another life we go in to after we leave this one, and to be in this life we had to come out of another one. We have come out of another live to be in this one. God showed me that back in my other life I left three little girls and a husband behind. Now you may not believe what I am saying but that is ok. God told me one day in heaven is a year on earth. He showed me heaven looks just like earth but the air smalls so good and the day is so bright. He showed me my house, which is pink with white trimming around the windows and doors. In addition, people or working there just like on earth so there no free rides there. He showed me that I walked up the street to the store and hasn't returned yet and my husband is waiting for me. Three little light skinned girls with long black thick hair sticking up on top of their head looking just like their father or in their bedroom. In addition, people wear the same clothes on earth they does in heaven. Therefore, you see we just enter in to a better life. This life is our learning tree. God showed me this and I was not asleep. God also told me before we or born he prepares a life book for each one of us and if it is not in our life book it want happen. I am saying that to say this stop blaming yourself for thing that you have no control of. So when thing happen to us it is meant to happen.

Chapter 50

The chain has been broken

THE OLD SAYING like father like son: Like mother like daughter the chain done been unbroken: you your own person. You do not have to be any way you do not want to be. If your father or mother is the kind of people you cannot be proud of then you can be the kind of person your kids can be proud of. You can be anything you want to be. You just have to work hard at it and put time and effort in it. It does not take effort to make a mess of your life but it does take effort to make the most of it. When you or doing, positive things with your life do not look for support. If you get it, fine if you don't let that be fine also. They're going to be people telling you that you never make it. They hope you want make it. You can get more people by your side when you or doing negative thing in life. However, when you decide to clean up your act and do the right thing your want have all that support. Therefore, I am telling you this so you want look for it because you or not going to get it. You can get a positive lover, what I mean by this is a person who is positive they love you and only you. In addition, will do positive by you. In addition, they want only the best for you. People will take a fool into negativity surrounding because they have nothing positivist going on in their life because if they did they wouldn't have time for you and wouldn't want to be with you. Now if this person had what you had and if they had sense they would be home with the person. Since they do not have a good person at home, they do not want the best for you. So when you loses your good person because it takes a fool to stay with a person somebody else can control and get them to do anything ageist the one who love and care for them. In addition, I do mean love not lust something you can get in the streets. Now when you lose your lover and you or alone nobody has time for you then. Everybody have his or her own life now and you or not welcome in it. Only two people can make a relationship work and it takes works and you must keep other people out of your relationship. To make it work and some people don't do that and some don't take up much time with the person they say they care for. You can buy a person things and you never spend much time with them when you know you can things want mean nothing and it want keep your relationship together believe me.

Chapter 51

being in abusive relationships

THERE SO MANY women in an abusive relationships and abusive relationships will take your pride away because it make you do anything just so you want get beaten and you don't want to be around people with bruise on your body and you have to make up some lie to tell people why you have the bruises like they believe you and you only making yourself look like a fool. And if you with a man that beats you no matter what you do or don't do you're going to get beaten. Somebody may ask you the wrong question that calls for a beating and sometimes people will push a man in to beating you. You get to the place where you don't want to go anywhere in hopes that will keep him from beating the hell out of you. But that don't get it that man going to find something to beat the hell out of you about anyway and it could be about something he sees on TV or something somebody else does to him and you have nothing to do with it but still you get the hell beaten out of you about it. A man will tell you he's beating you because he can. They will beat you for something somebody else done because that person was a woman too and he will tell you a women ant nothing and start in on you. Still a woman will find reason to stay in relationships like that and the number one reason women use is they wanted their kids to know their father. Now any fool knows this is a lie. Because what good is it doing a child to see his father beating the hell out of his mother. He will hit you too hard one day and that will be the death of you. He may not meant to hit you that hard but sometimes they don't realize how hard their hitting you. You're not fooling anybody everybody knows the real reasons your staying in that relationship do not have anything to do with the kids you just love that man or afraid that man is going to kill you or your family if you leave. When your love is gone that is that you want be coming back. Because there's no way anybody can keep on living a person that keep abusing them even a dog will turn against you if you abused it and sometimes he'll leave. Abuse is never good and there is no reason in the world to stay with a person that abuses you not even for the kids. The kids will start hating their father. Because some kids loves their mother more than they do their father anyway. Some fathers done left the home and the mothers or the only one the kid has. Mothers or not doing their kids any justice by staying in abusive relationships. And the kids grades will start dropping from A's to D's and they will developed mental problems like bed wetting and them not wanting to come home or develop problem with their speech or not wanting to eat and can't sleep or have problem with their peers at school when they use to be a kind and happy child now they starts fights. Sometime when the boys see their fathers fighting their mother they too will grow to be abusive to women.

The kids may become very depress and withdrawn. Now see this used to send a child to a mental hospital, see how easy it use to be. This is depression a mental problem but in the sixth's if you stayed depress for some time you was conceder a mental. I'll person. Now things has change, most everyone you see is dealing with some form of depression. So it is so common now that when you tell somebody, they can tell you about the kind of medication their own for it, and tell you the name of their doctor. Now days there or nothing to be ashamed of. It shouldn't have been a big deal back then because it's something you can't help. Getting back to abusive relationships, if you or in an abusive relationship I am going to give you a number to call to get help. In addition, you call it and get out of it. Love yourself enough to move on, there or better things in life for you. Women do not ever feel that you need a man to be a woman. You were a woman that day you turned 21.The best thing you could ever do for yourself is to move on. Staying in that relationship will beat you down and it will take all your pride and yourself-worth and your motivation. You will start looking older than you or and you will stop keeping yourself-up and you will start putting on weight or losing weight. In addition, the strangest thing is you want even realize how bad you look until somebody tells you. However, you will be lucky because you will still be alive. And another thing if a man give you VD please don't believe he gotten it from a toilet set or he got it from wearing his friend clothes you don't get it that way you get it through sex, now bugs you can get them from a toilet set but nine time out of ten you got it from sex. So if a man gives you VD the first time leave him alone because he will be giving it to you again. So if you love yourself enough to get out of your abusive relationship please call this number before it is too late: Violence against women Hotline at 1800-799-SAFE or 1800-787-3224.

Chapter 52

Marriage it is not for everybody

I AM GOING TO tell you something and I know you going to think I done lost my mind but just like kids not in the cards for some people love and marriage also not. Now I am not saying that the person does not want either. It is just not in the cards for them. Some people leave this world without ever having anybody that really loved them and meant them well. It do not matter how many times they been in love but who they was in love with never loved them. So there for some people never get married. But that's to is ok and not a thing you can do about it any way just love yourself even if nobody else do and do what's make you happy and go places by yourself lots of people does, it's not against the law. Go get yourself a dog you can do whatever and say whatever you want and no matter what a person offers that dog it's not talking, a person can't make that dog tell on you, even if a person puts a gun beside that dog's head and tell it, if it don't tell on you they will pull the trigger, they just have it to do, because that dog not talking boy! I will tell you that is what you call man best friend.

Our strength comes with time

As I once stated earlier nobody is a strong person. Strength comes from time and a lot of it. Strength is like a newborn baby. When it first comes to the world, it is very weak. First year = weak. Now as time passing the baby will get stronger and stronger. Second year = stronger. Stronger plus time passing, you will begin to heal. Now you become stronger and stronger. Time= Strength: See like the newborn: When it is first born, it cannot hold it head up on its own. Weak= Time, time= strength. Only time can heal, there is no magic pill we can take. So if it takes you longer to heal than it do other so be it. Nobody is the same not even identical twins. In addition, if you never heal so what that too is all right. Nobody can tell you how long it should take you to heal from something. Do not live your life for other people because their sure not going to live their life for you. In addition, live for yourself. Make yourself-happy. Do people try to make you happy? I do not think so. Now I am not saying only think about yourself and no one else. I am just saying love yourself to. By loving yourself meaning, do not put yourself in harm's way to get yourself hurt to satisfy nobody. If a person has your best at heart they won't try to talk you into going places that might get you hurt and also a friend want try to turn you on to something that's going to harm your body and mind a real friend cares about all of

150

you. If your friend want you to go somewhere with them and your mind tells you not to go do not go, a real friend will respect your feeling. However, you have to love and respect yourself enough to say no. Stop doing things you know you do not want to do to please other people. When you are able to tell others how you feel and by not letting people walk all over you they will respect you. Now telling people how you real feel will make you feel better about yourself. In addition, always feel that you just as good as anybody else no matter what anybody tells you. Parents have to start with their child at a young age teaching them that their just as good then anybody else. In addition, the first start is not putting them down no matter what. If they gets D's and F's it is not always that they do not try. Some time a child mind wonders as mind do and mind did when I were in school. In addition, never! I do mean never! Tell your child about another child is smart and your child is not. I am not what you would call a smart person and believe me a child has enough to go through at school with being call dumb and they do not need to hear it at home. In addition, if you have other kids at home, which are smarter than one child do not let them call the not too smart child dumb. The not too smart child may grow up to be the president of the USA or a famous inventor you never know. So do not let anybody call your child dumb. In addition, on top of it all I was benign abused at school, which even made it worst on me trying to learn. And I was on my own out there alone with all the kids picking on me and the teachers not doing a thing to stop them.

We were richest people in the world

When we first stayed on watts drive, I say first time we stayed on watts drive because my first year of high school we move back on watts drive but in a different house. Now we didn't have anything but we were the riches people in the world. It doesn't have to be what you have that makes you happy it can also be what you don't have that makes you happy. Some may say what? That woman is crazy, how can she say what you do not have makes you happy. I tell you. If you thought you had cancer and the doctor told you, you did not have cancer would you be happy, Even if you do not have money, and maybe you didn't have a house to live in, but you in good health. In addition, would you be happy if your love ones were in the same good health? See what I mean. Now the person with everything you do not have just might be the unhappiest person you ever have seen. Sure, he has money and things but he's sick, he has cancer; and don't have long to live, what good is money and things when he don't have long to enjoy it.

Good things come to those who wait

I remember when I was thirteen good things come to those who wait was a song I love and it was Song by this woman I didn't understand the song back then I had no idea what she was talking about, in this song she said now let me tell you people here's what I want you to see he said girl you're just what I'm looking for please come my way. I do not have much to offered but what I do have you can have it. Then she says but the foolish girl said no baby you are not the right one yet. How well do I understand that song now? That was her good thing but by him not having much, she did not want him. She wanted a man with more. Now the man with more may not even have given her a dime. However, the poor man loved her, wanted her, and was going to give her all he had. However, that was not good enough for her. See some people do not know when their good thing comes alone. One of the reasons why relationships do not last long is some people is just out to use others, Sometime the first day they meet you they want to know what your job pays. If a man asks me something like that, if I had any intention on giving him a play, it is over, done with, good bye. No, he is not for me. Another thing some people thinks sex is all what a relations is about check this out. I hear some women telling men's you have heaven had any good this and that until you had some of hers now what decent woman are man going to put their self on display like that? What may be good to one person may not be good to the next. Like my grandmother always said, there is good and there is better. In addition, the only time when something is the best is when you have not had anything better. Nine time out of ten, if a person goes around bragging about how good they are I can tell you they not all about nothing. If you are good in something, it sounds crazy to go around bragging about it. If you good yours good and that's that now let it go. Most people like and respect people who do not brag at all. Ladies don't think all men just want what's between your legs. That's fine when it's time for that but remember that don't pay the rent no matter how good you think it is. When a person is under stress because of the bills and you cannot or will not do anything to help, that sex not so good anymore. I have been there. In addition, when a person can't work the penny stops there, dam some sex. Addition, you done been on your jobs for some years and you knows your job well. However, you want to get a head because the jobs you have do not pay enough. You could move up if the other person got up and help but want. That sex not going to satisfied you. In addition, you want some of the load taking off you. That is what a person does that care for you. They will do something to help if it is just babysitting at home are taking in laundry there is something they can do to help you. However, if the person has kids they can do the things above at home to make money that is if they care. When you do not do anything to help, no matter how hard the person having it, the love they has for you not going to last very much longer. My love for both my husband is gone like it never been there at all. They never helped me no matter what I was going through. I could be sick in bed and can't work they would leave me. How can you love somebody like that very long? You cannot. No ways can you. This why I say if you have a person who love and care for you, you should do everything in your power to keep them loving you. Never think no matter how bad you treat a person they going to keep loving you and be there for you. You must think that person is crazy. Believe me nobody has it that good ant nothing on your body is that good that you can do a person anyway you want and they never stop loving you; nobody have it that good and never will, it's just not that good people and never think it is. Whatever that person liked about you that made them fall for you it will soon be over In addition, once it is over, there is nothing you can say are do to make that person fall back in love with you. Once the love is gone, it is gone and that is that. So now it's time to move on it takes a fool to misuse a person who loves and care for them since true love is hard to find. A good kind loveable person is so hard to find. When I first met my husbands, he was homeless with nothing. No job, no place to stay where he was welcome; I took him in and would let him used my only car thinking he would find a job and help he. Never did he, everything was on me. In addition he laid up on me than here come his family and friends and he would go out and find homeless men and bring them to my house, yes I will say my house because if you don't pay the bills it's not your house. Every woman that had a house and let him stay he would not pay any bills but still call his crazy self the man of the house. I do not understand how some people can be so low down and good for nothing. I hated some people in the beginning and I soon begin to feel the same way about him. Everything I had to do I had to do it alone no matter how sick I was. I never had any help from my husbands. In addition, all the hard times I went through. I went through it without them. That's another thing when a person is there for you when you're going through your trials and tribulations that bring you two closer together. A person that you love not there for you through your trials and tribulations and a person you don't love is that make you start thinking about that person in a positivity way and that person you love wasn't every there for you, you will start thinking Lesser of them till there be no love at all. Therefore, my hard ships had passed and I come through the hardest times without any man by my side. Therefore, I said the hell with them the love gone and nothing they can say are do for me now but leave me alone. Everything is long over with now. I made it without them. I did not care if they went to hell and never came back. I did not care what happen to them just as they didn't about me.

In addition, for as depression I know it all so well. However, I look back and what I went through I am happy I went through it now. I do not depend on nobody. If I need something, I can go out and get it all on my own I am so happy to be able to say that. I do not need any man to make it. There is not anything I cannot do on my own and that is a lost to say being a woman. However, I can say that with pride. In addition, I am a woman with pride and have pride in everything I do.

We all have a gift

I want you to know that GOD done given all of us a gift, but some people may be like I was it has not been discovering yet. See what my gift is. I am writing my own book. In addition, I been told I am a good talker. I'm an inventor. Then to if GOD did not give you a gift you just as good as a person that has one hundred gifts. It do not matter if you cannot sing nor dance like myself. It had to take time for me to realize that it did not matter. It is all right to have two left feet's when it comes to dancing. It is all right if you cannot sing like a bird. Whatever gift you do not have it is not meant for you to have it. It is not your fault that you do not have it. It's all right what you can't do as long as your heart is true a true heart just might be your gift after all because that's something everybody does not have. And do not let anybody take that away from you. See whatever decisions you make in life good or bad you the one have to live with it. Your decisions may not satisfy everybody because you cannot please everybody all the time so do not try. And if you make mistakes along the way just remember erasers where made on pencils because it's a known fact that man going to make mistakes and then to do you know that some of the best known inventions is here because of somebody's mistake. So I hope I done cleared up some things you been wondering about. I just explained them to you the way GOD explained them to me. Now I know it may seem like I'm out of my mind must been out of my mind telling about these thing happening to me and you may say it cannot all be true. But it is and if it didn't happen to myself and it happen to somebody else I can say myself I wouldn't believe it either. It's all kinds of thing happen in this world every day that doctor's cant explained. They just dismissed it as the person being crazy or something. However, there are ghosts and hunted houses whether people want to believe it or not and GOD does talk to some people and show them things. I know what I am talking about when I say I have seen ghosts and GOD have showed me things and those five boys come to me in sprints. However, I cannot make anybody believe me. In addition, I know sure people going to say all hell she been in a mental hospital she must be nuts. Say what you want but I do know my story is true so I'm getting back to it I just wanted to clear this up about my story and later on at the ending of my book I'm going to ask you again what is my gift and without looking I want to see do you remember so here more of my story enjoy.

There is no dumb child

That is one thing I hope I never hear and this a parent calling their child dumb. There is no dumb child. Some children just has a learning disability And when the teacher asks, does every one understand the assignments?

The child not going to raise he's or her hand to say no I do not understand. They know them teachers can be and most are very impatient with a child that is harder to learn. See I been one of them kids myself. In addition, I remember how I was treated for it. I would be afraid to raise my hand to say no I didn't understand in case someone would say I knew old dummy over there had her big fat round hand up she never understand anything now you put that fat hand down. I knew you didn't understand do you ever? In addition, I would get beat up after school for been dumb they would call me. In addition, if I told the teacher I would be told to sit down. Never, and I mean never talk about your child been dumb or having a learning disability when other kids or around. That is no one else business. For some children's it just takes longer for them to learn and teachers do not have the time or patients to be bother with them. Nobody do not have to tell me how they or I been there. And a child can tell when a person don't want to be bother with them or don't have patients for them and they don't want to be laugh at or called names which kids wouldn't go for that to day. In addition, I do not blame them at all. Now I do not say kill anybody or take a gun to school. I do not blame them if they sue the hell out of the school for the teacher letting the child be picked on by others kids and doing nothing about. Therefore, I went through school never raising my hand and admitting that I did not understand the assignment. I am sure there were other kids like myself. However, at the time it seemed that I was the only one in the hold school that never understood anything. I would get so nerviest when I had to get up and go to the front of the room to speak that I would stutter. However, to my surprise nobody ever made fun of me. I just learn not to long ago just before my father died that I got a brother on my father side of the family that stutter also. Just as I used to stutter and sometimes, I still stutter a little now. So just have patient for your child because you never know what your child may grow up to be one day because some of the most successful people have a learning disability believe it or not. Do not think your child just at school playing around and not trying to learn. That may not be the case at all. In addition, do not let anybody compare his or her child with your child. That is not fair to your child. Their child may be younger than your child is and maybe they can spell words your child cant. That don't mean nothing someday your child may grow up to be something special and the child that could spell may grow up to be a bum you never know because they didn't have the get up and go it takes to be successful. So you never know how children going to turn out. We just never know. Children or laughed at in school when they have a learning disability. It may take some kids longer to learn something. However, once they do learn something they want forgets it and they're going to be good at whatever they learn. Therefore, a learning disability may not be very bad. It just makes you better at something once you learn it that is all. In addition, some people just cannot learn at all. That still does not make them dumb. That just makes them disable to learn. We all have some kind of disability some people or more noticeable then others.

Chapter 53

On the wings of them snow white doves

IREMEMBER WITH MY first ectoped pregnancy which I had no sign that I was pregnancy at all. One day I was on my way to the store, which was up the street from where I live. The woman hated black women because her husband had sex with a black woman and she said he told her that black women were better in bed then she. She was so stupid he said that black woman was better in bed then his wife not all black women it didn't matter about the race of the woman she just happen to be the one he liked. Anyway, this day I was on my way to the store when these doves flew down on top of my head from top of this laundry matt. That frightens the hell out of me I was screaming and trying to hit them off my head. Therefore, when I looked up to see were the doves were I did not see them. I say about a month later I started hurting badly below my stomach I would lay down then the pain would stop. The hold time I was still working in the rest home lifting patients weighting three and four hundred pounds. One day I was getting ready for work when I start hurting again each time the pain came back they was harder than the pain before. Therefore, I had to catch the bus to go to the hospital they told me I were not pregnancy so they sent me home. Two weeks later the pain came back. So I asked what I thought was a friend to take me to the hospital he told me no. Therefore, I caught the bus and went I started bleeding on the way to the hospital. When I came in, I fainted that is all I remember. Then when I came to the doctor told me I had a pregnancy growing in my right tube and the baby alone with my tube had to be removed. So doing my operations both of my lungs claps and I woke up on life support the doctors call my family and told them they had done all they could do for me and I was in GOD hands now. They called in a preacher to give me my last rights and they gave my things to my sisters because they all though I was dying but I knew I were not because on the wings of them snow white doves GOD had sent down my healing with his pure sweet love.

How I am doing now

How I am doing now, well I take it one day at a time. In addition, I have to admit I am not that same woman I use to be to men anymore. In addition, I do not care about them the way I use to. See when a person tries to treat people decent they just used and abused them every time. People do not seem to appreciate decent kind people. So when mothers and fathers tries to rise their children to be a fine kind caring respectable person all their doing is sating their children up for people to abused and mistreat and use the hell out of them because where you trying to teach your child right from wrong their going to fall for the person who was rise to use people and get over on them and to get all they can out of good people if the person give it to them. And the user parents tell them if a fool takes you in their house without you having any means of support you take them up on the afford you let them take care of you and don't be in a hurry about getting a job because honey you done found yourself a good fool so you had better hold on to them because child you can't find a sucker like that every day. A sucker like that only comes around once in a lifetime so you bet not let them get away. Therefore, you see that is what other people or teaching their Childers so it takes a fool to mess over a good person and to think that person want get tired of them.

> They said I wouldn't make it out in the world on my own: Well from 19 years old to years old
> I'm still out here on my own.

Nobody ever thought I could do anything, not even make it out on my own, nobody ever treated me as I was a human being with feeling; they would say anything to me and tell me anything about my old man and it weren't for my own good. You don't tell people things that was told to me when you just getting out the hospital from almost dying and you just lost your child and you feeling down as a person can get, and the father of your child pass by your house with you setting out side all huge up with a woman and he should be with you. People telling you things your baby father said that kills you inside; people such as the people I had in my life a dog don't need them around them. We must not take everybody for our friend; we must learn who our friend is. Just think, when a person tells you things to hurt you it's not love and never believe it is because it's not. And when people hurt you never let it show, see people like that it make them feel good when they hurt you, keep your head up never let them see you cry. Well it done been thirty-seven years now since I done been out on my own and everybody said I would not make it. What people was saying I didn't have sense enough to make it out in the world on my own. However, I provided them all wrong. My job was talked about when I was working at the convalescent hospital, it was a job I didn't ask anybody for anything I had my own place I wasn't staying with people like over half the world does, I was standing on my own tow feet's. I was doing the best I could I didn't have the education it took to get a good job but I did my best even if I never was told anything to brighten up my day when I was feeling down, just a kind word or two would had meant so much to me but I never did get that. What people did was steal from me. In addition, it always was said I never would amount to nothing. Well I done invented stands and carriers and bags for amputees and I have invented four pairs of tennis shoes. See to make a long story short you can make it if you try. In addition, please never forget when you make one step God makes two. And another thing that's why I tell you don't look for people to be supportive when you're trying to do something positive for yourself because you will be on your own please believe me.

However never thing people going to have feeling for you, I didn't tell you how we was treated when my grandmother was in the hospital on her death bed, this dam woman ask me if she cod did we want CPR done on her? With me I wanted anything done to save her life that woman told me if she was her grandmother she wouldn't have it done because it could break her ribs. Then she told me now I don't care as though I thought she did. I never said anything about it because I knew the only thing I would had been told was she didn't mean it that way because some people can say anything they want to say and nothing ever said about it. Now if that had been me and I, said that to somebody I would have been without a job. I had to use the restroom that same day and didn't know where it was there for I asked this lady she just pointed at the door there for I thought she meant the door she was pointing at. A nurse seen me opening the door and told me you can't be going all over this hospital you going to be made to go out, that the way she talked to me while my grandmother was dying. Look what I been through with losing my baby and with my grandmother death. There for if I seem cold now you know the reason why; because of the way I been treated in my life, that's what made me the person I am today.

Don't forget

Now don't forget what I said about not letting it get you down if you and somebody else has an accident at the same time as yourself or if your accident was before theirs and it seem like they doing better then you or because you don't know how their really feeling inside. We all heal at our own pace. In addition, like I stated earlier in my book religions have a big part on our life and it plays a big part on our healing process. We must take our healing process one day at a time and if that don't do take it to the lord in prayer. Never think about how well the other person doing because that can be a setback for you just think about how well your doing and what you can do to get better because it's all about you now and nobody else.

Chapter 54

Where are we all now?

EVERYBODY MOVED TO Sacramento California, my mother and my two sisters and my brother. My mother is looking good and doing well, Dana is married with a good husband and she has one child a grown daughter name Marquita she is twenty-five with a college education she has one big fine baby boy name Jesses she has a good boyfriend which is the father of her baby. Her baby father world is his baby and his baby mother. His family is crazy about Marquita and her little son. Louryette has five children's and she is a grandmother with three grandsons. She lives up the streets from my mother and Dana. My brother JR is married with a nice wife and they have five children between them both and he has a good job he likes, everybody is blessed. In addition, myself, well I am still in Bakersfield California; you know I grew up to be the author of look to the sky.

I have moved on

Now I must tell you when I was in high school I use to get discouraged when I had to walk those miles to school when I was in that foster home and I would be so cold but I went on and there had been times when I thought I could not go on, but I know our mother had went without clothes herself so we kids could have clothes to look decent in to go to school. She would wash on her hands till they bleed because the water was so hot. She wouldn't have clothes to put on to go to the kids gradation. I would feel so bad, that's why I had to go on and finish high school; after all she had went without for us to go to school looking half way decent, I just had to, no way could I drop out; lord knows I had to keep telling myself. No matter what, I had to go all the way and god knows I had it hard. However, along the way I could hear my mother saying, nothing worthwhile comes easy. I would remind myself of her words every time things got harder. I shed tears and lord knows I shed many of them. But that day I graduated was worth every tear and more I ever shed. Now that day has been so many years ago which was the six day of June of nineteen seventh three, looking back if you asked me what did those days teach me, I would have to say; we all are somebody no matter what we may or may not have and people treat you the way you let them treat you. And when you let people treat you anyway they want to treat you, they don't have any respect for you. If you love and respect yourself you want let people just do anything to you and not say anything about it. Even with your husband don't let him treat you just anyway he wants. You have to let him know where to get off. And you know what? He want leave you if you stand up for yourself. Most men like a women with an attitude, no man like a pushover for a woman he like a woman that can take care of herself. Just like no woman want a pushover for a man no man want a pushover for a woman. No woman wants a man that she can push around. The more you take off a person the more they will give, a person will try you. Even on jobs a pushover don't get anywhere, an aggressive person that speaks up and speak out and with some attitude always makes it. That kind of person will soon be over you if you're the kind of person that let people walk all over you. I can recall when I would let my old man fight me and I run from him crying he run behind me until one day I got fed up with him fighting me and I got me a sick, when I picked up that stick and started hitting him all over his head with it and everywhere else I could find, I thought he would kill me; he just smile and pull me to him and kiss me and told me it's about time you fight back he respected me for fighting him back, he didn't hurt me for beating him with that stick; he told me he was going to beat the hell out of me till I fight him back. A doormat is for walking on not people and people weren't meant to be beaten on and mistreated. However, don't be a doormat for nobody. You know men love a woman that puts her foot down, a man going to at times act like a dog so you must tame him. Another thing about the way woman dresses, most men like the Betty Crocker look for a wife and a woman that knows how to cook and clean. Now he loves to look at women showing it all and leaving nothing to the imagination, but he doesn't want you for a wife. And he like for a woman to smell nice and sweet. And young ladies if you want a young man to respect you respect yourself. You must give respect to receive respect. Act like young ladies in talking and carrying yourself about. I'm going to tell you to do something for yourself please, always keep yourself a nickel handy at all times when you're with a young man and he will respect you for this in the long run. You take that nickel and put it between both knees and hold it there and he will love you for it. See older men will tell your young man, why buy the cow when you can get the milk free. What that mean is why married that woman when you can go to bed with her without being married to her. Before I end here's something I want you to always remember and that is no matter what you may have and no matter how high you may get never burn the bridge that carried you over, such as your mother I said mother because most black families that's all they have is they mother. Your mother was the person that laid down the foundation for the bridge to be contracted and what I mean by that is she's the one that gave birth to you. She's the one who pretended so many times that she was not hungry so you could have the last bite of food. She's the one who wouldn't buy herself clothes so you could have clothes to put on your back. She's the one who would ware her poor knees out from being on them so long praying for you to come home when you're out in the street not even thinking about her. She's the one who couldn't sleep when you was out but when you come home she would pretended that she was sleeping well because she never wanted you to know how much she really was worried about you. Now the bridge was billed by the people that were there for you when you were away from home and you needed to hear you can make it and the bridge was made strong when family stepped in and carried you over it. So never burn the bridge that carried you over. I must tell you before I end one day I went by that old blue home we lived in on watts drive the first time we moved back to Bakersfield after living with my aunt and her husband and kids, yes the old blue house is still standing and I just got off the bus and walked up two blocks up the street where the bus driver let me off and I just looked at the house, and still in my mind I could see two little girls faces up to the living room window looking for the mailman, the mailman that pass their house by that sad day that was so many years ago. I just couldn't move I just looked at the house, yes the little blue house I loved, the house I was so happy in, the house I called home. Yes our house, the little blue house where my mother and my sisters and I once lived. We was bless even if we had nothing still we had everything. We had god we had our heath, we had each other and we had our family. Some rich people didn't have what we had and still have. I can't forget about Camarillo the long and sad days I spent there, yes it was hell all the way but god as always sent his angles to carry me through hell I can't help but cry some times when I think about how good god been to me because I know there been times when I would say god don't love me

159

because if he did he wouldn't had let things happen to me like he did and he would had let me have children. Well I still don't know why god never bless me to have children and he let other women have them to break up homes and give them to women who kill them I never will know the answer to that oh yes just as he told me he had nothing to do with that my how fast we can forget what god says. As I said I can't forget about old Camarillo State Hospital, you know that hospital was once the biggest psychiatrist hospital in the world I hear. I still can remember the times when my mother would come to visit me whenever she got a way up there how I would stand and look out the window seeing them going around them lonely looking mountains and I would cry lord at that time nothing looked so sadder to me then seeing my mother leaving and going around them mountains I tell you I thought them days would never end but that was all in my mind because they did end and now I'm no longer that twelve year old girl now I'm a fifth six year old woman so now I'm proud to say with a smile those days at Camarillo State Hospital are so far behind me now. Camarillo is no longer a state hospital. It was close March 23, 1997. The community said goodbye to old Camarillo State Hospital for good. It was one of the most famous institutions in California. Because it use to house Charlie Yard bird Parker a jazz player who had a nervous breakdown in 1947 who stayed there for six-months.

Camarillo State Hospital opens in the 1930's until the late 1990's. It's said to have been Hotel California the song the Eagles was singing about because one of them had been a patient at Camarillo and he wrote a song about it Called Hotel California. Camarillo State Hospital was a Psychiatric Hospital for both developmentally disabled and mentally ill and schizophrenia patients.

Also Camarillo State Hospital was the first units of any hospital to deal with autism patients. Now the old sun-bleached building stands as the First California State University in Ventura County. Looking back I think about them days in Camarillo State Hospital and what it taught me and you know what? Nothing, I cannot think of anything I learn from that place other then how to put eye brow pencil under my eyes other than that nothing. The places do not help anybody believe me when I tell you. The only thing they do is I will say if you have a little sense you will use what little you have to get the hell out of there if you have no sense at all are in a coma than you can stand it and that's the only way please believe me.

Now I would like for you to take a moment to think about the things you learned the hard way plus the things you learned the easy way now which you remember the most? See those things in life we learn the hard why hardly do we ever forget. And things it takes you a long time to learn when you do learn it your will be a pro at it because you'll know it so well. Now you see a learning disability no matter how crazy this may sound could turn out to be your gift after all. And things that we come by the hard way we will appreciate it. In the medical field a person can get all A's on all the written exams but when it comes to the hand on field exam meaning do they understand how to do what they learned in class on the field, check it out they may not now they gotten all A's in class but they can't do on the field exam but the person that gotten all c's gotten A's on the field exam. Just because a person can pass a written exam don't mean they can pass the hand on exam. On the other hand, a person that gets c's on the written exam may get all A's on the hand on field exam. See what I'm saying. Just because you pass something that doesn't mean you will do well on the job doing it and it don't mean you understand it. On the other hand just because you don't do well on a written exam doesn't mean you want do well on the job. There for never think just because a child grads not to good the child going to grow up to be a nobody because that may not be true at all, that child may fool you one day.

Now I will write down 150 saying back home people still uses till this day, I hope you enjoy reading them and I will be explaining some of the meaning to you then I will go into some of the wise tales that back home people uses and some live by them till this day. However before I do I just like to tell women that's jealous of other women with men in their life, I'm going to tell you something I once was one of them women other women was jealous of little did they know they had nothing to be jealous of because I never had a man no other women couldn't get and when you have a person in your life like that you don't have yourself nothing little did they know that. The men was good in the beginning but the same thing you do to win a person heart you have to do to keep their heart. People think just because they have you the job is over no, how wrong they are the job is never over the job is just beginning. Even with men what it took for a woman to get a man it will take that to keep him. Let's say if a woman kept herself looking nice and smelling nice and kept her house clean and cooked things he like to eat and once he married her, she let herself go. She stops keeping herself looking nice and stop bathing often like she use to. She stop cooking she stop keeping her house clean all this she stop because she feel she got her man however she never think about what it took to get her man it takes that to keep him. If you were everything he wanted in a woman and once you were his best friend now you put your girlfriend before him and if he wants loving you talking on the phone to your girlfriend. I can bet you your girlfriend don't have a man and if she does he goes out on her and never take her with him. He got somebody else on his arm. However your man want you everywhere he goes and love showing you off to his friend but you don't have time for him it's your girlfriend. Well how long do you think he going to put up with you. Any woman man that wants to take her places and want to be seen with her should be happy because so many men don't take their woman anyplace and don't have time for her he's either with the boys he say anywhere other than with you. There for if your girlfriend had a man that wanted to be seen with her and wanted to take her places she wouldn't have time for you there for if you ladies that's bless to have a good man please keep him loving you because so many women don't know what a good man is and they so hard to find.

Chapter 55

one hundred and fifty of the old saying back home people would use. Some of them I'll be telling the meaning to because

Some you will know, and also not all of them I agree with, however they just old saying.

1. Vengeance is mine said the lord: This means when someone do you wrong don't get them back because the lord will take care of them and you should keep on loving them.

2. A blind man has the best sight: because he sees with his heart and not with his eyes: This means a blind man can't see you to judge the way you look there for he goes by the way you talk and the little things you do such as help him across the street just little things means so much to the blind man.

3. To build a house you start at the bottom then work your way up. This means you have to start at the bottom of anything then work your way up.

4. Always treat others the way you like to be treated. This means always treat others the way you want to be treated.

5. Together we stand divide we fall. This means when family is together their stronger but when their apart they at their weakest.

6. Loving eyes can never see. This means when you love somebody you can't or will over look their faults. Other people will see their faults before you will because you're blind to them.

7. Hell has no fury as a woman scorned. This mean nobody is angrier and want to take revenge more than a woman that been hurt by somebody she love.

8. Little or much always be thankful for what you got and you may be bless with more.

9. Watch the dog that brings the bone. This means watch the person that telling on others.

10. You cannot buy love. This mean no matter how much money you spend on a person you want to love you or be your friend you want win their heart over. Love and friends comes free you cannot buy ether.

11. Be appreciated for what a person does for you. This means say thank you I really appreciate what you done for me and show by doing something for them. Just don't take and take and never give.

12. If you live by the gun, you will die by the gun. This mean if you live a bad life you usually die a bad death.

13. You will leave this world the same way you come in it. This means. You come with nothing you will leave with nothing.

14. It is in GOD we trust. This means don't put your trust in man because man will deceive you.

15. Mother may have and father may have but god blesses the child that has his own. This means even if your family have things after your grown go and work for what you want don't depend on your family any more.

16. The world was not built in one day. This means it takes time to do things.

17. don't put off what you can do today and think you will be here to do it tomorrow, because tomorrow not promise to anyone.

18. He who laughs last laugh best. This means he who laughs last laughs the longest because he have save his wind while the other people was laughing they was laugh out.

19. When you or digging a hold for somebody else you had better dig one for yourself. This means when you trying to do somebody else wrong it may fall back on you.

20. What goes around, come around and sometimes buckers under. This means what you do to others will be done to you and sometimes twice as bad.

21. What goes in must come out. This means when you're a child what you hear and see you is learning things and good or bad later in life it will show. However another way to put it is take a person that get drunk and they do and say things and blame it on them being drunk the reason why they said and done what they did. That's not true; if that wasn't in them they wouldn't have said nor done what they did. Other words if it wasn't in them it would have never come out.

22. You can lead a horst to water but you can't make him drank. This means you can't make a person do anything they don't want to do. This one I don't know about because a person can beat the hell out of you if you don't do what they want and make you do what they want.

23. Every dog has his day and a good one has two. This means When you do somebody wrong your day will come when something bad going to happen to you. When you do good thing for people good things happens to you and sometimes twice as good.

24. Love doesn't love anybody. This means love don't care who it hurt because it's just a word with no feeling.

25. Take pride in what you do. Whatever you do, This means do it at your best have pride in it as you do yourself because what you do speaks about you if you have pride on yourself it will show in the work you do if you do not it to will show in the work you do.

26. Understanding is the best thing in the world.

27. When you pray, put others first then yourself.

28. Too many cooks will `spoil the soup. This means when you let too many people in on what you got going on somebody bond to mess it up. A better way to put it, say you're cooking soup and you put in a cup of water, the next person puts in a cup and on and on now it's a mess too much water.

29. Smiling faces sometimes don't tell the truth. This means a person may look friendly put you can't go by the looks because you can't see what's inside, they may be a bad person.

30. The bigger the tree the harder the fall. This means the bigger a person is when they knocked down that harder they will fall.

31. You cannot lose what you never had. This means if you never had anything you will not lose it. Other words: if you never had any money to lose you want lose it, you have to done had it to lose it.

32. You can't miss what you can't merger. This means love, you can't merger it there for why would you miss it.

33. A whistling woman and a crowing hen never come to no good end. This means just be yourself.

34. Love to a tennis player means nothing. This means this the only time love doesn't mean a thing and this in a tennis game.

35. You cannot keep a good man or woman down. This means you can take everything a good person owned and walk off and leave them with nothing and somehow they always seem to come back up and sometimes even higher than before.

36. He that without sin let him cast the first stone. This means whoever was doing no wrong throw the stone. Other words this means in Christ days there was this *prostitute* and the people wanted to stone her and they told god what they wanted to do to the lady, and god spoken he without sin cast the first stone now do you think anybody cast the stone? Then to over eating is a sin.

37. <u>Oh what a tangled Web we weave when first we Practice to deceive. Nobody really knows</u> the meaning we just said it.

38. The only three things in live that's a guarantee is #.1 you will die, #2 you will pay taxes #3 and if you live you will age.

39. When you pointing a finger at somebody else three pointing back at you.

40. Saving for a rainy day. This means putting back money for hard times to come.

41. Leave well enough alone. This means if something going well for you let it be enjoy it.

    A better way to put it let's say you're a woman that always prayed for a good man and finally your prayers was answer. Now instead of you being grateful to god you say he's too fat or too skinny, too short or too tall too young, too old he's black, he's white, you just ask for a good man and you was sent one. You never said god send me a man that's perfect in every way you just said send me a good man. When god sends you somebody he doesn't go by looks because as we all know looks can be deceiving. He just goes by what's inside a person heart and we should also be that way, that way we will hardly ever go wrong in a relationship.

42. Easy come easy goes. I say it this way when something comes easy to you, you usually don't appreciate it. Other words when you work hard for something that make you appreciate it. I will say again when a woman play hard to get once a man happen to get her he will feel special and he will have more respect for her and he will feel she worth having. However no matter how much you want a man ladies play hard to get because every woman is worth getting there for act like it.

43. Do not let your left hand know what your right hand doing. This means don't let people know your business.

44. Take time to know them. This mean what it say, don't rush in to a married or relationship take out time to learn something about the person first and learn something about their family tree, other words learning where a person come from can tell you something about them. Such as did they come from a dysfunctional family or did they come from a family where there was incest or drugs and abused. If boys did the father cheat on their mother or did he abused his wife. You just check that family tree before you marry a person.

45. If you can't say something nice don't say anything at all. This means if you don't have nice things to say about a person don't say anything about them.

46. Don't rush to judgments. This means just because you think something about somebody don't think it's true until you learn the facts.

47. People treat you the way you let them. This means if you let a person walk all over you they will do just that.

48. Self-preservation is the first law of nature. This mean to take care of yourself first before you take care of somebody else.

49. Put GOD a head of everything you do. This mean always say if its god will I will do this or that because he may have other plans for you such as calling you home that day.

50. It is not always, what you say, but the way you said it. This means if you're telling a person you love them, you would say it in a way to make them believe it such as sounding sincere.

51. It takes a village to raise a child. This means if the child not at home if friends or neighbor sees them doing wrong they should tell the child right from wrong.

52. Together we stand divided we fall. I put it this way; take a car with all four wheels on the car, as long as there's all four wheels on that car it will stand take off one don't matter if it from the front or back that car will fall. A family that's together they can overcome most anything, god will bless their home, that's a home that's together but when a home is divide your home will fall it want be bless no matter how hard you try god won't come into a divide home.

53. Everybody plays the fool. This means when you love somebody sometimes they will take advantage of you this when people say they playing you for a fool. If that's the case everybody plays the fool and there's no exception to the rule.

54. Never burn the bridges that carried you over. This means never do others wrong that helped you because you might need them again. A better way to put this is to say it's so easy for some people to forget about the people that help them when they was down and out, now god blessed them to get on their feet now they don't have anything to do with the people that once had their back and was there for him which they was the bridges that carried them over, now god may fix it so they may have to cross that same bridge again and if you burn that bridge you can't cross it, so don't burn it you may need it again.

55. Don't count your chickens before them hatches. This means

Some of your eggs may not hatch. Say you have ten eggs, and you invest in feed and a cage large enough to feed and house 10 chickens, but only 1 egg hatches. There goes your money. Other words things may not work out the way you planned.

56. Why buy the cow when you can get the milk free?

    Now this means why a man would want to marry a woman when he can go to bed with her without being married. This older men will tell younger men. Man why buy the cow when you can get all the milk you want for free? 56. Don't lose your head over teal. My grandmother would tell me a story about this dog that was crossing the railroad track when his tail gotten caught between the tracks and he the dog had his head down trying to see his tail so he could find a way to get his tail out of the track, there for by the dog not looking to see where the train was the train knocked the dog head off there for the dog lost its head over tail. The real meaning of this is don't let nobody used you and make a fool out of you just because the sex may be good other words don't go crazy over it and lose all matter of reasoning over it.

57. Look before you leap. This means don't jump in the pool without checking to see how deep the water is. The real meaning is don't do anything without checking it out first.

58. Always remember: the other man's grass is always greener. This means that the other man takes care of his grass that's way his grass is greener then yours. Other words take a man that takes care of his home his family going to look better then the man family that's not being taken care of.

59. They like night and day, this mean how different they or for somebody you had better dig one for yourself.

    This means if you do evil to somebody it just might come back to you. There for when you dig a hole for somebody else to fall in you dig a hole to fall in yourself.

60. Take care of your own house. This means to take care of your business and mind your own business and when you do you don't have time to mind other people business. When you see a person that's have time to mind other people business you can very well believe their business is going undone and they should be taking care of their business.

    If you mind your own business that's a twenty four hours per day seven days a week three hundred and sixty five days a year job no time do you have to be up in other people business. When you mind your business you have things to do such as work clean house just making sure your business is done.

61. it's like finding a needle in a haystack. This means why bother trying to find something because it's imposable to find no need to search for it.

62. You don't miss your water till your well runs dry.

    This means you don't miss something or somebody till it's gone. Other words say you have this person in your life and they love the hell out of you and they bent over backwards to make you happy but you take them for granted because in your weak mind you think they love you so much that you can do just anything to them and they want leave you because you think what you got is so good to them. You think you have them for life and this when they up and leave you and they show you they want be back. Now you miss the hell out of them more then you ever knew you would. See you may be good but there's always going to be somebody better then you and somebody going to be better than them and it goes on and on so never think what you got is so good to a person that you think you can do them anyway you want and they never leave you because you can mistreat a dog long enough and it will leave you and never come back.

63. Pull one string the hold heaven ring. This mean if you bother one person in somebody family the hold family be out to get you.

64. Blood is thicker than water. This mean the bond between family is thicker then the bond between nonfamily.

65. Monkey see monkey do. This means a person that do what other people do to try to fit in with the in crowd or to impress somebody instead of being themselves.

66. Don't judge unless you want to be judge.

67. Action speaks louder than words. This mean I can show you better than I can tell you.

68. Never do to others that you wouldn't want do to you. Other words if you don't want something done to you don't do it to others see what goes around come back to you there for if you don't want it to come back don't do it.

69. it's a thin line between love and hate. This means don't think you can keep on mistreating somebody and they will keep on loving you and stay with you no matter what you do to them because sooner or later that person will no longer love you.

70. Rolling stone gather no moss. This mean when a person always moving around they want accomplish anything you must stay in one place other words when you move you lose.

71. You have to crawl before you walk. This mean you have to start at the bottom.

72. Practice what you preach. This mean when you tell a person something right make sure your doing what you telling the other person to do. Other words when you tell a person not to mistreat their spouse and all the time you're mistreating yours that's no good.

73. Good thing come to them that wait. I will say take a woman that looking for a man now you shouldn't go out looking for a lover if you do nine time out of ten you want like what you get. You must wait and see if somebody out there for you if so you don't have to go looking they will come to you when you're least expecting it.

74. A bird in the hand is worth two in the bush: this means what you have means more then something you don't have other words you have the bird in your hand but it can fly away if it's in the bush or somebody else can get it.

75. You can't have your cake and eat it too, however I know what this mean but it don't make much since to me I say what the use in having cake if you can't eat it? However this means you can't have it both ways.

76. Still water run deep. This another way of saying look before you leap, other words the water is still and you may not know how deep it may be there for you must check it out before you get in the water because the water may be too deep for the best swimmer.

77. It takes one to know one. This means the pot calling the kettle black or it takes a thief to catch a thief.

78. You will leave this world the same way you come in. This means you come here with nothing and you will leave with nothing.

79. Don't keep up with the Jones. This means don't go out and buy thing you know you can't afford just because maybe your friend bough it.

80. Loose lips sink ship. This means your mouth can get you in trouble by telling things or talking about things you shouldn't.

81. You can catch more flies with honey then with vinegar. This means you can get farther in life by being nice to people then you will if you mistreat others.

82. What's good for the goose is good for the gander. Now what's a gander you may ask? A gander is a mature male goose. This means if a person goes out and plays around on you it's only fare to give them a test of their own medicine. Not all of these saying I agree with such as this one. Now to me two wrongs don't make a right. If somebody mess up on you and you mess up on them to get them back you're really not getting them back because nine times out of ten they don't know what you're doing anyway. Then to you know deep down inside you're not enjoying messing up on your person anyway. Then to the only person your hurting is yourself because if you have a conscious it going to bother you.

83. TKO. This means tactical knock out. Such as another love TKO, which means you was knocked down by love again. Other words you got disappointed or hurt by somebody you were in love with. You never learn love don't love nobody.

84. TLC. This means, tender loving care which is something the heart doesn't get enough of.

85. ASAP. This means as soon as possible do it now it can't wait.

86. TCB. This means taking care business. Making sure your business is being taking care of.

87. You can't teach old dog new tricks. This means you're older now and your mind can't comprehend. This one I don't agree with because you're never too old to learn as long as you have some portion of your right mind.

88. What you smell is not cooking. What this means is what you think is so is not so.

89. If you lay down with dogs you will get up with fleas, this means be careful who you go to bed with because they may give you VD.

90. I just look this way. This means I just look stupid, dumb, silly, crazy, naïve, I'm not this way.

91. Its every man for himself and god for us all. This mean everybody has to take care their own self. A better way to put it is say you're on a boat and the boat began to sink and there's only a few lifeboats and somebody yells out the boat is sinking! There or only a few lifeboats every man save himself and god save us all.

92. The early bird gets the worm. This means the person that gets up and out early usually be the one that gets the job or other things that's to be gotten.

93. That's the proof is in the pudding. This means the proof is as planed as the nose on your face its right there.

94. The family that prays together stays to gather. This means through praying together no negativity will enter that family home there for they will stay together such as husband and wife.

95. Step up to the plate. This means to take on your responsibility.

96. They like them from eight too eighty blind cripple or crazy. This mean this person being in a relationship don't care what age the person may be don't matter what medical conduction the person is in they like them any way.

97. Mama's baby papa's maybe. This means it's for sure it's the woman baby because she's the one that gives birth to the child however for as the man you don't always know because a child don't have to look like his father to be the father's child there for that might and might not be the man' child.

98. it's raining cats and dogs. This means it's pours down.

99. No skin off my back. This means I'm not getting in trouble behind it because it doesn't concern me.

100. He beat her for breakfast, lunch and dinner. This means he beat her all the time.

101. Don't sale yourself short. This means don't talk like you can't do anything worthwhile and don't talk down about yourself.

102. Your getting the short end of the stick. This means you're not getting what your worth.

103. Seek and you shell find. This mean when you go looking for something you shell find it. A better way to put this lest say you goes out looking to see if a person is fooling around on you if they is nine times out of ten you will find out and even sometimes when you're not seeking.

104. Don't take any wooden nickels. This means don't believe anything's that's not real.

105. You believe that fried ice cream. This means you believe anything if you believe ice cream can fry.

106. If the left one doesn't get you the right one will. This means. It you don't have something bad happen to you now you will later.

107. Beauty is in the eye of the beholder. This mean where one person may not see the beauty in you another person may see you as the most beautiful person on earth.

108. Let sleeping dogs lie. This mean leave the problem along

109. Don't cry over spilled milk. This mean don't let nonsense things upset you. If you spill the milk just wipe it up.

110. You can't judge a book by its cover. This mean you can't tell whether a person is a good person just by their outer appearance.

There or three sides to every story. This mean when two people or telling a story there's bout of their side of the story which is two sides and the truth which makes three sides.

111. To kill two birds with one stone. This mean to get both things done at once.

112. The pot can't talk about the kettle. This means they both the same thing. A pot is a kettle a kettle is a pot.

113. Nothing likes a bone but a dog and he buried it. That's what people would tell their overweight child to tell other kids that call them fat. It never worked.

114. A closed mouth doesn't get fed. This means if you don't speak up you want get what you want. Other words keeping your mouth closed not going to get you anywhere I had to learn this the hard way and as I said anything you learn the hard way as long as you have your right mind you never forget it. I was wrong when I said keeping your mouth closed don't get you nowhere it do an early death, disrespected and people want never feel your even human. As I stated before a man like for his woman to stand up and speak out to him no man want a pushover. If you let people walk all over you that's what they will do. A door mat is for walking over not people so never lie down so people can used you for a doormat.

115. You jumped out the frying pan into the skillet. This means you got out of one thing and gotten back into the same thing. A better way putting it is say you're a woman and you got a no good man and you leave him and gets with somebody just as bad now this when people say well hell you jumped out the frying pan into the skillet a frying pan and skillet is both the same thing.

116. You make a mountain out of a mole hill. This means you take something small, which a mole hill is a small hill of dirt and make a mountain. Other words let's just say a man tells a lady he like the dress she have on, now he have a wife at home and it's her birth, he like the lady dress for his wife. The woman go home and tells her husband some man was hitting on her and shows the man to her husband now her husbands the man, the man have no idea what's going on, the woman husband tells the man you was hitting on my wife, the man say hitting on your wife? Yes says the husband, I weren't hitting on your wife, I just told her I liked that dress she has on and I think my wife will like it so I will buy it for her birthday. Now see how this woman turns an innocent compliment which is a mole hill and started something.

117. You can't get blood out a trump. This means a trump has no blood there for you can't get it. A better way to put it the person doesn't have any money their dry there for they saying you can't get any money from them if they don't have any.

118. A man home is his castle. This means a man home is a big thing to him well it should be some men has an open house for the public in their home and gives smoke outs just don't have respect for the home and I you don't respect your home you can't look for other people to have.

119. like father like son. This mean if the father no good the son want be any good however this not true and never been true you don't have to be anyway you don't want to be this just one of them old wise tales.

120. Only the strong survived. However as I said nobody is strong what happens is sometimes a person gets not caring confused with a person being strong. A person can grow to become hard through the years that don't mean them a strong will person and there's the one that do the best they can in the presence of a situation.

121. Wake up and smell the coffee, this mean to open your eyes and see things as they or.

122. I'm going to tell you the way the cow ate the cabbage. The way the cow ate the cabbage was the way it is. There for they going to tell you the way it is.

123. You like the dog was by the hay. What that means the dog couldn't eat the hay and he didn't want the hay but he didn't want the horst to have it, other words that how some people or about another. They don't want you but they don't want anybody else with you.

124. Stitch in time save nine. What this means is, if you do something right the first time you do it, you save yourself time from having to do it over

125. Monkey see monkey do. This means when a person sees somebody else do something they have to do the same.

126. One monkey doesn't stop no show. This means one person can't stop nothing, let's say if a show was going on and a person was going to do their act and they don't show up the show must go on without them. In some ways one monkey can stop a show depending on what kind of show it is and how many monkeys should be there. If the act was for two monkeys and one didn't show up and no other monkey can do the monkey act then the show can't go on.

127. One bad apple doesn't spoil the hold bunch. This means take men just because one you date may be bad don't look at all of them being the same way.

128. Charity starts at home then spreads abroad. This means when you get money before you give to charity take care of home first. Never neglect home for nothing if you have anything left over after making sure home have been taking care of them you can give to charity.

129. Bin the cype while it's young. Cype is a small tree growing and you can only bin it while it's just a twig you can't bin it when it's a full grown tree. This saying the same thing about a child you have to put value in a child while they young when they teenagers and grown it's too late.

130. It takes two to tango. This means it had to take a pair for the activity, there for one is no more to blame then the other one.

131. You have to crawl before you walk. This means you must start at the bottom of something before you make it to the top.

132. They like two peas in a pod. This mean the people or similar or identical; in their action or ways. Take sweet peas they in a pod, don't the peas look identical? Take people that's friends usually they has ways similar to each other.

133. Leave no stone unturned. This mean to go out your way. Lest say you have tried everything it is to try to get rich, you saved every penny, you worked three jobs, you live outdoors, you begged for food, and you still not rich, you left no stone unturned.

134. Why rock the boat. This mean if you have something good why risk it. Take a man that got a good woman and he goes out and fool around on her, he's rocking the boat because she may find out and leave him.

135. Rocking in the same old boat. This mean you and others have the same problem,

    Such as you have nowhere to stay just like everybody else don't have anywhere to stay

136. Two can play that game. This mean whatever one person can do, the other person can do it. Lest say if a man fool around on his woman, his woman can fool around on him.

137. Where's there's smoke, there's fairer. This means if the evidence there, that's usually the proof.

138. If you miss one bus, another one coming. This means if you love somebody and they leave you, somebody else will come alone.

139. I been there and done that. This mean, that person have experienced what you experiencing now.

140. I pass this way before. This mean I went through this before.

141. Beware of false prophets. What this mean is beware of people claiming they been sent by god to do his work, such as healing you.

142. Turn the other cheek, what this mean is, if a person slaps you, not to slap back just turn the other cheek so they can slap the other cheek. Some women teach their sons if a woman hit them not to hit her back. Now look what can go wrong, let's say a woman been with a man for years that mother taught him not to hit a woman. Therefore, she always hitting on him, and he never once hit her, now she think all mothers teach their sons not to hit a woman, now her man can't take her hitting on him any longer now he leave her. She meets another man not knowing he was taught to knock the hell out a woman if she hit him. There for one day she slap him and he get up and lay her out, she on the floor looking up at him and wondering why she's on the floor from being knocked down, and asking her man; why he hit her, didn't his mother teacher him to turn the other cheek when a woman hit him? He answers hell no! My mother taught me, if a bit-h hit me to try my best to knock her brains out and that's what I did, you must be crazy if you didn't think I wouldn't knock your brains out for hitting me Bit-h ;I mean you hit me, you want hit me again now will you?

171

143. The bigger the tree the harder the fall, this mean when a person that's bigger than you is picking on you, don't be afraid of them because; the bigger they or the harder they will fall if you knock them down.

144. Where there's a will there's away. This means if you want something bad enough if you have the determination which is the will, you can find the way, because there is a way, and this only means if it's in reasonable. Take like if you want to be the first person with your home bullied on the moon now you know that's not in reasonable.

145. You are judge by the company you keep. This means whatever kind of people you be around, people judge you by them. If you not on drugs why be with people who or.

146. The wolf in sheep's clothing. This mean when a bad person pretending to be a nice person, such as the wolf, he had on sheep's clothing because everybody know a sheep is harmful.

147. A snake in the grass. This means a snake crawls on its belly it's as low as the snake can get, and he hiding in the grass to bite you, this is sneaky he hides in the grass so you want see him; there for snake crawling = low down, crawling in the grass to bite you =sneaky if a person is said to be a snake in the grass, this means they low down and sneaky; and can't be trusted, you cannot trust a snake.

148. The apple don't fall far from the tree, this means like father like son like mother like daughter.

149. Never bite that hand that feeds you. This means never do a person wrong that's there for you. Now a dog will bite the hand that feed it because it doesn't know any better.

150. Heads will roll. This means people will get in trouble.

Back home people believe in many old wise tales and many people live by them. Here or 30 of them.

1. One of the old wise tales that people back home believe in is when you get married after the preacher announce you man and wife when you're leaving out the door never walk ahead of your husband or wife because that's splitting and if you split that day you will forever remain split.

2. Another one is when a woman marry give her at least one gift with a ribbon on the box that way she will unite it and she will have children if there's no ribbon to untie on her gifts its said she want have children.

3. Never give a couple knifes for a wedding gift because what you do with a knife? Cut, split, there for they will be split.

   Give people bread when they move in a new house that way they never is without food they will always have lots of good things to eat.

4. If you want a person to go to jail just take a broom and sweep their feet. If they spit on the broom and leave they want go to jail.

5. If you cut a person hair on the wrong Side of the moon they hair won't grow back, now what's the wrong Side of the moon I don't know. However there must be something about them old wise tales because I never gotten a ribbon on my wedding gift and I never had kids.

6. If you want a couple to break up just take a rotten egg and throw it agents a tree and repeat three times I want this couple to break up like this egg brakes.

7. If you want a man to stay away from your house just take salt and throw it over his feet's or put salt at your door and he want be able to inter your house.

8. When you dream of fish this means somebody in your family is pregnant.

9. A holing dog means death.

10. If a bird fly in your house this too means death.

11. If a baby stands on its head this means the baby's mother is pregnant again.

12. If a sore on your body and a dog licks it, it will soon heal.

13. If you break a mirror you will have seven years of bad luck.

14. If you split a pole walk back around it saying bread and butter if not it will bring bad luck.

15. Never walk under a ladder if you do it too will bring bad luck.

16. Never eat peanuts while riding in a car if you do the car will break down.

17. If it rain on your wedding day that's a good sign.

18. If you get out of the wrong side of the bed your day will be a bad one all day.

19. If you're left ear itch it means somebody is talking good about you.

20. If you're right ear itch somebody talking bad about you.

21. If your noise itch somebody coming over.

22. If your hand itches you're getting something in it.

23. If your left hand itches you're getting a letter.

24. If your right hand itches you're getting money.

25. If you throw your hair out and a bird takes it and make a nest with it you will have headaches for the rest of your life.

26. If you cut your hair on a bad moon it want grow back.

27. Whatever you be doing when the new-year come in that's what you be doing all year.

28. If you cook black eyed peas for the New Year it will bring you good luck.

29. When you move in a new house throw a broom over the house for good luck.

30. Never cross a black cat because it will bring you bad luck.

I don't believe in any of this as I said all this is, just old wise tales no truth in it there for ladies if you don't want a man at your house just tell him to stay away I know this something that don't work for some men because I had them however just call 911.

Chapter 56

This telling about my inventions

What! You mean I didn't tell you I was an inventor to? Yes I am.

BELOW IS A write up about me that was in a book called motions this book has amputees doing different activities and it shows different things amputees such as myself done invented. If you want you can check it out you can contact motion amputees book by calling 411 and getting they phone number. Therefore, here is my story.

Hello my name is Dorothy Ann Darrough (Johnson), I'm a fifty six year old female of Bakersfield California, I was an innocent bystander wounded in a drive-by shooting back in 1993. The unfortunate incident caused me to lose my right leg above the knee. During my fitting process, I would frequently visit my Prosthetics by bus, carrying my main prosthesis leg with me. What I mean by saying my main prosthesis leg is the one I wares all the time. When I first had my leg amputated, I gotten my first prosthesis leg. Then my stomp shrink, after that I had to get another prosthesis, now if something happen to my main prosthesis I have a standby to put on while I bring my main prosthesis in to my prosthetics. This is where my stands and carriers come in. If you're taking your prosthesis on the bus you know how silly people or and how they stare at you and if you're anything like me you get mad when people stare at you. This why I have invented carriers to put our prosthesis leg in, so people can't see it and that give you more privacy; people don't need to know your business, and the carriers come with thick straps and the stands comes with a handhold handle, four wheels that can be change to two to none, and it can be lifted up or down and tipped backward and frontward; and moved to side to side, when something happen to what I call my main prosthesis leg I have something to carried it in. I have to put back on my standby prosthesis leg.

This what gave me the idea to create a leg carrier so we can transport our

Prosthesis in, The Carrier also has a stand on wheels to transport the prosthesis in, and if you don't want to used the carrier you can put the prosthesis leg on the stand or if you don't want people seeing your business like I don't then you can put your prosthesis in the carrier then put it on the stand on wheels so you can roll it so it want be so heavy. The wheels can be taken off depending on if you just want two wheels. The carrier also keeps the leg warm. My prosthesis is often cold in the morning. The carrier comes in above and below the knee. No stand for the below the knee they not as heavy as above the knee prosthetic however there is a carrier for it. I also created an arm carrier with the stand for above and below the elbow extremity amputees. The leg, and arm carrier, and leg stand and arm stand comes in a variety of fabric and designs.

And also I created prosthesis shoes, prosthesis foot and hand case, and a Prosthesis pillow case bag so you may put your personal in. I have gotten calls like you wouldn't believe however I don't have them for sale at this time but hope I will one day. I also invented four pairs of tennis shoes I call the skyrockets original and high tops and the sky walkers the original and high tops. I thought I save this for last. My senior year in high school as you all know we have to take them final exams however, if you don't pass them you don't graduate, as always everybody just knew no way in hell would I pass the final exam, once again old dumb old me, now don't forget I been in a nut house; there for me passing the final exam, no way in hell would I. Now I never believe I would ever graduate anyway. However when final exam rolled around now here we all set taking our exam and for yours truly here I sat crying as usual and praying and asking god not to let my mind wonder off like it always have so I could pass my exam. However, my mind would wonder off and I would find myself daydreaming. In my mind I heard my math teacher telling me so clearly that day, Dorothy your mind just wonders off that's all; you're not dumb Dorothy, and you must forget about what people have told you about you will never amount to nothing and Dorothy you will graduate with your class of 1973. Yes I could hear him saying those exact words to me. I prayed all through my final exam that day and like everything else it was over. I didn't have faith that I had passed. A week later our names and scores was up on the board and I knew mine wouldn't be up there. However, to my surprise there it was! My name was there! I was jumping up and down and crying once again as usual. I went and had a set because I was crying so hard. The next thing I knew somebody was asking me was I ok? Before I could say a word my math teacher was there and saying you bet she's ok! She's not only ok, she's a graduating student of the class of 1973! Yes, old dumb me! Was marching in with the graduate class of 1973! On 6-6-1973 to this day I still look at my diploma and I can't help but cry and say to myself I did it!

This goes out to everybody that having sorrow in life.

There's going to be times when you feel there's no hope, but just remember god don't give us anything we can't cope. If I should ever cross your mind and you think of me, just think how sweet god can be. Now I must tell you, there's still times when I feel depressed, but I know to take one-step and god takes the rest. You will have days when you're going to feel blue, just think of me and what I done been through. One thing I done learn that I know is true, if I can make it you can to. You're going to have good days, and bad ones to, but don't you ever give up, you're going to make it through. There's going to be times when nothing goes your way, but don't forget you always pray. Now when there's something you don't understand, pray about it and leave it in god's hands, if there's something you love that you can't do, just think about it, that may not be meant for you. Never let life just pass you by, always remember you can make it if you try. Now do you know what my gift is? If not I will tell you I am an inventor and an author! Therefore, you see god did give me not one but two gifts, I just had to find them. I am going to end my book now I hope it will help somebody out there. GOD BLESS You.

Well we done come a long ways from them little girls on Watts Drive, we all grown up now and we have a brother and he's a man. He was not blessed to be with us through them days. You notice I never said hard days because they weren't to me, to me those were the best days of my life. We didn't have anything but still we were rich with love and care in each of our hearts and we had each other to lean on. Looking back I have to say them days for some unknown reason were the happiest days of my childhood. A lots of things we didn't have but we never miss counting our blessing and we was so happy and people would wonder why, I will tell you why; because we never forgot to LOOK TO THR SKY.

My family left to right my brother Micheal, my mother my sister
Louryette my brother wife.

Dorothy Me at 16

In Loving Memory
Diane Fisher

Sunrise:
July 23, 1962
Bakersfield, California

Sunset:
January 9, 2006
Bakersfield, California

St. John Missionary Baptist Church
1300 E. Brundage Lane
Bakersfield, California

Rev. Tyree D. Toliver, Officiating
Assistant Pastor St. John M.B.C.

Friday, January 13, 2006 10:00 A.M.

Marquita graduation picture from high school

The day I got married
to my first
husband
James L. Williams

Me at 23

ME AND MY FIRST HUSBAND WILLIAMS

Women hated me over my husband

James and me the day we got married.

This is my brother Michael and his wifle two daughters, Necole holding her baby sister we we.

My big day graduation day 6-6-1993 a day I will never forget still to this day I look at my picture and I say I did it!

This me a week before graduation.

the scene.

DOROTHY ANN DARROUGH (Johnson)

Shooting Investigated

Kern County sheriff's deputies are investigating the shooting of a woman in the Cottonwood area.

The shooting occurred late Monday night at 3137 Cottonwood Road. The woman was identified as a 38-year-old. She was shot in the leg and taken to Mercy Hospital.

The assailant used a shotgun in the shooting, sheriff's reports stated.

This telling when I was shot.